ETHICS
FOR
PUBLIC
MANAGERS

ETHICS
FOR
PUBLIC MANAGERS

Harold F. Gortner

 PRAEGER

Westport, Connecticut
London

Library of Congress Cataloging-in-Publication Data

Gortner, Harold F., 1940–
    Ethics for public managers / Harold F. Gortner.
        p.   cm.
    Includes bibliographical references and index.
    ISBN 0–275–93847–6 (alk. paper)
    1. Civil service ethics.   I. Title.
    JF1525.E8G67   1991b
    172'.2—dc20   90–47540

British Library Cataloguing in Publication Data is available.

A hardcover edition of *Ethics for Public Managers* is
available from the Greenwood Press imprint of
Greenwood Publishing Group, Inc. (Contributions in
Political Science, 272; ISBN 0–313–27586–6)

Library of Congress Catalog Card Number: 90–47540
ISBN: 0–275–93847–6

First published in 1991

Praeger Publishers, 88 Post Road West, Westport, CT 06881
An imprint of Greenwood Publishing Group, Inc.

Printed in the United States of America

The paper used in this book complies with the
Permanent Paper Standard issued by the National
Information Standards Organization (Z39.48–1984).

10 9 8 7 6 5 4

To my Father

CARL KLINE GORTNER

who always practiced what he preached

It would seem as if the rulers of our time sought only to use men in order to make things great; I wish that they would try a little more to make great men; that they would set less value on the work, and more upon the workman; that they would never forget that a nation cannot long remain strong when every man belonging to it is individually weak, and that no form or combination of social policy has yet been devised to make an energetic people out of a community of pusillanimous and enfeebled citizens.

Alexis de Tocqueville

CONTENTS

FIGURES AND TABLES

PREFACE

There has been a revival of interest in the subject of ethics in public administration over the last decade. While there was a burst of interest after Watergate, that event was seen, rightly, as a unique phenomenon unlikely to repeat itself in anything like that form in the future. The spate of writing about that event and its ethical dimensions died away relatively quickly; however, the nagging problem of ethics in public service did not go away. Instead it has continued to grow in importance as we have gone through a series of events such as the Iran/Contra scam, the General Services Administration procurement and contracting scandal, a similar event within the Department of Defense, the Robin Hud scandal within the Department of Housing and Urban Development (HUD)—the list could go on for quite a while without even beginning to include the situations uncovered at the state and local levels.

Quite appropriately there has been a continuing, growing interest in ethics within the field of public administration. There is a recognition that: (1) if public administration is to be a profession, it must address the issues of service in the public interest and the kind of decisions and actions therein prescribed; (2) if the schools of public affairs and administration are to play their proper role in developing a professional attitude among public managers, there must be an emphasis on the subject of ethics in public administration; and, most importantly, (3) if the democratic process is to function properly, the government is to remain strong and able to address societal problems, and the citizenry at large is to have faith in their government, the public bureaucracy must play a central role in creating the atmosphere or environment that encourages that trust and faith. With these factors in mind, several individuals in the field of public administration have addressed the problem of administrative ethics over the last several years.

I hope, through this book, to add to that debate some new insights that will make the study of public administration ethics more meaningful to the students and practitioners of *public management*. Much of the literature in public administration ethics is generic, or addresses the field as a whole, not zeroing in on any one set of actors within the policy process; therefore, much of the discussion ends up being addressed toward policy makers—those individuals at the elected and appointed levels plus the top echelon of bureaucrats whose role is primarily that of formulating public policy or interpreting the law into processes and systems of implementation. That literature is extremely important; however, it does not directly address the needs of the much larger number of individuals who work at non-policy-making levels within the public bureaucracy.

This work focuses on the issue of public administration ethics theory and how it applies to the lives of managers operating in the middle ranges of the public bureaucracy. I focus on those who normally fall within the GS 12–15 level of the federal service, or program management levels within state and local government. This is the level at which most individuals are currently working and will work throughout most of their lives. Through a general review of the literature on public administration ethics and a comparison of that literature to cases drawn from the real-life experiences of over forty civil service managers (who shared with me a detailed description and analysis of a critical ethical dilemma they faced during their careers as middle managers), I have attempted to categorize the literature and measure its relevance to the thought processes, decisions, and actions of individuals within the bureaucracy.

The result of this exercise is twofold. First, the literature on public administration ethics does seem to divide into five meaningful categories. Each of the five approaches to public administration ethics is discussed at some length within this volume. An understanding of these five approaches to public administration ethics is helpful in understanding the arguments that are presented even though much of the literature includes more than one of these categories. Once the five categories are understood, it is much easier to comprehend the arguments of the writers.

Second, by examining these categories against the real-life experiences of public managers, we can begin to comprehend which of the various ethical arguments are most recognizable and meaningful to the individuals who are practicing managers in the public bureaucracy, and to understand why those particular approaches are useful or applicable to their ethical dilemmas. Some of the approaches used by academics are not readily translatable into "rules to live by" within the bureaucracy. This does not mean that these approaches to ethics are not useful or necessary—they are—but it does mean that we should not expect immediate and positive responses from public managers at the same level of sophisticated interest that we might get from other academics. Other approaches more directly address the public manager's environment and daily life. These approaches to public administrative ethics are recognizable to practitioners and are used by them as they try to deal with the difficult situations they face while keeping up with the routine of daily life in the bureaucracy.

It is often easy to forget that the life of the public manager usually goes on in a relatively routine way and that new and exciting situations occur only occasionally in an otherwise workaday world. We should not kid ourselves into believing that managerial work is always exhilarating and fulfilling. The description of police work as 98 percent boredom interspersed with 2 percent terror may, with some translation to fit the situation, be applied to most managerial positions. It is the situations where ethical dilemmas arise, not the majority of everyday events, that we focus on here. We are not going to change the work environment nor the everyday functions of public management; however, we must sensitize public managers to the presence, more often than they realize, of ethical dilemmas, and help them to deal successfully with those problems so that they can fulfill their duty to operate in the public interest. That kind of public service may not be eternally exciting, but it is never banal. It is the basis for successful, fulfilling careers that achieve the goals of government established by the citizens through the political process. The ultimate aim of this book is to help public managers achieve this goal.

Numerous individuals must be thanked for their help in this effort, but a few must be mentioned specifically. Brack Brown and Julianne Mahler, two of my colleagues at George Mason University, have read parts of this manuscript, and being academics, they were generous with their comments. My students in the ethics course in the MPA program at George Mason University have, over the years, helped to focus my thinking on the subject through their questions, discussion, criticism, and encouragement. Finally, Ric Mayer read the entire manuscript and, through his creative criticism, contributed greatly to my ability to make sense out of all of the material I had collected. In spite of all their efforts— they did their best—I must still take credit for any errors in fact or argument. As usual, my wife, Sylvia, was the world's best research assistant as well as a special friend when I inevitably faced onslaughts of discouragement.

Finally, one last group of individuals must be thanked for their help in this endeavor. I cannot note the names of the numerous individuals who volunteered their time to be interviewed as I prepared this book. There were many more than appear as specific cases in the text. Many of these individuals still continue their public careers. However, let me express to all of them my gratitude for their time and help.

One individual I do wish to recognize specially. David Weathers, the friend whose case appears first in this book and who started me on this intellectual journey, did not live to see the book completed. I owe him a debt of gratitude that I cannot pay.

ETHICS
FOR
PUBLIC
MANAGERS

CHAPTER 1

ETHICS AND PUBLIC MANAGERS

Political systems can fail for many reasons. External forces may bring them down. Major scandal can certainly lead to the loss of power by political leaders, and may ultimately cause the demise of a political system. Or systems may simply limp along and find it impossible to meet the expectations and fulfill the desires of the people even though the problem never becomes critical enough to lead to revolution or radical change. Whatever the situation, perhaps the most common cause of failure is the weakening of the system, much like cancer working in the human body, because the component parts are unable to fulfill their roles in efficient, effective, and ethical ways. If the bureaucracy fails to fulfill its role in an ethical, equitable way seen as fair by the members of society, they will become increasingly distrustful and frustrated with the government, and serious problems for the political system are almost inevitable. We often point to this question of equity as central to the problem of many third-world countries and argue that it must be corrected before significant improvement can be made in their social/political/economic systems. However, the problem of ethics and trust is also at the center of failure in political systems among the more advanced societies.

There has been an upsurge of interest in public administrative ethics over the last two decades. The flames of the theoretical, academic debate rage. However, practicing public administrators often find it hard to warm their hands, much less their hearts and minds, at these flames because the heat of the debate is often totally dissipated by the time it passes through all of the ivy-covered walls of academia. Theory building, semantics, paradigms, and ''ultimate truths'' are seldom directly useful in the real world of the public servant. (This is not a charge against such work. These issues must be addressed in order to understand the foundation on which society is constructed; however, broad generalizations, even though they set the context within which actions will be taken, often are almost useless to the individual dealing with a specific problem.) On the other hand, academics tend to dismiss practitioners' lukewarm attitudes toward the ethical debate as another example—bordering on proof—of the fact that public bureaucrats are quickly turned into insensitive, value-indifferent, amoral automatons. In fact, it is not uncommon to hear the charge leveled that many public administrators do not even recognize ethical problems, much less know how to deal with them, when they appear among the routine decisions and tasks of the bureaucratic world.

Such charges are not true. The vast majority of practicing public administrators are interested in the ethical aspects of their tasks; however, the subject becomes alive to them only when the discussion moves to the level of operation and/or application with its implications for the decisions and actions that affect their lives. The issue of most importance to practitioners is whether or not public administration theory is, in some way, meaningful to them as they try to do their jobs in the ubiquitously political and organizational world in which they work. In other words, the discussion of ethics must be relevant. The situations faced by public administrators often present not one but several ethical issues simultaneously, with each issue creating divergent and contradictory problems and solutions. Let me give you an example.

While on temporary assignment in the Department of Commerce, I often met a friend for lunch. David Weathers took delight in helping me, a professor, to experience and comprehend the opportunities and frustrations of working in the Washington federal bureaucracy. As a GM–15 who had spent some years in "The District" as a successful bureaucrat—measured by productivity, promotion, and self-preservation—he was a sensitive, able, and willing instructor. On this particular March day, however, Dave approached the table with a troubled look on his face. Upon being seated he quietly informed me he had a serious ethical problem that he had to deal with in short order. Over the next few days I discussed the problem with him and observed as he worked through to his ultimate decision and action.

Dave was a contract administrator in the Department of Energy, which had been in existence for only a couple of years, having been created by President Carter as a reaction, in large part, to the energy crisis of the early 1970s. The contracts Dave administered were specifically related to developing a national energy plan, and numerous contractors were involved in piecing together studies that would spell out: the kinds of existing reserves, the current status (domestic and imported) of energy supplies, the preparation for any future crises, and the required steps to achieve the long-term goal of energy self-sufficiency. It was in relation to these contracts that Dave had discovered he had a problem.

In order to carry out the studies that were currently under way, it was necessary for the contractors to have access to information about energy reserves and production that was considered by the energy corporations throughout the United States as top secret and highly sensitive within the industry, and probably within the total world community. No corporation trusted any other with that information. They wanted assurance, above all, that no data would leak to any competitor; nor did they want anyone to use it to their personal advantage on the stock market or any other way. This information had been released, rather reluctantly, to the government only after repeated assurances that the information would be secure and that those who did receive it would not be allowed to use it for their own advantage. The information was stored in computers under contract to the Department of Energy and could be accessed only by use of an extended series of key words and commands, known only to a few people in the department, the White House, and by those contractors who were currently utilizing the information. All contractors had to sign a disclaimer that they would not release the information to anyone and they would not use the information for personal gain. Breach of this trust carried a very heavy penalty.

Dave discovered that the most important of the rules and regulations pertaining to handling this information had been broken. The opportunity for serious mischief was extraordinary. A consultant, who operated a firm that was not under contract to the department, had been given the access code. While Dave could not be sure how this had happened, he suspected that it had occurred outside the department, most likely by a member of the White House staff, but there was no way to find out. The suspicion, however, reinforced the sensitivity of the problem. There was tremendous pressure from the White House to produce a national energy plan quickly while there was equal reticence on the part of the industry to cooperate. The fact of illegal activity was clear; Dave's problem was to correct the effects of the illegal activity in a way that would allow the program to continue and, at the same time, protect his career.

Dave felt that it was impossible for him to speak to his supervisor about the problem for two reasons. First, his supervisor did not want to know about such problems. When, a few months earlier, some fellow employees had brought a problem of a similar nature to this superior, they had been berated, received no support, and given less than satisfactory ratings at evaluation time. Second, Dave's superior was under direct political pressure from the White House to "get the study done as quickly as possible by any means available." Any intimation that such a breach of security had occurred would make the White House contacts either angry, negatively influencing the supervisor's personal career because of the "ineptness" of the operation, or defensive and/or threatening, if the perpetrator feared that he might be discovered.

Nor was it possible to go around Dave's superior in the chain of command. Above his immediate supervisor was a political appointee in the SES [Senior Executive Service] who was closely identified with both the Carter administration and the individuals in the White House who were probably involved in the situation. This administrator, Dave was convinced, would try very hard to stop any action and to cover the indiscretion, even if it meant letting a few bureaucrats "dangle in the breeze" to accomplish that goal.

It was impossible to announce the breach of security publicly because of the difficulty of supporting the charge in a hearing or court of law if the consultant fought back—which he most certainly would do. Of equal or even greater importance, any public announcement would destroy the possibility of gaining further cooperation from the energy companies—it would prove their worst fears were fulfilled. And Dave felt strongly that the program should move forward to achieve its stated goal.

Dave decided that his best first attempt at solving the problem was to approach the consultant and see if he would admit he had the information. If so, the problem could easily be resolved by noting that an "error" had led to the breach of security, changing the access codes, and making no charge of impropriety; hence, no one would be injured, and the information could be kept within the department. However, when confronted, the consultant denied the allegation even though enough evidence existed to verify the breach of security. Dave came away from the discussion with the consultant (it had turned into a rather nasty confrontation in which the threat of both hierarchical and political pressure was made if Dave did anything) more convinced than ever that the person did have the information and frankly worried about how the data might be used if some way could not be found to force the individual to admit he had it.

Finally, on the fifth day of the crisis, Dave joined me at lunch with a rueful smile on his face. He had made his decision, and the problem was "solved." Bidding on a new set of contracts had just occurred, and the contractor had bid on one of the smaller jobs in this batch of studies, apparently in an attempt to "get his foot in the door." His bid was a few thousand dollars higher than one of his competitors, but Dave gave him the contract.

My initial shock at his action was quickly alleviated as he said to me, "Public administration, just like politics, is sometimes 'the art of the possible.' If the contractor accepts that contract [and he did], he will have to sign the same disclaimer that everybody else does. If he uses any of the information in the data banks in an improper way, I can and will nail him to the wall. It also gives me additional time to verify my strong suspicion of his cheating; therefore, I can go after him for an illegal act if it proves necessary. Finally, I can force him to deliver a useful product to the department or withhold his pay, and I do not have to agree to give him any additional contracts if he doesn't deliver. It may not be the prettiest solution in the world, but I believe that it meets the test of working in the public interest. I am satisfied that I have done the best I can in this situation."

Dave's choice of action seemed to be the most rational and ethical way to resolve a very serious bureaucratic dilemma. This is ethics in the real world of the public administrator. The mid-level manager in the Department of Energy's Office of Macro-Economic Analysis does not worry about "the socio-pathology of the peer group and its effect on his or her ability to form a pre- or post-bureaucratic understanding, based on a pre- or post-conventional moral perspective, about the modern multi-national, military-industrial complex." However, that individual may be desperately searching for ways to analyze and decide upon the proper approach to the problem of guaranteeing that the current administration's desire for quick action in the development of a comprehensive energy policy is achieved while not releasing privileged information (the property of major oil companies) that might speed up the decision-making process but cause other serious repercussions.

The ethical problems faced are complex. The solutions discovered by the public administrator must take into account *at least*: (1) the general public interest; (2) the goals of policy toward which he or she is working; (3) an understanding of the major actors in the larger scenario; (4) the dynamics of the organization(s) with and in which s/he must work; and (5) the personalities of the specific individuals with whom s/he must interact. During all of this, the manager wishes to keep his or her job—a perfectly normal desire at which some may sneer, but civil servants are human and they usually can be martyrs only once.

With this real-life introduction to the everyday world of ethics in the public bureaucracy, I began to think seriously about the ways mid-level public servants deal with these kinds of ethical dilemmas and situations. While this kind of ethical problem is not as newsworthy or exciting as the multi-million-dollar C5–A scandal or the Iran/Contra scandal, it is much more representative of the world of the career civil servant and the kinds of situations dealt with almost daily. No single case may have the system–shaking impact of the big news-makers, but the sheer number of situations faced by career public administrators ultimately means that the proper understanding and resolution of these cases are equally as important as the cases examined and debated on television before congressional committees.

The basic assumption of this study is that ethical questions faced by public servants take on a special importance because of the unique place of public administration within our society. Therefore, the first task to be completed, in the rest of this chapter, is to describe the unique and critical nature of the public sector and the special challenges faced by public administrators as they manage "in the public interest."

Not only must we understand the unique nature of public administration and the environment thus created within which public administrators must work, we must also comprehend how the history of our attempts to deal with the problem of ethics in government has brought us to the point we have now reached. Chapter 2 lays out that development and brings us up to date, summarizing current thinking about ethics and the impact of that thinking on the everyday world of the public administrator.

Once the unique nature of the world of public administrators is clear, that "essence" becomes a central factor throughout the rest of the study. The last six chapters examine the experiences of public managers—individuals in the center of the public bureaucracy—who have been successful in recognizing and dealing with ethical dilemmas. These public servants were successful in dealing with ethical problems, to a great extent, because they were aware of this "democratic essence" and it served as the focus and anchor for their analysis and action. Democratic values are assumed to be the most basic values necessary for the study of public administration ethics as we examine the efforts of these public administrators to act ethically. However, the study also focuses on a set of questions that help to clarify why these managers were successful: How do mid-level civil servants and public managers recognize, analyze, and resolve ethical problems in their everyday work? What is unique about the environment that affects their ability to go about this task when ethical problems appear? Are recurring themes apparent as public administrators deal with ethical dilemmas? Are there universal questions that need to be asked in almost every situation, given the nature of the world in which public administrators work?

In examining these questions, a series of interviews was completed with current and retired federal merit system employees. While the cases describe a variety of situations,[1] five common threads run through them, and they make up the core chapters (three through seven) in this book. First, in almost every case the appearance of an ethical dilemma led to a period of serious self-searching. In order to resolve the problems they faced the individuals in the cases had to come to grips with their own personal character and values in order to guarantee that these factors did not improperly influence the decisions and actions that were ultimately taken.

Second, everyone felt constrained by the law. As public servants they had to be sure their actions met the statutes, rules, and regulations that made up such an important part of their bureaucratic life. Beyond simply complying with "the statutes," however, there was the sense that something bigger than specific statutes—generally known to us as "the law" (the body of rules governing the affairs of man within a community or among states and essential to the social order)—existed and this larger entity sometimes required them to seriously question specific statutes, rules, or regulations. The presence of both statutes and the law is an ubiquitous aspect of bureaucratic life, and this was recognized as especially true by these public servants. The presence of the law either limited, or served as the basis for, action depending on the situation and the individual, but its existence was always recognized.

Third, there was a common desire to serve the public interest. Whether acting in a managerial capacity, as a professional fulfilling a specific function in government, or as an individual worker filling a standard position in the bureaucracy, whether the case involved their career alone, the career of a single subordinate, or the lives of larger numbers of people, these individuals sensed their obligations as public servants. They knew they ultimately served the people at large and they had to act in ways recognized as fair, equitable, and representative of the values and expectations of society.

Fourth, since all of the individuals in these cases worked in bureaus, they thought about the limitations and opportunities created for themselves by the organization. The attitudes of and roles played by superiors, peers, and subordinates created vital factors that had to be taken into consideration as decisions were made and actions taken. For example, in spite of the formal hierarchy, these individuals were often on their own in dealing with their ethical situations since, for one reason or another, their superiors were not available for help and advice; yet it was recognized that those superiors would be the primary judges of the public servant's ultimate actions. Organizations were one of the most critical elements to be considered as the dilemmas were faced.

Fifth, whether or not they fell into the usual definition of a "professional," the vast majority of these individuals shared a desire to meet and apply professional standards to their work and the situations they faced. Many individuals in government do belong to professions, and the values and sense of purpose they bring with them help to guarantee that everyone will be represented and served in the total policy process. The individual managers in these cases could not be considered professionals by any current standard; however, they attempted to realize what would be the "professional" approach to their work. Both managers and individuals "just doing their jobs" attempted to borrow the basic values suggested by the concept of professionalism and apply those principles to the decisions and actions they faced because they sensed this would create the result best suited to the public interest.

After discussing these five themes, the last chapter summarizes the findings from the research and approaches the issue of how to deal with ethical dilemmas when they arise. It is obvious that no single approach is meaningful in all situations; however, there do appear to be some general rules that might help to lessen conflict, with its corresponding trauma, when ethical dilemmas are faced. The concept of limiting conflict becomes important when one examines what happens to individuals when they take a stand and act in what they believe to be an ethical manner.

PUBLIC ADMINISTRATION'S SPECIAL CONTEXT AND ITS IMPACT ON PUBLIC ADMINISTRATORS

It has become increasingly difficult to define "public administration" over the last few decades. This may be partly the result of a growing sophistication on the part of those attempting to define the phenomenon, but it is also caused by a widening of the arena within which public administration takes place. We used to define public administration as that work carried out by the government bureaucracy; now, however, many public administrative activities are carried on outside the confines of the halls of government. In order to include all of the relévant actors, the definition of Michael Harmon and Richard Mayer (1986) is borrowed here:

[P]ublic administration deals with decisions that

• Affect people's lives,
• Are made in the name of the public and
• Use public resources. (p. 6)

All three elements must be included before a decision falls within the public sphere, and if all three are present the decision is public whether it is great or small. The decision may be as small and noncontroversial as whether or not to strictly enforce the twenty-five-miles-per-hour speed limit near a local school or as large and inflammatory as the attempt to define a new national policy related to the availability of abortion-on-demand, but both meet the requirements to classify as public administration. Especially when we deal with the more controversial decisions we become aware of the full implications of this set of conditions for public administration.

While we normally consider public administration to be related to the *implementation* of public policy, it also includes activity related to public policy formulation. Neither formulation nor implementation is easy because public administration always occurs in a "political" world. If issues can be resolved privately by individuals or groups working outside the general political system and without their resulting decisions having an impact on society, they do not become political. Issues become political when they cannot be resolved privately for a variety of reasons (inability to arrive at a common definition of the problem or issue, inequitable distribution or inability to determine the distribution of costs or benefits, variance in values among interested parties, etc.) and rational calculation is no longer possible.

The political world in which public administrators act dictates the existence of a volatile environment. In the political world, at least within our society, there is a general agreement on democratic values and procedures (although our understanding of specific values and procedures varies between individuals and changes over time). Public administrators, as actors within this political world, are expected to serve in "the public interest." They are given guidance through statutes, rules, and regulations, and they are given sufficient discretion to carry out their responsibilities if the directions are not clear or complete. The difficulty comes from implementing the concept of serving in the public interest in a world of plural, conflicting definitions of and prescriptions for specific issues. For example, in the pro-choice/right-to-life battle surrounding the abortion issue, one group's definition of the public interest is diametrically opposed to that of the other, and which opinion is in ascendance within society changes over a short period of time. Nevertheless, public administrators must make decisions and act. And they will be judged as to their service "in the public interest" no matter how complex and difficult the situation faced.

Public administrators often must deal with problems referred to by Guido Calabresi and Philip Bobbitt (1978) as "tragic choices." *Tragic choices* come about because scarce goods must be distributed by society and

the distribution of some goods entails great suffering or death. When attention is riveted on such distributions they arouse emotions of compassion, outrage, and terror. It is then that conflicts are laid bare between on the one hand, those values by which society determines the beneficiaries of the distributions, and (with nature) the perimeters of scarcity, and on the other hand, those humanistic moral values which prize life and well-being. (p. 18)

When dealing with the apportionment of life and death (Calabresi and Bobbitt use as an example the determination of who gets to use kidney dialysis machines when there are more patients than there are machines available), it is nearly impossible to make decisions and carry out actions in a way that satisfies everyone in society. Our values related to these issues vary dramatically.

Even when not dealing with issues as volatile as tragic choices, the kinds of problems faced by public administrators tend to be especially difficult. Governments also must deal with issues defined by Horst Rittel and Melvin Webber as "wicked problems."[2] *Wicked problems* have no generally accepted definition or formulation either because it is impossible to discover one due to the complexity of the issue and the environment, or because there are numerous definitions espoused by different interested groups or actors in the process. Given the inability to define the problem we cannot agree on a way to formulate the questions so that we can arrive at mutually acceptable alternatives for action, and both of these difficulties make it impossible for us to decide when we have resolved the issue. In fact, in many cases there is no "solution" to the problem; instead we try to deal with a manageable part of the question, such as recognized symptoms, or we address those parts of the issue on which we can agree. In such situations only a portion of the problem is addressed—therefore the larger problem continues, although perhaps somewhat abated or changed, or we discover that the solution causes new problems because of unanticipated consequences.

Harmon and Mayer (1986) present unemployment as an example of a wicked problem.

The Bureau of Labor Statistics uses seven different definitions of the concept (and therefore the problem) of unemployment. These definitions differ depending on whether part-time workers are counted, or whether it is only heads of household, or dependents too, who are counted. Thus, in April 1977, the nation's unemployment was, variously, 1.9, 3.1, 4.4, 6.5, 7.0, 8.6, and 9.9 percent. (p. 9)

The "drug problem" is another example of a wicked problem that everyone recognizes, but no one knows how to clearly define or solve. The lack of a clear definition leads to an inability to choose an alternative for action; even when we act we do not know if or when we will solve the problem, and the solution often becomes part of the next problem.

While not all situations involve tragic choices and wicked problems, a significant level of conflict is still involved because public servants must make decisions determining who gets scarce resources (not necessarily critical to life but often related to "quality of life") or deciding whose interpretation of "right" will be accepted and who will have to live under an interpretation of law they dislike. In the political world of public administration someone is going to win and someone is going to lose. A major factor in maintaining the confidence of society in such difficult situations is the historical good will developed over time by the public bureaucracy, or society's firm belief in the fairness and trustworthiness of their public servants.

Public administrators are on the "hot seat." In all cases, contending with wicked problems and tragic choices or lesser variations on the themes, public administrators are not given the luxury of avoiding decisions, an action sometimes taken by politicians. When they are mandated to make decisions, to regulate, to act, they must do so or fail to carry out their public responsibility. Table 1 offers a classic example of a wicked, tragic issue with which public administrators have to cope.

Table 1

A Public Administrator Deals with the "Wicked," "Tragic" Issues

A classic example of a bureaucrat faced with the problem of dealing with these volatile issues can be seen in the career of Dr. C. Everett Koop, the Surgeon General of the United States. The two commentaries below, written upon Koop's retirement as surgeon general, point out the impossibility of satisfying everyone and the kind of opposing views generated about those in public life.

USA Will Miss Koop, a Man of Principle

It is rare these days for a controversial official to leave government with his integrity and credibility intact.

It is rare that the departure of one person is considered any real loss to a government so big and so impersonal.

And it is rare to yearn for more public officials like the one departing.

C. Everett Koop is that kind of surgeon general.

It took 10 months to confirm the appointment of Koop by President Reagan in 1981. Liberals condemned his anti-abortion crusades. They called him "Dr. Kook."

Conservatives, like the writer across this page, thought Koop would represent their views. He didn't march to their drumbeat. So they called him nasty names like "Dr. Death."

Sadly, that's the price some pay for doing a good job.

Operating with a staff of five and a budget of $500,00, Koop used his obscure office in the Washington suburb of Rockville, Md., to become the health conscience of a nation.

He reassured a people near hysteria that AIDS couldn't be spread by casual contact.

He recommended early sex education and contraception to prevent unwanted pregnancies.

He reported evidence linking tobacco and cancer, called nicotine addictive and endorsed public smoking bans.

He attacked drunken driving, recommended more taxes on alcohol and tougher standards to measure drunkenness.

And he resisted White House pressure to say that abortion caused psychological damage. The facts, he said, didn't support the claim.

USA Won't Miss Koop; He Abandoned Principle

C. Everett Koop is no longer surgeon general. Liberals considered him a model civil servant. Conservatives breathed a sigh of relief. Nobody has ignored him, try as one might; his narcissistic drive demanded recognition on a grand scale.

When Disraeli said of Gladstone, "He was inebriated by the exuberance of his own verbosity," he could have been describing Koop. He was nominated for public service after a brilliant career in pediatric surgery, but some colleagues considered him "an academic bully." When Koop spoke, people were mad, sad or glad.

Koop came to President Reagan's attention because of his unbending opposition to abortion. His confirmation hearings were described by Newsweek as "a prolonged three-ring circus." He was stridently opposed by Sen. Ted Kennedy, Rep. Henry Waxman and other liberals who now praise and applaud him.

Conservatives who tirelessly championed his cause became distressed, disbelieving and disillusioned once he was confirmed. He pushed sex education in the lowest grade possible. He wanted to condomize America. He urged distribution of needles to drug users. He simply wimped out on abortion. Many were stunned by his frankness and pontifical tone in his AIDS report and pamphlet that went to every home.

When challenged, Koop steadfastly claimed he held to the basic fundamental Christian positions that he had always had. But the Free Congress Foundation's Connie Marshner explains Koop's 180-degree turn as intimidation by the left's superhostility.

Koop is a hard worker who interprets criticism as hate. His philosophy is, "You don't have to agree with me; you can be wrong if you want to."

Table 1 (Continued)

How did that happen? Did Koop change?

No. Koop kept his beliefs. He's still a conservative. He still opposes abortion.

But he refused to put politics before principle. He refused to bow to pressure, even from the White House.

If more public officials put principle first, we would have been spared the long investigation and bitter resignation of House Speaker Jim Wright.

Attorney General Ed Meese wouldn't have had to leave.

If more officials put public responsibilities ahead of personal beliefs, there would have been no Iran-Contra scandal. And Oliver North wouldn't be a convicted felon.

If more officials put the public first, well-placed politicians couldn't have ripped off the poor at the Department of Housing and Urban Development. And former Cabinet officials wouldn't be appearing before Congress.

With so many moral and ethical lapses, so many weak public officials around us, it is refreshing to find one who made a difference without sacrificing principle.

One who did what he thought was right, despite his personal beliefs, despite political pressure.

There are others like Koop who may not get the recognition they deserve. They make government work.

Public service means serving the public. Not serving political expediency, not serving personal interest, not caving in to those who call you names.

We just need more public officials with the guts to do what is right.

An enigma full of inconsistencies, Koop fights smoking vociferously but has a diet that makes the American Heart Association recoil. He eats omelets, potato chips, peanuts and steaks. He is overweight and doesn't exercise. Like the smoker, when people comment about his bad habits, his excuse is he feels good.

A self-proclaimed folk hero, his policy was one of conquest and domination. He mastered the art of what U.S. News & World Report called "bureaucratic trench warfare." In a largely symbolic job, he managed to catapult himself, vice admiral's uniform and all, into the spotlight. No one questions his ability and his accomplishments, but his ego is as much on display as the gold braid on his uniform. He has talked so much on both sides of most controversial issues that many magazines end up quoting Koop against himself.

Koop has Papa's problem in the delightful Pennsylvania Dutch play Papa is All: Papa says it's God's will that Jane does not go to the party. When Mama arranges for her to go, Jane is guilt-ridden, but Mama whispers to her, "Sometimes, Papa gets his will and God's will mixed up.'

Sources: "Will Miss Koop": Lead Editorial in *USA Today*, July 17, 1989, p. 8A. Copyright 1989, *USA TODAY*. Reprinted with permission. "Won't Miss Koop": Tottie Ellis, in *USA TODAY*, July 17, 1989, p. 8A. Reprinted with the author's permission.

Nor are they allowed to be "wrong." Public administrators are accountable for the consequences (social, political, economic, etc.) of the solutions which they espouse or carry out. Their *actions* affect people related (and often people thought unrelated) to the issue being resolved; *inaction* also affects numerous people, often the same ones. There is no way to avoid affecting the lives of citizens. And the action or inaction of public administrators will be second-guessed; thus, it is important to maintain an ethically sensitive bureaucracy *and* an image of ethical purity and adherence to the basic values of the larger society, just as it is important to remember that not only must the bureaucracy be ethical, it must be *perceived* as ethical by the public. Trust by the populace—politicians, members of interested groups, involved citizens, and citizens uninvolved and uninterested in the current issue—is essential to effective service if not survival.

Another important historical factor leads to the importance of public administration within society. The number and type of people involved in "doing public administration" have changed dramatically over the last couple of decades. Before that time, when we talked about public administrators we meant individuals known as public servants or civil servants—hired by the government and working within the structure of the public bureaucracy at the national, state, or local level. As government has become increasingly "privatized," with much public policy formulation based on research and recommendations from individuals and firms considered to be part of the "private sector," and much public policy implementation likewise being contracted to organizations outside the "normal" government structure, it is increasingly hard to determine who is a "public administrator."

Anyone who is creating or carrying out publicly mandated policy that uses public resources to have an impact on individuals or groups of society is functioning as a public administrator. This must be understood. It may be confusing for individuals working in a private firm, for instance, who spend part of their time working on projects contracted by the government and another part of their time working on "private" contracts (between two corporations).[3] It may be difficult to remember, but when one is carrying out work related to public policy, he or she is "doing public administration." In this study the focus is on those working full-time within the public bureaucracy because the confusions as to roles do not exist; however, the findings of the study are of equal value, maybe more important, to those who must move between the public and private worlds as they work.[4]

In either case, there is one common characteristic of extreme importance for all public administrators. They work in an organizational setting which always has three arenas: inter-organization relationships, intra-organizational relationships, and organization-to-individual relationships. The predominance of this feature of public administrative life is well-known to all successful public administrators. To give an example of these three arenas, let us return to David Weathers in the example presented earlier in this chapter. In solving his ethical dilemma, David had to deal with all three arenas of this world. First, he had to consider the *inter-organizational* aspects of his problem. He had to be representative of and agent for his organization in relations with major private corporations, other powerful bureaus of the government, and private contractors working for his agency. His calculations had to measure the impact of any action on each of these groups, and he had to consider the probable results of his actions on future cooperation.

Second, David had to recognize the *intra-organizational* arena and the probable effect of any action on his relationship with individuals above him in the organization chart. Third, he had to deal with the *organization-to-individual* aspect of his task. He had to, as an agent of his organization, confront, interact, and work with individuals who had a variety of personalities, powers, and other characteristics that influenced how they must be handled. As David resolved the problem he faced he was aware of and responsive to the values central to each of these arenas; these included some values common to all public organizations, some specifically related to interpersonal relations, and others related to the goals and procedures of the Department of Energy.

In all situations public managers must be aware of this ubiquitous environment in order to be successful. The importance of this environment is increased when *public managers* face *ethical dilemmas* because of the special location of the managers and the nature of the problems. Let us clarify these two terms so that everyone understands the nature of the phenomenon being examined in this book.

Public managers, on whom we focus in this study, must constantly make ethical decisions. Not only do the ethical dilemmas place them under tremendous personal pressure, but their ability to resolve these issues is vital to the long-term health and viability of the public service. However it is only within the last few decades that literature on public administration ethics has recognized the significance of this group of public servants and attempted to develop guidelines and procedures for ethical behavior in the middle and lower ranges of the bureaucracy.

Most early writing on public administrative ethics was aimed at individuals in the appointive/policy-making levels—those at the very top of the bureaucracy who were expected to play the role of leader. Managers generally play a different role but may decide to play a leader's role on occasion. If we define leaders and managers it may become easier to see why the ethical dilemmas faced by the two types of individuals differ and why the discussion of ethics aimed at one level may not apply to the other.

Leaders play at least nine roles within the organization according to John Gardner (1986): envisioning goals, affirming values, motivating, managing, achieving a workable level of unity, explaining, serving as symbol, representing the group, and reviewing both the organization and the individuals within it. Other writers (Barnard [1938] 1979; Burns 1978; Sarkesian 1984; Zaleznik 1966) generally agree with Gardner that leaders primarily focus on creating new ideas and images within the context of organizational goals and/or missions, and that the leader's critical considerations are values, commitment, and human resources. These functions or roles are performed formally from the apex of the organization (usually at the political appointee/senior executive service level in the federal bureaucracy). Obviously people at lower levels within the organization may perform the leader's role occasionally, but the formal leaders who must address the role all of the time function primarily at the executive level.

Managers perform a variety of functions also, but these functions tend to focus on solving problems relating to organizational goals, resources, processes, and structures. Remember the acronym POSDCORB developed by Gulick ([1937] 1973a), which stood for planning, organizing, staffing, directing, co-ordinating, reporting, and budgeting. This was Gulick's attempt to focus on the functions of the manager and to make a skeletal set of those functions easy to remember. The goals are "given" and the manager strives to guarantee predictability in procedure, resource allocation, time usage, and other elements leading to efficiency and administrative effectiveness. Public managers in the public bureaucracy usually hold merit system positions, supervise employees and/or other supervisors, and answer to a superior inside the organization (Gortner et al, 1987).

The ethical dilemmas faced in managerial situations are primarily related to *competing values*. Each individual interviewed during this research was asked at the beginning of the interview to define what they meant by the term "ethical dilemma," and their cumulative response was an excellent definition: An ethical dilemma is a situation where two or more competing values are important and in conflict. If you serve one value you cannot serve another, or you must deny or disserve one or more values in order to maintain one or more of the others.[5] While one may feel she has a clear legal or professional duty to do something, there is an internal pressure telling the individual to do the opposite of what the legal or professional requirements say she should do; or she may believe that she should do something different than what is being imposed on her from above. In all cases the major factor that had to be dealt with in ethical dilemmas was that different values held by the individual came into conflict. Thus we are discussing a conflict that is generated by values held *within the individual*. An ethical dilemma is a uniquely personal experience. We can turn to others for advice and help in analyzing the problem, but ultimately we must resolve it ourselves and then live with ourselves and the after effects.

But what is a value? Values play an important role in our lives and are central to our determining what is ethical or unethical. According to William K. Frankena (1967) in *The Encyclopedia of Philosophy*, the concrete noun "value" refers to "what is valued, . . . thought to be good, or desired."[6] People, organizations, and societies have "value systems" which determine what they think is right or obligatory and often serve as the basis for what they believe to be true. Behind this widespread usage lies the covert assumption that nothing really has objective value; "value" simply means being valued and "good" means being thought good. Obviously, if this assumption is held, there is much room for difference of opinion and controversy.

Likewise, every individual, organization, and society have many values, some of which conflict. In order to deal with this problem, there inevitably develops a "hierarchy of values" so that those making and acting on decisions can avoid gridlock when faced with competing or conflicting values. The hierarchy may be implicit or explicit, but it exists and heavily influences perception and behavior.

The competing values, and the definition of one's hierarchy of those values, is a recurring theme in the resolution of the ethical problems of mid-level civil servants. Anyone in a mid-level position must deal with ethical issues as both an individual and manager. We must be sensitive to our own value system; yet, while it is true that we must be able to live with ourselves, we must be true to the organizations in which we operate, and above all, as public administrators we must recognize the values of the larger society/political system we have sworn to uphold.

It is this last point that must be stressed when dealing with public administration ethics. One of the basic assumptions of this work is that public administrators, when serving as instruments for accomplishing the public will, must accept the ultimate centrality of the democratic ethic and the values related thereto. These values will be discussed later, but let us here briefly note that they include such values as individual liberty, equity or fairness, and the rights guaranteed in the Constitution. In spite of the competing sets of values, public administrators do not operate in an amoral or purely situational environment. There are strict guidelines at the general level. It is the interpretation and application of those general guidelines to specific situations that create ethical dilemmas. Successful managers are sensitive to these values; however, the way they apply them and the resulting actions may vary depending upon a variety of factors that arise in the heat of everyday activity where numerous situations must be faced, each with a different set of facts, and internal and external pressures, and decisions must be carried out under pressure of politics, time, and limited resources.

Therefore, public administrators work in a unique environment where ethical issues are of special importance and where the way those ethical dilemmas are handled is critical to the overall health and welfare of the political system. In summary, public administrative ethics are important because:

- these are decisions (the presence of discretion) made by

- individuals in a position of public trust (personal commitment to achieving the public interest, however amorphous)

- operating in an organization (with bureaucratic values including, but not limited to, authority, rationality, and efficiency)

- existing in a political environment (with its conflicting goals, values, and perspectives)

- yet expected to implement public policy (be "effective")

- while practicing, maintaining, and supporting society's values (economic, social, political, e.g., ideas such as decentralization, participation, openness, etc.),

- especially *democratic values*, which include but are not limited to

    —individual dignity

    —liberty/freedom, and

    —fairness/equity/due process.

Obviously public administrators have their work cut out for them. Let us look at how they do it.

NOTES

1. In almost all of the cases presented to the researcher, the individuals ultimately resolved the situations in a positive manner—as they related to the public interest—and satisfactorily—from an individual perspective. It is difficult to collect firsthand descriptions of unethical behavior. This kind of case must usually be pieced together from secondhand accounts (e.g., newspaper descriptions and stories related not by the actor but by those who knew him and/or the case). An interesting recent example is the story of Marilyn Louise Harrell, referred to in the newspapers as "Robin HUD" because of her practice of stealing from government property sales and donating at least part of the money to charity (see, for example, *The Washington Post*, June 18, 1989, and subsequent issues, where the difficulties of HUD and the specific abuses of Marilyn Harrell are discussed as front page news). Such cases do exist, and much of value can be learned from them; however this book focuses on ethical behavior and how individuals have succeeded in such situations.

2. Wicked problems can be compared to "tame problems," which can be solved because they can be defined and separated from other problems in their environment, and one can tell when the problem is "solved." Building an interstate highway system is a tame (although complex) problem while creating a good transportation system is a wicked problem.

3. Numerous efforts have been made to describe the difference between the environment of the public and private sectors of our society. I have attempted to do this in summary fashion in earlier writing (Gortner 1981, 8–12). Among other factors, there is a variance in:

• the locus where goals are established (private organizations tend to have greater internal control of goals while public organizations more often have their goals established externally).

• the type of services delivered (private organizations tend to offer more competitive services while public organizations tend to offer monopolistic services).

• the measure of efficiency and success (private organizations measure success in profits, public organizations seldom do).

• the level of public scrutiny (higher for public organizations).

4. Some critics of the "privatization" of government functions argue that the inability to change perspectives is one of the great weaknesses in contracting out some public policy activities. For example, these critics believe there is a great danger, in fact there is strong evidence, that individuals do not change from a private to a public perspective in carrying out public policy studies; therefore their perspective is wrong. The solutions proposed are preordained to failure because the analysts' definitions were wrong and, therefore, the alternatives considered were inappropriate.

5. The term "dilemma" is deliberately chosen as the term most often used throughout this book to describe the ethical situation faced by a public manager. John D. Aram (1976) defines dilemma very well when he says that it may be viewed as similar to a paradox.

A paradox is a statement or situation containing a logical contradiction. . . . Although a paradox conveys a logically contradictory state of affairs, it offers no choice to be made, no action to be taken. A dilemma, on the other hand, is a predicament—a complicated and perplexing situation—that requires choice between equally valued alternatives. (p. 9) Even after a decision . . . has been made and the situation has passed, there is no way for a person to know conclusively if the actual choice was "correct." The ambiguity of a dilemma remains even after an action has been taken. (p. 2)

6. According to Frankena (1967), the word "value" is used:

1. in a narrower sense to cover only that to which such terms as "good," "desirable," or "worthwhile" are properly applied.

2. in a wider sense to cover, in addition, all kinds of rightness, obligation, virtue, beauty, truth, and holiness.

3. to describe what might be said to be on the plus side of the zero line.

4. as the generic noun for all kinds of critical or pro and con predicates, as opposed to descriptive ones, and is contrasted with existence or fact. (pp. 229–230)

CHAPTER 2

THE GORDIAN KNOT STILL TIED: ETHICS AND THE PUBLIC MANAGER

Public administration has been recognized for approximately a century as an independent field worthy of study. During this time scholars and practitioners in the field developed many schools of thought concerning ways to organize and manage public agencies. People were quick to take sides and argue vehemently on such issues as how to structure offices, motivate individuals, and evaluate programs, and the predominant attitude regularly changed as new theories arose. However, during this same time the subject of public administrative ethics remained an ambivalent issue at best.

In most cases and with most individuals the question of ethics in public administration was avoided, at least in part, because it was seen as a Gordian knot—so complex that it could not be untied. For many public administration theorists the knot did not need to be untied because it was *inappropriate* and *unnecessary* to do so. For the others, the ethical question was not only unsolvable by any standard method, they also felt that the solution of Alexander the Great was inappropriate; the problem could not be resolved by simply severing the knot by sword stroke, or—as we often refer to such activities in the current day—the meat cleaver approach. Both of these attitudes discouraged efforts to examine the role of ethics in public administration. (In spite of these pressures, a small but important flow of thought on this subject did appear all along. This explanation is not meant to be a charge that nothing was done in the area of ethics, only that the level of effort related to this subject was much less than one might expect.)

To focus on ethics was *inappropriate* because public administration was separate from politics. Public administration scholars and reformers were advocating an apolitical public bureaucracy where hiring and promotion were based on merit. Ethical questions were asked and answered in the political sphere. Any admission that the public bureaucracy was involved in making ethical choices (which often become political choices in the public sphere) could be used to refute the merit principles that were being ardently proposed and supported. Politicians were expected to deal with ethical/political issues; once the decisions were made it was simply the job of the public administrator to efficiently and effectively carry them out (Goodnow [1900] 1967). Such, according to Charles G. Dawes, is the life of those who "are down in the stokehole of the ship of state, and are concerned simply with the economical handling of fuel" (Dawes 1970, 95).

In addition to the insistence on the separation of politics and administration, there were two other problems related to the discussion of individual ethics. First, when one discussed "*responsibility*," the term usually attached to personal ethics, it was ultimately necessary to deal with the problem of personal interpretation; once it was admitted that ethical questions were open to personal interpretation, the door was open to individual perspectives that might lead to misinterpretation and aberrant conclusions. While individuals with healthy personalities and ethical sensitivity could usually be expected to make appropriate choices, there was no guarantee that even the most conscientious person would make the right choice every time, nor was there any guarantee that separate, equally conscientious individuals would arrive at the same decision when considering the same factors. There was no scientific way to study and define "correct" personal interpretation: No agreement could be reached among any large group as to a universally proper way to view issues; therefore, it was impossible to scientifically examine ethical responsibility.

It was also necessary to recognize that not everyone had a healthy personality and ethical sensitivity. Hence, the idea of personal responsibility in ethical dilemmas was recognized but seldom dealt with because there were no definite answers and it was generally believed that individuals should not be encouraged to make independent decisions (although the possibility, even the necessity, of occasionally doing so was always recognized).

The second reason the discussion of personal responsibility was inappropriate must be traced to the philosophy of the individuals who made up the practitioner and intellectual groups in the discipline. Prior to World War II, public administration was philosophically rooted in the reform movement and the myth of science and progress. As was stated earlier, the dichotomy between politics and administration was firmly accepted. Ethical problems fell in the arena of politics. One of the major theses of the reform movement was that democracy would produce "good" leaders if the process could be properly constructed; at that point the "right" ethical decisions would be made by the political leaders.

In close conjunction with their faith in the political system was their conviction that problems of administration could be resolved through use of the scientific method. Much of the pre–1940 writing in public administration was filled with attempts to find the "one best way" to carry out tasks. A part of the faith in the scientific method was an assumption that there would be no disagreement on the results of "scientifically achieved improvement." This simplistic view was possible because almost everyone's focus was on economy and efficiency; the debate about how to interpret these two concepts was yet to come.

Not only was the consideration of public administration ethics inappropriate, it was also *unnecessary*, because the institutions of government and the structure of the bureaucracy guaranteed that there would be an ethical administration. This traditional view was addressed under the title of "*accountability*," and it meant that there were formal controls, both external and internal to the public bureaucracy, which guaranteed that the objectives of, and processes used by, public managers would be appropriate.

The Constitution's founders thought that accountability from outside the bureaucracy was achieved by the political rules (such as the separation of powers between the executive, legislative, and judicial branches of government) created at the national and state levels. James Madison, in the *Federalist Paper No. 51*, argues that the aim of the Constitution is "to divide and arrange the several offices in such a manner as that each may be a check on the other—that the private interest of every individual may be a sentinel over the public rights" (Hamilton, Madison, and Jay 1961, 322). The most specific control included in this system is executive control—the accountability of the members of the public bureaucracy to the president and his duly appointed officials—but the separation of powers also guarantees an observant congress that is quick to check the bureaucracy if it gets out of line.

The development of political parties and interest groups throughout society made the guarantee of external control even stronger. And, of course, the underpinning behind all of the political and governmental structures was the most magnificent edifice of all, "*the law*." From the Constitution to the legislation passed by the lowest body of the federal system, the law placed carefully prescribed limits on the actions of public managers. When doubt arose the judiciary clarified these points.

There was also an internal formal control that took care of the problem of maintaining an ethical public administration. The inherent *hierarchical authority* pattern guaranteed that accountability was maintained (Weber 1947; Appleby 1952). Each individual within the bureaucracy was required to answer to a superior, and superiors were held responsible for the actions of their subordinates. The bureaucratic system guaranteed that someone was not only always available to see that everyone acted ethically but also to clarify any questions about the definition of proper behavior. At the pinnacle of the hierarchy in the public sphere were either political appointees, who could be held accountable by elected officials, or elected officials themselves who could be held accountable by the citizens through the power of the ballot box. The citizens, therefore, served as the ultimate authority through the democratic/republican principles and procedures on which the government was based. With such a thorough system of control over personal or collective behavior, it was considered unnecessary to spend much time studying the issue of public administration ethics.

Observations about public administration began to evolve as President Roosevelt brought large numbers of highly educated people into the government to run the New Deal programs, and this evolution gained momentum as more people were involved in administering the World War II bureaucracy. As academics, on a large scale for perhaps the first time, crossed over into the world of policies, programs, processes, and deadlines that makes up the everyday environment of the practitioners, the simple dichotomies and stereotypes of the role of public administration beat a hasty retreat. By the end of the 1940s, politics and administration were recognized as two related fields with large areas of contiguity and overlap.

With the arrival of the 1960s, and the turbulent events of that decade—especially the civil rights movement and the Vietnam War—the inability of public administrators to separate themselves neatly from ethical issues became increasingly obvious. Then with the 1970s came the single incident—the Watergate scandal—that created an almost universal acceptance of the need to include ethical considerations as part of the discipline and study of public administration. The Watergate scandal emphasized the fact that even if one cannot be taught to be ethical, one should be made aware of ethical issues and how to give them proper consideration alongside technical concerns as decisions are made. With the Iran-Contra scandal in 1987, it was forcefully brought home that things had not changed much in spite of more than a decade of talk.[1]

Two major factors helped to create this new attitude toward ethical issues. First, the development of experimental, research-oriented social science has led to a recognition of the obvious; it is impossible, no matter how sincere the effort, to separate technical and ethical issues. At some point values intrude on even the most scientific of social analyses and decision processes. While Luther Gulick argued at one time that "in many of the subsidiary but fundamental fields of social knowledge it is possible to put values and ends to one side, or to assume them as constants, just as is done in the pure sciences" (Gulick [1937] 1973b, 192), and thereby believed that he was removing values from the administrative process, he was actually making a value statement. There are always certain subjective, value-laden ideas attached to terms such as "efficiency." When traced to its ultimate meaning, and especially when applied to human beings, scientific terminology has highly significant value connotations. These value connotations cannot be avoided.

Values also enter into the questions that are asked and the methodologies used to answer them. The type of questions Robert Moses asked when he ran the Triborough Bridge Authority in New York influenced the answers that were received from the analysts and, therefore, influenced the type of transportation systems and the location where they were developed as well as who benefitted or suffered from the development (Caro 1974). Supporters argue that Moses accomplished the unattainable by getting the highways built in a state where almost nothing had been accomplished up to that time. Detractors argue that Moses rode roughshod over small home and farm owners and that he destroyed neighborhoods on a wholesale scale because he worried *only* about building highways and bridges and never considered the human factors related to his projects, the personal desires of individuals (those most basic elements considered in the American democratic creed).

Likewise, the way in which data are analyzed and answers to questions are sought leads to dramatically different conclusions. One example of this phenomenon is presented by Sam Adams (1988) when he discusses the difficulty that he got into by "correcting" the statistics on enemy force levels produced by the military and the Central Intelligence Agency during the Vietnam War. Both the Department of Defense and the Central Intelligence Agency wished to "put a good face" on the war; therefore, their statements about the number of enemy (Vietcong and North Vietnamese) soldiers in South Vietnam were consistently underestimated. When he, by asking the questions about troop strength differently and then analyzing the data in a more thorough way, showed that their estimates were extremely low, he was ignored, shunted aside, and ultimately reassigned so that his numbers could be ignored. It was not until the Tet Offensive that anyone was willing to listen to his facts and figures.

Regularly the Federal Drug Administration, drug companies, and patient advocate groups look at the same data, analyze it, and arrive at three sets of totally opposing conclusions about the safety of a new drug and whether it should be released to doctors for prescription. The difference in conclusions is based on the questions that are asked and the way the data is "massaged" and interpreted by whoever is doing the analysis. When values are involved—in the questions asked, in the definitions of terms, and in the analytical tools used—ethical dilemmas are inevitable and must be treated equally alongside technical questions.

The second reason for the increased interest in the ethical aspects of public administration is the realization that leadership has failed to act as an "ethical anchor" for public employees. Formal authority can be accepted as the ultimate power—or the linking pin between society's values and bureaucratic action—only if the leader can be trusted to (1) know what is "right" and (2) carry it out regardless of the adversity. During the last two decades the possibility of maintaining such a view of formal leadership has been severely damaged if not lost. President Johnson demolished the public's view of infallibility by getting the United States ever more deeply involved in the Vietnam War; President Nixon managed to destroy everyone's belief in the incorruptibility of the presidency with the Watergate affair; then the Iran-Contra scam damaged the public's faith in the wisdom of a very popular President Reagan.

Several other recent presidents (including President Carter and many would argue President Bush) have been guilty of a third serious error—which may be the culmination or logical conclusion of our acceptance of political pragmatism:

They have failed to "lead through an idea" (Gulick [1937] 1973a, 37–38). Gulick argues that if everyone shares an idea, that fact alone will often serve as the primary motivation for cooperative effort and, ultimately, success in achieving a goal. Individuals naturally want to see something constructive come from their effort, and the leader can harness this power by presenting the followers with a vision toward which they can strive. Since these leaders have failed to have a goal or a rallying idea (as Martin Luther King called it, "a Dream"), they have appeared to tack aimlessly with the ship of state, and people (both common citizens and bureaucrats) wish to have a sense of direction, or to feel that there is a goal attached to their efforts so that they may experience at some time in the not-too-distant future a sense of accomplishment. These incidents have pointed out that assumptions about formal leadership and its ability to serve as an ethical anchor or ethical guide were too simplistic if not wrong; therefore, new solutions and directions had to be sought for dealing with the ethical issues related to governmental authority and action.[2]

ATTEMPTING TO UNTIE THE KNOT: APPROACHES TO PUBLIC ADMINISTRATIVE ETHICS

It is impossible to separate technical problems and ethical concerns. Neither can we depend solely on the structure nor the leadership of public organizations to provide definitive ethical guidelines and checks. Where then can practitioners turn for guidance? And how can ethical behavior be guaranteed? Scholars studying public administration ethics have been attempting to answer these questions by looking for methods whereby bureaucrats can be induced and/or helped to maintain an ethical posture toward their work. The various approaches to ethics that have arisen recognize the difficulty that faces anyone who attempts to resolve these two problems. They also point out the relationship that always exists in public administration between theory and practice; in some cases theory is developed as an attempt to explain practice while in other cases practice either develops or changes as a result of new theory.

Perhaps the different types of general theories about ethics can be best described by showing how they are related to two different characteristics: type of, and source of, guidance and control. As for *type* of guidance and control, at one extreme guidance and/or control is formal, often appearing as a written statement of what is or is not appropriate action (see Figure 1). These formal controls are enforceable to the extent stated within the law (the common way of stating formal controls in the public sector), and one cannot avoid that enforcement which is carried out by individuals and/or offices outside his or her control. At the other end of this continuum are informal, often unwritten, codes of behavior or conduct. Even though pressure for conformity may be great, an individual may choose to ignore it. (However, there is a positive correlation between individual responsibility and informal control.) Once this continuum

Figure 1
"Guidance/Control" Continuum

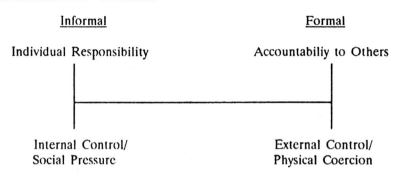

Informal   Formal

Individual Responsibility   Accountabiliy to Others

Internal Control/   External Control/
Social Pressure   Physical Coercion

Figure 2
Theories Relating to Ethical Guidance and Control

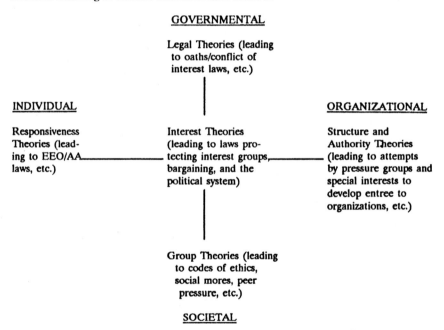

GOVERNMENTAL

Legal Theories (leading
to oaths/conflict of
interest laws, etc.)

INDIVIDUAL   ORGANIZATIONAL

Responsiveness   Interest Theories   Structure and
Theories (lead-   (leading to laws pro-   Authority Theories
ing to EEO/AA   tecting interest groups,   (leading to attempts
laws, etc.)   bargaining, and the   by pressure groups and
                        political system)   special interests to
                                                   develop entree to
                                                   organizations, etc.)

Group Theories (leading
to codes of ethics,
social mores, peer
pressure, etc.)

SOCIETAL

between informal and formal control is recognized as ubiquitous we can examine the source of guidance and control.

The *source* of guidance or control may also vary, but the theories related to ethics seem to argue that it comes from one of five sources. Figure 2 presents a visual map of the theories related to the source of guidance and control for public administration ethics. It must be remembered that the type of guidance and control may vary from formal to informal in any of these five major categories; however, some of the theories depend much more heavily on one or the other type. For example, legal theories are intimately related to the government, and the government is generally recognized as the ultimate formal authority in society, with power over our lives and fortunes. Perhaps the theories at the other extreme are those related to responsiveness, where the basis of ethical analysis and behavior is the individual's understanding of and sensitivity to the values of his/her self and the relevant other groups.

Formal governmental theories of ethical control are based upon the idea that there is a need for a legal foundation to governmental activity. This was the theoretical basis of the reform movements—pushing for civil service reform and structural reform of local government—during the latter half of the nineteenth and the early part of the twentieth centuries.

Two ideas are central to theory and activity of this type. First, the laws are an expression of the will of the people, created by their chosen representatives, and the laws are therefore held in high esteem by everyone; second, when activity takes place that is detrimental to, or frowned upon by, the people, the best way to stop such activity (and to give some guidance to action) is by passing a law. When, for instance, it is found that members of government (elected/appointed officials or public employees) are making decisions on matters in which they have a personal interest, the legislature attempts to deal with this problem by establishing conflict of interest laws. Such laws spell out with great specificity what are considered to be conflicts of interest and also establish procedures whereby these conflicts can be controlled.

The establishment of these controls over behavior through the law lends the full weight of the political system's prestige to the ethical control; most people try to obey the law because they logically believe that such behavior is best for society and because they are socialized into such behavior from early childhood. In addition, such legislation often includes structures and procedures, as noted above, to help individuals in interpreting and reviewing their actions if they are covered by the law. This allows a great deal of specificity in the areas of conduct covered and makes sure that the intent of the law is carried out. However, there are two major difficulties with these laws. To the extent that they are clear they are also narrow in focus; therefore, only a limited number of activities can be covered by law. This leaves many ethical dilemmas faced by public employees and officials outside of the realm of the law. In addition, this approach, as discussed by John Rohr, reduces ethical behavior primarily "to staying out of trouble. . . . (This approach) is innocent of any reference whatsoever to the influence that career civil servants might have on . . . policy" (1978, 54). He argues the result of such a negative approach may be the creation of "pharisees" rather than mature, thoughtful, well-balanced decision makers.

Two examples of the results of such legislation are major offices established at the federal level, the first to deal with conflicts of interest, the second to examine such charges and other claims of illegal behavior after the fact. First, the Office of Government Ethics has been established to help policy-level appointees create a personal situation where they are free to act without fear of claims of special interest or personal bias. This is done by very carefully helping the appointees to file all of the personal financial information necessary and to meet all of the conflict of interest requirements. It is hoped that the careful disclosure of information and removal of any question of personal gain (through the establishment of blind trusts, etc.) from decisions made while in office will allow these individuals to carry out their policy-making tasks without hesitation or fear of second-guessing by the public.

The second kind of organization created by legislation looks at those actions after the fact. The Inspector General Offices, as these organizations are called, exist in all major federal departments, and have the right to examine any charges of fraud, waste, and abuse, as well as other issues such as conflict of interest. Again, the government has built into the bureaucracy, at least to an extent at public insistence, a specific structure that has as its primary function the policing of bureaucratic activity.

Part of the vacuum left by the governmental approach to ethical questions is covered by the group theories of public ethics. These theories place responsibility for guidance and control upon various sectors of society. Ethical standards are established and sustained by a wide variety of organizations and groups—ranging from religious organizations to garden clubs, from political parties to street-corner gangs, and from labor unions to professional associations. For example, an ongoing debate within the American Society for Public Administration has culminated in the development of a code of ethics (Chandler 1983), and debate still rages over what role that code should play within the lives of members of the society.

Regardless how widespread the institutional attempts to control the behavior of public administrators, there is no way to achieve either adequate guidance or control through such approaches. As was noted earlier, it is impossible to cover all activities in such a formal way. It is also impossible to establish a law or rule that can be easily interpreted in all cases. Therefore, informal systems of ethical control have also developed, based upon theories of human nature and social and political systems. An example of a responsiveness theory that is so widely accepted that it became the basis for a major personnel system in government is the idea that the best way to (1) deal with everyone wishing to work for government and (2) guarantee that all parts of society would be represented and responded to by the bureaucracy is through guaranteeing equal employment opportunity to all citizens. Not only is everyone, regardless of sex, race, religion, or national origin guaranteed equal treatment as they seek employment in the various civil services (in itself an attempt to make personnel decisions based on what are considered "ethical" or appropriate values, e.g., objectively, on merit, rather than on any other basis), but this program operates under the value assumption that good government requires a responsive bureaucracy, and that the best way to achieve that responsiveness is by having a representative bureaucracy, that is, one in which the composition of the bureaucracy represents society as a whole (Van Riper 1958). This idea, as old as the Jacksonian presidency and as new as the civil rights movement and the New Public Administration theory of the 1960s and 1970s, implies that one result of representativeness will be a civil service which is an ethical mirror of the society it serves. For this reason, some individuals went one step beyond equal employment opportunity and argued that affirmative action (action beyond simple equal opportunity) was necessary to achieve such a bureaucracy representative of the values and ethics of society.

While individuals and their values and ethical standards are addressed on the one side, structures and authority patterns and their impact on ethical behavior are addressed at the opposite extreme. This fourth set of theories argues that the form of the organization and the positions available to specific individuals will have a major impact on organizational values and what is considered ethical or unethical. It does not matter what the values of an individual are if that person cannot wield power, and if the structure of the organization places a person in a position of power s/he can have influence far beyond what would seem possible in other situations. It is suggested by some theorists, for example, that leaders set a moral tone (Burns 1978). It was on this basis that, during the Reagan presidency, Attorney General Ed Meese was held by his opponents as an unfit leader for the primary legal office of the land.

For this reason nongovernmental groups in society are interested in the way government departments and agencies are organized, and whether that structure allows the interests and ideas of employees, clients, and the interested public to be considered. External groups attempt, for example, to influence governmental recruiting practices so their organizations' ideals will be given full consideration as decisions are made. Many professional groups have been able to gain at least partial control of the recruiting process of particular government agencies; in order to be hired for certain positions in the agencies, it is necessary to hold a license or other credential from a particular profession. They feel that it is certain, in such situations, that the ethical perspective of their professions will be given a central place in the decision processes of those organizations.

There are also organizations specifically interested in helping public employees who are facing an ethical dilemma and who cannot achieve a satisfactory resolution of these problems within the bureaucratic structure (Mitchell 1979; Bowman 1983). Organizations such as the Institute for Policy Studies, the Ethics Resource Center, the Washington Ethical Society, and the Government Accountability Project specifically try to help whistle-blowers in the civil service (and in corporations, where the problems for whistle-blowers are often worse).

These and similar groups have also been active in pushing for new structures and organizations in government that can aid employees who feel they are caught in an ethical bind by their agencies. Out of this effort has come the Office of Special Counsel (within the Merit System Protection Board) which as one of its duties deals with the cases of whistle-blowers. Outside groups watch carefully to see if structures such as this have an impact on the conduct of business by the federal agencies and on the ability of federal employees to publicize ethical problems that they are not able to get resolved within their organizations.

Finally, a fifth group of theories has developed that does not see ethical conduct as guaranteed by any set of laws or input from any particular group. Instead, supporters of this approach, known as public interest theory, value the democratic process. They believe that the best way to guarantee an ethical and responsive public bureaucracy is by making sure that the processes of government are open to all actors. The only way to achieve a balance of needs, demands, and values within our very diverse society is by making sure that all interests are represented in the arena where public decisions are made. Then it is possible to decide how and what should be done by the government. The goals and procedures established by public participation can serve as an ethical anchor for the public bureaucracy. Therefore, this theory leads to action by its followers that is geared toward adjusting the political system so that the public's will can be discovered.[3] This approach to ethical questions spills over into the other four areas of theory/ activity that have been spelled out, therefore it is graphically portrayed in the center of the group of theories related to ethics in public administration.

FROM SYSTEM ATTEMPTS AT CONTROL TO INDIVIDUAL ETHICS

The above theories relate to public administration in its general social/political scope. They take a broad, systemic view. It is essential to understand this background, but our interest here is to apply this more general theory to particular individuals in the middle of the bureaucracy facing specific situations where ethical issues must be addressed. Public administrators work in varied situations at different levels of the bureaucracy. Nor do they remain in stasis—some move up and down in the bureaucracy as elections come and go; others, especially at the policy-making level, move laterally between public and private positions. Each move requires a change in perspective to match the new environment. The ethical problems faced by any public administrator also combine types of situations and levels of consideration. When trying to serve democratic values, what is a right answer in one situation may be wrong in another context. Therefore, the attempt to deal with analysis of ethical issues by grand formulas often leads to overgeneralization or speaks to a very small group at the apex of the bureaucracy. In this discussion we are seeking to address the ethical dilemmas faced by public managers in a narrower but more meaningful way. The questions we are asking are: In what way can these grand theories be reduced in scope so as to help individuals in the middle levels of the organization? and from the opposite and pragmatic side: What do public managers currently use as guides for dealing with ethical problems?

In order to achieve a final clarity of discussion, it is necessary to consider one additional approach or perspective to our analysis. We must briefly emulate economics and utilize the "micro/macro" concept. After that we can zero in on a series of variables representing perspectives that, while not necessarily giving us absolute answers, appear to help public managers, as individuals, to clearly analyze ethical issues.

Micro and Macro Aspects of Ethical Dilemmas

Discussion of ethical considerations must at least recognize the difference between those dilemmas that involve major segments of a community or a society and dilemmas that primarily have an impact on the careers or well-being of the individuals who are faced with the choices (but do not have a broad impact on society).

At the macro level, and this is the level of most ethical theory building to date, the concern is the "impact" of decisions on society, in a material and spiritual meaning of the word impact. These decisions often involve large groups of people and even complete institutional systems. In this case the administrator's activity is carried out in a context that requires loyalty *at least* to the organization one heads and its clientele, the chief executive one serves, and the basic values on which our democratic society is founded. The result is an amalgam of roles and identities; therefore, ethical dilemmas are infinitely complex because of the "open system" type of interaction involved. Spillover, or ripple effect, continues outward in an unrestricted way, and this means that it becomes extremely difficult, if not impossible, to comprehend the ultimate results of a choice or set of choices.

Any decision at the macro-ethical level has both positive and negative impacts. At the extreme this problem generates what Calabresi and Bobbitt (1978) call "tragic choices," where there is no way to avoid, for instance, determining that someone will die while another individual lives. If money is put into highway safety it cannot be spent on cancer research. The classic example is that of deciding who gets the use of kidney dialysis machines when there are not enough to go around to potential users. No matter how these questions are answered, and depending on the particular segments of society who are being considered or who are judging the decisions made by the public administrator, a "right" decision according to one individual may be "wrong" when judged by an opposing person. Such a situation can cause schizophrenia in all but the most secure egos.

Hugh Heclo describes the antithetical nature of the demands made on public administrators when he refers to the relative dilemmas of "obedience and independence, stability and adaptability, power and restraints on power, cooperation and resistance" (1977, 5) that require changeable balances rather than absolute solutions. The political appointee, as the top official of a federal department or agency, must achieve this changeable balance, especially in his or her relationship with the White House and the organization being administered because

too close identification with the White House restrict[s] the very effectiveness that . . . motivate[s] their appointment in the first place. [This creates] the inevitable dilemma of overcentralization. . . . "For the guy to be worth controlling, he has to know what is going on in his department. If he knows what's going on there, he's less likely to be amenable to central control.". . . . In short, to be of use to the White House, appointees had to be of use to the department. Their effectiveness depended on a selection process that permitted divided loyalties, or at least room to maneuver as both the President's man and the department's advocate. (1977, 97–98)

While they are resolving the problems of identity and role they must also remember that their ultimate loyalty should be attached to the goals and processes of the democratic system. In fact, many students of public administration argue that herein lies the answer to the dilemma of identity and role—if public officials base their identity and role on loyalty to democratic ideals this will tell them how to act. (This answer, however, is of limited utility because each situation is different and the answer is so broad that it is trite—as is often true at the macro level.)

The macro level of ethics applies formally, however, to a relatively small portion of the total bureaucracy. The micro level of public administrative ethics relates to the much larger number of bureaucrats—the careerists—who usually operate from the middle or lower levels of the public agency, and who exercise some power, but this power does not extend far beyond the individuals and their immediate environments. (What happens, of course, is that there is a shift in perspective; the change from macro to micro emphasis is not an either/or phenomenon.) The decisions made by this bureaucrat influence her perception of herself and her personal worth, and they also have an impact on the effectiveness of a segment of the overall organization; however, it is doubtful that the success or failure of the agency is in the balance since organizations often have built-in redundancies that guarantee overall success even though a single element fails in its mission.[4] Therefore, the level of ethical consideration is relatively limited, and usually includes the values of the decision maker and a recognizable set of factors surrounding the individual and the situation—the "ripple effects" do not appear to continue outward interminably. While the dilemma may be quite complex, it is more likely to be comprehendable and, to a certain extent, calculable because of its recognizable limits.

People at the middle levels of the bureaucracy seldom have great influence on the policies of their organizations; instead they are expected to carry out their tasks in an efficient and effective manner. The ethical problem that these individuals usually face are of three types: (1) they are pressured to carry out tasks that they consider to be wrong (for whatever reason); (2) they are asked to overlook wrong actions by someone else; or (3) they gain information that appears to be useful to the government in general or their organization in particular but cannot get anyone to listen to them. While these problems may have an impact on organization policies, the primary conflict that is created is one of personal integrity versus organizational pressure to conform; the results of these conflicts usually cause only minor ripples on the sea of public policy, although a large number of such cases might have a deleterious effect on the overall morale and sense of values among public employees and on the trust and respect for government held by the citizenry at large.

The analytic exercises and tools required for micro- or macro-ethical problems are quite different. When dealing with specific dilemmas, the situation is further confused by the fact that issues seldom fall at the two extremes of the continuum but instead fall somewhere along the continuum and thus require a combination of analytic styles and tools. For the larger questions that involve society as a whole, economic and/or quantitative approaches are useful because they allow one to deal with complexities in a way that cannot be accomplished by qualitative analysis. However, the quantitative approach to macro-ethical problems is woefully inadequate by itself; in every case there will be vital issues that are non-quantifiable and must be dealt with in the less esthetically pleasing but more realistic mode of value-laden debate about characteristics, attributes, causes, and cures. That is why the issue is political in the first place.

For the micro-level questions faced by the individual public administrator, the utility of economic or quantitative analytic approaches is practically nil. These types of analysis never arose in the interviews carried out with public managers for this research. Such an approach would have been totally inappropriate for such issues. In every case the issue had to be faced, analyzed, and resolved with very little help from other people as well as from any scientific tools. Nor are there ready-made answers for the analyst. In the cases discussed, the best—perhaps the only—help that was available for our protagonists was an increased sensitivity to the presence of an ethical dilemma and help in asking the right questions. This inherent sensitivity, and the ability to ask the right questions, came from personal preparation to deal with such issues. We turn next to this "set of questions" that proves so valuable.

TRYING TO COPE: THE QUESTIONS PUBLIC MANAGERS ASK

Since there are no "answers," public administrators must be especially sensitive to the presence of an ethical problem so that they may recognize and try to deal with it quickly and effectively. They are also looking for guidelines that determine how much analysis is necessary. Those public managers who were successful in addressing and handling ethical problems tended to have "sensitive antennae" that immediately tingled when a problem appeared that might have ethical overtones. They also had a basic, automatic response that guaranteed they would give such a problem at least minimal thought and analysis. The ultimate amount of time spent dealing with any particular ethical problem was determined by the importance of the issue, the impact that it had on them as individuals or on some larger segment of society, and the role they felt they must play. (Could they deal with the problem from their managerial role or did they have to shift to a leadership role as defined in Chapter 1?) However, immediateness of response was a vital factor in determining the seriousness of the problem. (Could they resolve it before it became a larger or major issue?) Immediateness was important in guaranteeing that their response got off on the right foot, thereby not complicating any future analysis or action. Their goal was to keep from making the matter worse than it had to be.

There is, of course, no clear-cut set of questions that should be asked in any ethical situation. Only one point can be made with a strong sense of assuredness: Any approach to analyzing an ethical problem that includes only one perspective, or the viewpoint of one part of an individual's personality, social setting, or professional life is doomed to be too narrow. We are complex individuals and we live in a pluralistic society; therefore, we all have multiple views of any problem, even if we are sometimes not willing to admit it. This recognition of "multiple selves" was, in fact, at the center of many of the ethical dilemmas faced by the practitioners. They recognized that answering a problem from the perspective of only one of their "selves" was almost certain to create serious problems for other parts of their identity. They had to take into consideration all parts of their personality, and that often meant working out a compromise so that the various parts of their psyche could live with whatever action was finally taken. This problem was multiplied by the fact that they had to move outside themselves and their individuality in order to consider their place in the bureaucratic and political world.

Since about 1950, shortly after most students of public administration rejected the politics/administration dichotomy, there has been steady development of a framework for individual ethical analysis. This framework has attempted to clarify the limits or boundaries of analysis, or to help individual public administrators understand what facets of the total "ethical picture" most be included in order to minimally address such questions. Kathryn Denhardt (1988) successfully and succinctly presents a summary of the development of this framework starting with Wayne A. R. Leys ([1952] 1968; 1952) and ending with a series of comprehensive treatments of ethics in the public sector by John Rohr (1978) and Terry Cooper (1986). This increasingly complex and sophisticated theory (see Table 2) started out with the recognition that an administrator must go beyond custom and tradition of the day to the core values of society. It also was apparent that external guidance and control could not fulfill all the needs of individual public administrators or the larger system. Part of the answer to ethical behavior must come from within the individual. In looking for appropriate guidance and control, a number of theories have been espoused, and each has emphasized a different facet of life, thought, and action in the public sector. The next five chapters deal with the issues raised by all of these theorists, but the discussion also tries to test these theories against the reality of management in the middle of the public bureaucracy. In other words, this study compares theory to reality and then tries to reconstruct, based on that comparison, a viewpoint toward ethical problems that will allow an individual to cope with them in the real bureaucratic world of insufficient knowledge and limited time.

Table 2
Stages in Development of Ethics Framework in Public Administration Literature

Once it became clear that ethical behavior must focus on individual action and analysis, a series of writers developed a continuously more complete and sophisticated framework for use in making and judging ethical decisions. The framework recognized that:

I. To be ethical requires that an administrator examine and question the standards by which administrative decisions are made rather than relying exclusively on custom and tradition (Leys [1968]; 1952).

II. Those standards should reflect to some degree the core values of society (Anderson, 1954).

III. Administrative standards will change as we achieve a better understanding of absolute moral standards (Golembiewski, 1965).

IV. There must remain a commitment to societal core values. The administrator must realize that ultimately s/he will be held professionally accountable (social check) for both the standards which inform decisions as well as for the decisions themselves (Hart, 1974; Henry 1989).

V. Social values must be personally understood and responded to by the administrator (Rohr, 1978); however, personal understanding of, and response to, the values of the organization within which the administrator works must be given equal weight in our organizational society where many of the basic values are interpreted and realized (Cooper, 1986).

THUS, we end with a definition that says, "Administrative ethics is a process of independently critiquing decision standards, based on core social values which can be discovered, within reasonable organizational boundaries which can be defined, subject to personal and professional accountability (p. 26)."

Source: This framework is condensed from Kathryn G. Denhardt, *The Ethics of Public Service: Resolving Moral Dilemmas in Public Organizations* (New York: Greenwood Press, 1988), pp. 4–27.

NOTES

I wish to give recognition to my colleague, Jeremy Plant, for his contribution to the ideas presented in this section.

1. It should be noted that the Watergate scandal and the Iran-Contra scandal were classic examples of what can happen to the bureaucracy. In both cases the individuals involved were appointed officials *outside the regular civil service*; however, the general public does not recognize this fine point and makes no differentiation between political officials and civil servants in the merit system. Therefore, public distrust of all public bureaucrats tends to carry over from such headline cases. There is much talk about "bureaucracy run amuck," which means "all those bureaucrats in Washington" to most citizens.

2. One wonders if a part of the responsibility for the loss of faith in our institutions of government, and leadership in particular, must not go to another institution of our society—the communications/news media. Would Lincoln have survived if the instant-communication system of today had existed in 1861–1864 and shown the carnage of the Civil War to every home each evening? Could Roosevelt or Kennedy have survived our current cynicism about the disclosure of the private behavior of leaders? It is unlikely. On the other hand, perhaps current leaders have simply not discovered the proper approach

to the new means of communication. The answer is debatable, but it raises another perspective, or interpretation, of the problems faced by leaders in the current society and of the difficulty in making controversial decisions.

3. One of the major areas of concern for the Federalists as they established the Constitution of the United States of America was the guarantee of procedures that would not only allow (limited) majority rule but would also protect the rights of minorities. Current Public Choice theorists, while they approach the issue from a specific and narrow perspective, are also addressing the issue of how to guarantee that interests can express their views and that those views can be weighted in a way that allows "proper" decisions about public policy.

4. If the failure is repeated throughout the various subsystems, or pieces, of the organization, the total agency may fail; but even then it is probably impossible to trace the failure to any one part of, or person in, the organization, so the level of personal responsibility for larger program success or failure is relatively limited.

CHAPTER 3

LOOKING IN THE MIRROR COMFORTABLY: PERSONAL ASPECTS OF ETHICAL DILEMMAS

The most important factors underlying the success of anyone attempting to operate in an ethical manner within the bureaucracy are the individual's personality (or characteristics), his or her self-understanding, and the ability to apply that understanding to the ongoing organizational context. This fact was unrecognized, and therefore not adequately dealt with, by the early writers on ethics in public administration.

Even now the discussion of public administrative ethics is often couched in terms created by the civil service or professional mentality; this, in turn, limits ethical discussion to issues such as avoiding conflict of interest, the nonacceptance of gifts, or protecting professional neutrality and objectivity. These issues are important, but they only begin to deal with the smaller, yet larger, ethical matters that must be faced by individual management decision makers (These issues are "smaller" because they relate specifically to the individual rather than broader segments of society; however, these issues are "larger" in that they are of utmost importance to the individual when he or she looks in the mirror and has to respect and like the person seen there.)

Public managers will be buffeted by numerous cross-pressures of varying strength. This is not an indictment of the world in which they work, it is simply a statement of fact. Public administration is inherently political and *must* be so. Self-awareness and self-understanding are essential in order to maintain a rational and effective stance in such an environment.

In such a political world, ethical dilemmas require objectivity, understanding of the costs and benefits involved in pursuing and resolving the issue, perseverance based on a clear commitment to the cause, and a willingness to accept

responsibility for their personal actions. Individuals may start on a moral crusade
before carefully analyzing their own capabilities and motivations in the particular
case, realizing what personal costs may be involved, and calculating whether or
not they want to and can withstand the pressures that will almost inevitably
follow from their actions. In order to answer these questions it is necessary to
know and clearly understand one's self—the kind of personality one has, the
individual values held and how they influence one's perceptions of the issue at
hand, the development of those values, and the way all of these factors influence
one's choice of when, where, and how to take a stand on ethical matters. Without
an answer to these questions, an individual may start a process of negotiation—
which can lead to confrontation—over an ethical issue and then find out she has
opened a can of worms with repercussions far beyond the expected and from
which she would like to withdraw. However, retreat often may be possible only
at considerable cost to one's dignity and/or career.

Self-understanding is probably the most difficult task *ever* placed before a
person, and it takes time. It does not occur through a blinding flash of sudden
illumination. Because of the difficulty of the task, it is essential not to wait until
an ethical problem has arisen to attempt self-analysis; the only way to be prepared
is to carry out this type of analysis prior to—in preparation for—the occasion
when it is needed.

It is impossible to be totally objective in self-analysis, although some individuals are much more objective than others; nonetheless, no one can totally
accomplish this state. Herein is one time-consuming facet of self-analysis and
self-understanding. It is necessary to turn to outsiders, individuals who are trained
in measuring and interpreting a variety of personal factors, in order for us to get
a clear and unbiased picture of ourselves, what drives us, and how we handle
the many pressures and influences surrounding us at all times.

And all of this development of self-understanding must occur before an ethical
problem arises; when it occurs, a problem will not wait for the person on the
griddle to call "time," search out appropriate help, and then come back to face
the issue. Once the ethical dilemma appears it must usually be solved in relatively
short order. Even if it drags on, which is a distinct possibility, and is the reason
for a commitment to perseverance where needed, it is still impossible to develop
the kind of understanding about one's personal values, perspectives, and habits
that is needed in the heat of a protracted battle. People may learn much about
themselves in retrospective analysis of such situations, (this is part of the "wisdom" developed with experience and maturity). But hindsight cannot change
the previous situation nor solve the next; it can help next time, but the next time
will be different, so only a portion of the knowledge gained in retrospective
analysis will apply to the new situation.

What are the personal characteristics to be understood, to what kind of individuals do they lead, and why are they so important? Let us turn for illumination
to the ideas of Stephen Bailey, who summarizes the characteristics necessary

among public servants, and York Willbern, who answers the question of why those characteristics are so important.

Bailey (1965), in his essay on "The Relationship between Ethics and Public Service," notes there are three essential mental attitudes and three moral qualities that must exist in all civil servants if they are to be successful in facing the numerous ethical dilemmas existing in the public service. Bailey's three mental attitudes are the recognition of: (1) moral ambiguity in all men and all public policies; (2) contextual forces which condition or affect moral priorities in the public service; and (3) the paradoxes of procedures.

First, every person is composed of a mixture of self-interest and altruism. This was recognized by the founders of the Constitution who created structures of government they hoped would help to compensate for this fact. The separation of powers written into the Constitution used the desire for power by the incumbents in each branch of government to serve as a check on the other branches.

Public policies are established to meet the public interest; however, special interests are also served in almost every case. Public servants serve in the public interest; they are also cognizant of what is in their personal interest or the interest of their friends, and the two cannot be totally separated. Policies and actions occur in a "gray area" that is neither totally good, ethical, and public interest oriented, nor absolutely bad, evil, and self-centered. Coming to such an awareness sometimes can be disillusioning, but it also allows a public servant to view the world realistically, thus avoiding the penchant for discovering frequent "holy causes" and/or being used by others.

Second, contextual forces change and as the context related to any policy or program changes so may the priorities of values and actions. It is often necessary to trade off one value or set of values for another that is currently more important or more important in another context. (This is often called "situational ethics.") It also should be recognized that as the context changes the current correct action might be wrong at another time. In fact, this contextual problem gets at the essence of an ethical dilemma as we have defined it in this book (see Chapter 1). The recognition of the contextual nature of ethics does not mean one has no basis from which ethical analysis and decision commences, and one should still have definite long-term goals in mind. It does mean we must look beyond the moment in order to achieve the larger and longer-range goals of society, the organization, and/or the individual. Flexibility in achieving those goals is then necessary. Rigid adherence to a set of values may destroy the opportunity to accomplish the greatest good.

Third, there is a paradox in following procedures. While it must be recognized that standard operating procedures are necessary for order, predictability, efficiency, and equity of treatment for all, feckless adherence to such procedures may destroy individuals, programs, policies, and ultimately deny the ability to achieve the public interest. At the same time we want protection from individualized, subjective, sometimes irrational decisions and actions on the part of superiors and public officials in general, we cannot become slaves to procedures at the expense of responsiveness to individual needs and the public will.

These three attitudes must be matched and supported by an equal number of basic values or moral qualities that are constants. These values, according to Bailey, are (1) optimism (2) courage, and (3) fairness tempered with charity. Optimism guarantees public servants will not give up either the search for the public interest or the ways to achieve it. Optimism is not the naive belief that all problems can be solved and "utopia is about to break out." Instead, we are talking about the belief that government can operate constructively, competently, and for the common good. Without such an attitude the public sector will probably be seen as a cynical world of conflict between self-centered power seekers.

Courage consists of the ability to do what is right even though it is difficult. Courage allows a civil servant to resist powers that might be turned against himself by those individuals guilty of self-centeredness. When something is obviously right a public servant must be able to act without fear; likewise, the action should be taken without expectation of favor. Numerous forces try to influence our actions—for example, politicians, special interests, competing organizations—and such influence must be considered, succumbed to when appropriate, and resisted in many cases. There must be a commitment to objectivity, due process, the law, and the public interest even though there is seldom a reward for performing in this manner.

Finally, fairness tempered with charity is described by Bailey as perhaps the most important moral quality of a public servant. While objectivity and due process must be observed, it is also essential to recognize individual differences. It is essential to maintain a balance between fairness to all and reaction to individual needs. "The public" is made up of individual citizens, so there must be a sense of compassion and we must have empathy even when it is impossible to feel sympathy.

And why are these characteristics so important for public servants? York Willbern (1984) answers this question by noting the types and levels of public morality needed and practiced by public servants. His taxonomy includes six increasingly complex levels of "morality" (ethical behavior as defined in this work) which must be recognized and dealt with by public administrators: (1) basic honesty and conformity to law; (2) conflicts of interest; (3) service orientation and procedural fairness; (4) the ethic of democratic responsibility; (5) the ethic of public policy determination; and (6) the ethic of compromise and social integration. The first two levels, which Willbern argues overlap with private morality, need no comment here; but the last four should be examined briefly since they address the importance of individual characteristics in public service ethics.

An acceptance of a *service orientation and procedural fairness* must exist because of the nature of the public service function. "Attitudes and the tone and flavor of official behavior are morally significant" (1984, 105). Government officials having and exercising power can easily become arrogant, secretive, and concerned about their convenience rather than that of the clients they serve. This emphasis on authority rather than service can dangerously affect citizens' attitudes toward government.

In addition, public servants must remember they serve a complex society where agreement on policies seldom exists, groups commonly oppose one another, and winners and losers are inevitable. In such a case there must be a clear acceptance of the procedures as fair or once again there will be an erosion of faith and trust in the government.

The ethic of democratic responsibility requires public servants to carry out the will of the people; however, what the people want is often unclear, sometimes flies in the face of the knowledge of experts, and often conflicts depending on which powerful voices from the community are heard. In such cases the public servant must be responsive to democratic control and his political superiors, but such responsiveness will not answer many important questions about solutions. Both public servants and political leaders sometimes need to make decisions based on factors other than the latest Gallup poll. Thus public servants, in order to be truly responsive, must be able to balance public desires with the knowledge, standards, and values of society and their professions in order to achieve the long-term goals of society.

The penultimate level of ethical behavior is *the ethic of public policy determination*. Determining what a particular program attempts to achieve and how government will go about accomplishing it often depends very little on technical and quantitative information—indeed, if technical information is available and accepted by all sides public policy debate is greatly decreased—but instead depends on qualitative factors and their interpretation based on human values. This conflict continues at all levels of formulation and implementation, therefore the public servant must be an active participant in the debate. Decisions about interpretation of the general policy statement, procedures established to carry them out, and the equity with which benefits and costs are distributed are often made primarily by the bureaucrat, and these are inescapably moral judgements. We are dealing, at this level, primarily with how things are to be done, not with what cannot be done. Laws restricting conflicts of interest and guaranteeing proper procedures for expenditure of funds generally do not address these proactive questions (although they may place limits on what alternatives are open). Public servants must act in this value-laden environment.

Finally, Willbern notes that public servants must operate with an *ethic of compromise and social integration*. "To some morality means uncompromising adherence to principle" (1984, 107), but the difficult question often is "whose principle?" While some ultimate principle may exist, all parts of society have not discovered it even though they often think they have. Therefore, there is a danger of intransigence and fractionation by all of those different holders of the truth. Willbern, quoting T. V. Smith, puts it this way:

The world is full of saints, each of whom knows the way to salvation, and the role of the politician is that of the sinner who stands at the crossroad to keep saint from cutting the throat of saint. This may possibly be the highest ethical level of the public servant (1984, 108).

Politics, at least in our Western society, covers the areas where values are not unanimously held, and therefore "it is necessary upon occasion to rise above principle and make a deal" (1984, 107–108). However, one can make such deals only if s/he has a very sophisticated understanding of social, organizational, and personal values. The compromises must occur only when they are necessary, accomplish their mission, and protect the greater good of society.

Writers on public administration ethics have increasingly stressed the need to depend on the individual public servant. This was a major theme of the New Public Administration movement of the 1960s and 1970s (Marini 1971), and it continues as a focus of debate on ethics within the profession. But little time and effort on our part have gone into describing how that individual comes into being. We have left this consideration to experts such as the psychologists, sociologists, educators, and theologians.

While any list of individual factors influencing one's ethical nature must be incomplete, there are three particularly important theories: personal background (family, religious beliefs, and educational experience); personality characteristics; and ethical maturity, that are essential to understanding how we decide what is an ethical dilemma and how we make ethical decisions. We shall then see how these theories apply to our real-world administrators.

BACKGROUND INFLUENCES

Three background influences—family, religious beliefs, and education—determine much about when and how we perceive and react to ethical dilemmas. We refer to these as background influences because they work in subtle ways and are often not recognized. Even when we recognize these factors in our friends and colleagues, we forget these same characteristics exist in ourselves. Self understanding must start with personal history.

There is an old adage in politics, "If you want to know how a person votes, find out how his parents voted." While that is not as good a test as it once was, there is still a lot of truth in it; at least, there is no doubt our political perceptions and values begin from that base. The same thing may be said of family influence in determining how an individual perceives and handles ethical problems. Thus we should address the question of how our family background, and its influence on beliefs, perspectives, and habits, affects our current ability to face ethical dilemmas. Our reactions to law and authority, to situations that require an understanding of what is "right" and "wrong," and to opportunities for self-aggrandizement (especially at the cost of others), are created in the home. By watching those around us, especially our parents, and to a certain extent our extended family, we learn what is "accepted behavior" and "how one should act when placed in uncomfortable positions."

The ideas generated at this early age form the basis from which our moral development occurs. Actually development only peripherally depends upon the family, nonetheless, the family creates the "first impressions" from which we then develop as we move into our adult life (Kohlberg 1976, 104). For example, on the negative side, research has shown that battered children are more likely to grow up to be abusive parents, and children from broken homes are more likely to experience divorce when they marry. On a more positive note, those children who have observed an interest in, and an adherence to, consistently ethical behavior on the part of their parents are more likely to have the same kind of demeanor as adults. Such an environment certainly more often includes at least a rudimentary level of ethical training for the child. When discussing "moral development," a subject covered later in this chapter, Lawrence Kohlberg noted that "children who were advanced in moral judgement had parents who were also advanced in moral judgement" (ibid.).

The important point for an individual to examine when looking back at early influences on his or her personality is not the presence or lack of such examples and training, since both examples and training usually exist to some degree, but instead to attempt to understand how the nuances (differences that exist but are not blatant or whose presence may not even be easily recognizable) of family life may have helped to shape his or her sensitivity to ethical issues and may have created unexamined assumptions about how to proceed in dealing with them. In other words, we need to move back through our reasoning process to find out where we stop being aware of our stance toward ethical issues. Probably we can never uncover all of our basic assumptions; however, to the extent that we can, we have made a tremendous stride in being able to address the basic factors creating our perspectives, values, and personality.

Another source of basic assumptions is our individually held beliefs (e.g., religious, social, and political beliefs). These beliefs begin to develop early in life, and they create a "point of view" from which one looks at the world.[1] The stronger the beliefs the more specific and firm will be the set of basic assumptions about many kinds of issues including ethical ones. For example, in the United States, where we value the separation of church and state, it is quite possible for an individual who holds strong religious beliefs to be placed in a position of conflict when public policy differs from the tenets of his or her religious faith.[2] Reinhold Niebuhr ([1932] 1960), for example, argues that religious values and those required for political decisions and actions are often quite different. In such a situation an individual must decide whether political or religious tenets are higher on his hierarchy of values. If religious values come first, a decision must be made as to what role the individual can play in the public bureaucracy as it relates to the issue at hand.

Generally the problem is not that stark. Instead any influence from individually held beliefs plays a much more subtle role in determining how we view the world, but the influence is there just the same. The essential point is to be aware of the influence and to recognize how it might affect the way we think about ethical dilemmas and the way we react to them. What is discovered in such an analysis may be negative or positive. In the first instance the analysis should clarify one's value system in such a way that it is possible to avoid taking stances ultimately proven to be personal and outside the realm of public discourse. The second, positive result from analysis will guarantee that one can feel sure of his or her position and "hold on" even if caught in a protracted situation or struggle.

Popular views assume that home and religion are the primary factors in moral development; however, Kohlberg's (1976) studies found the most important factor was "the provision of role-taking opportunities," and these were presented in a number of social situations. While the home is important, one's peer groups, the school, and the wider society also present many such opportunities. "Religion and religious education . . . do not appear to play any unique role in moral development" (104–105).

Thus, it is necessary to complete our triumvirate of early influences on individuals by noting the importance (but again not overstating it) of the educational system in developing one's current perspective of the world and its ethical phenomenon. School experiences help to form our self-concept. According to Segal and Yahraes, "the teacher's impact on [a child's world view] can be enormous" (1978, 205). Early in the school experience children's perceptions of their capacities and competencies take hold, and those self-images may be explicit or implicit influences on people for the rest of their lives. Experiences with peers also help to determine how individuals handle various types of social interaction, especially pressures for conformity. This kind of pressure, both from teachers and peers, continues throughout one's schooling; in later life this is precisely what is meant by "the socialization process" that goes on in any professional school.

Any attempt at self-understanding, to be useful in helping an individual cope with ethical problems, must deal with peer groups, the school, and society; however, Segal and Yahraes agree with Kohlberg that

it is rarely mother alone, father alone, schools alone, friends alone—any one factor alone— that shapes the destiny of the child. From birth onward, children are affected by a mosaic of forces. While one or another element may stand out in the case of a particular child, it is typically a combination of them that ultimately leaves its mark. (1978, 303)

What is true for the child is doubly true for the adult. In fact Erik Erikson (Gale 1969; Schott 1986 and 1987; Bailey 1987), a leading developmental psychologist, claims that we progress through eight stages in becoming a whole, well-socialized person (see Table 3). Each step occurs at a different point of life, and the significant others change in each of the stages. Of course many people do not make it through all of the stages, and unless an individual has achieved the integrity of the eighth level it is likely that s/he will feel uncomfortable in a truly democratic setting. The hurly-burly of the democratic environment requires a strong sense of personal identity, independence, trust, and willingness to face new and challenging situations; if we do not have that kind

Table 3
Eight Stages of Socialization

Learning Trust Versus Mistrust: The well-nurtured child develops trust and security. The opposite result leads to insecurity and mistrust.

Learning Autonomy Versus Shame: While learning to deal with basic bodily functions the well-trained child develops self-assertion and some autonomy. The opposite result leads to shame.

Learning Initiative Versus Guilt: The healthy child learns to broaden social skills and imagination, to lead, to follow, and to cooperate. The opposite result leads to dependence upon adults and poor development of social skills and imagination.

Learning Industry Versus Inferiority: Upon entering school the successful child wins recognition for productivity, work becomes pleasurable and perseverance is rewarded. The opposite result leads to a sense of inadequacy and inferiority.

Learning Identity Versus Role Diffusion: While moving into adulthood, the individual develops an identity, a self-concept, that corresponds with others' ideas. The opposite result creates an uncertain confusion about one's place in the world, with an accompanying uncertainty of appropriate behavior.

Learning Intimacy Versus Isolation: Once assured of identity, the individual is capable of experiencing the intimacy of an enduring relationship. It is possible to completely abandon one's self with no fear of losing one's identity. The opposite result creates a fear of self-abandonment and a feeling of isolation.

Learning Generativity Versus Self-Absorption: The individual is willing to accept responsibilities and is able to work productively and creatively. The opposite result is self-absorption, stagnation, and perhaps regression to an earlier stage.

Integrity Versus Despair: Having faced the previous seven psychosocial crises, the mature adult reaches the peak of adjustment--integrity. S/he trusts, is independent, dares to explore new experiences, and can be intimate without strain, regret, or lack of realism. S/he has a well-defined role in life, and a self-concept with which s/he is happy, works hard, and is proud of what s/he creates. In essence, this individual is achieving the fulfillment of self. If one or more of the earlier psychosocial crises have not been resolved, however, one may view one's life with disgust and despair.

Source: Paraphrased from Raymond F. Gale, *Developmental Behavior: A Humanistic Approach* (New York: Macmillan, 1969), pp. 256–258.

of personal strength we tend to look for easy answers to hard problems, hide behind slogans, and bury ourselves in "causes" so that our world has sufficient stability, connectivity, and continuity to protect us from the perceived dangers of anomie and anarchy.

The work of other developmental psychologists (Gould 1978; Levinson 1978; Vaillant 1977) supports and builds on the findings of Erikson. Richard Schott, in a review of the work of these writers, arrives at the conclusion that

there must be a relationship between developmental maturity and managerial capacity. How can an executive who is mired in the frustrations of say, developing intimacy, understand and relate to the psychological environment and dynamics of an individual who has successfully completed the individuation process of middle-life? Good management is based on, among other things, a capacity for empathy and the ability to divine where an individual is "at" in terms of his or her needs and motivations. (1986, 665)

Schott's statement is strongly supported by Michael Maccoby's research in which he analyzes a large number of leaders in both public and private fields and in which he finds that successful leaders tend to share

a caring, respectful and responsible attitude; flexibility about people and organization structure; and a participative approach to management, the willingness to share power. Furthermore, they are self-aware, conscious of their weaknesses as well as strengths, and concerned with self-development for themselves as well as others. (1981, 221)

Analysis of these three factors is only a beginning step (albeit an important one) in developing the type of self-understanding that is required in order for individuals to comprehend their background and to understand how it might influence the way they handle an ethical dilemma when it appears. Self-understanding starts here, with a careful analysis of how we got to the present point in time and personality/character development. Once this step has been accomplished, we must move to two additional personal factors that provide a better understanding of individuals' abilities to comprehend and handle ethical situations. Bureaucrats are likely to bury themselves in their organizations, follow the rules, and seldom think independently about the important social, economic, and political issues facing their organization.

CURRENT PERSONAL CHARACTERISTICS

Just as ethical situations differ in complexity and seriousness, people are differently prepared to face ethical problems. Individual perceptions, thinking processes, temperaments, and action modes vary, which means no two people will face the same ethical dilemma in quite the same way. It is not necessarily true that "something is wrong" if we do not agree with or act like other people, nor can we automatically condemn those differences. For example, Keirsey and Bates (1984) emphasize that people differ in fundamental ways. They want different things and have different motives, purposes, aims, values, needs, drives, impulses, and urges in everyday life. People perceive, think, cognize, conceptualize, understand, and therefore *believe* differently. And of course individuals' manners, the way they act and emote, differ radically since they are governed by wants and beliefs.

Since this is true, students of personality, such as Keirsey and Bates, argue that it is necessary to understand one's self *and to understand how other important individuals may react when faced with a thorny ethical situation.*[3] This is the second major step in the project of "knowing ourselves." One of the ways several of the individuals interviewed for this research maintained their equanimity was by occasionally stepping back and analyzing the situation from an objective point of view—recognizing, upon analysis, the similarities in their own actions and in the overall occurrences, to those expected according to studies done by others who were expert in human behavior. At a point where they began to feel overwhelmed by the situation, it was comforting to realize that such occurrences were not totally unique and that, in most cases, the scenario was within "the realm of the expected." This even allows an occasional laugh at one's self, and such an experience can be especially healing to frazzled nerves. Such analysis requires, however, knowledge of several sets of personalities (one's self, significant others outside the organization, and one's peers, subordinates, and superiors within the relevant bureau), and such understanding must be developed *prior* to any crisis. Knowledge about personality and its influence on the handling of ethical crises may be extended during the crisis; but unless the foundation already exists, there will be no chance for expansion of understanding.

According to Jung (1923), all conscious mental activity can be classified into four categories, two dealing with perception (sensing and intuition) and two dealing with judgment (thinking and feeling). Everyone possesses all four types of capacity; however, each individual will have a preferred style of perceiving and making judgements. *Sensors*, as the name infers, tend to depend on the senses for perception and to focus on the immediate, real, observable facts of experience. *Intuitives*, on the other hand, use hunches and insight to perceive possibilities, meanings, and the relationships inherent in situations.

After the new information is assimilated through one's perceiving process, judgments about what has been perceived must be made, and the second mental function, the thinking-feeling continuum takes over. In psychological terms, *thinkers* use logical analysis and look at cause and effect when making decisions. *Feelers*, those at the opposite end of the spectrum, depend on personal values and convictions as the criteria upon which they focus when making judgments or decisions about that which they perceive (Hrezo et al. 1987).

Keirsey and Bates (1984) carry the idea of personality types one step further and present a set of "character and temperament types" (see Table 4) that are extremely useful in understanding not only how people will comprehend and analyze a problem, but how they tend to be motivated and behave in the work environment. It is not wise, they warn, to assume blithely that you are a member of any of these categories; instead, it is necessary to go through some self-analysis and perhaps seek the help of experts in the interpretation of the available tests in order to fully comprehend how you fit and what that means. It is especially important not to oversimplify the meaning of these kinds of categorizations and to place a normative emphasis on the results, while remembering there is no "right" or "wrong" category—each simply exists.

Based on the theories and concepts of Jung, and Keirsey and Bates, think of the difficulty that might arise in any organization if ten people were forced to work out a critical ethical dilemma together. Depending on the particular cross section of personality types present in the group, there might be a wide variety

Table 4
Personality Types

Dionysian: Impulsive, active and short-term oriented (living in the present) individual who values freedom and variation in life. Not so interested in the end product as in the process. Has a high esprit de corps and is fiercely loyal to compatriots, but in an equalitarian way.

Epimethean: Duty-bound individual who desires above all else the sense of belonging earned through service to the group. This sense of obligation leads to an acceptance of hierarchical authority and rules and regulations. There is a strong commitment to the group, but believes it is best served by maintaining the organizational heritage and tradition.

Promethean: Competence-seeking individual who tends to constantly question authority and seek new information. Expects the same search for knowledge and excellence in others. The emphasis is on finding the truth and achieving "progress," even if these goals may cause discomfort for others. Focuses on the future and desires to rearrange the environment. The focus on "knowing" often makes this person oblivious to the emotional responses of others. These characteristics make this individual appear to be less loyal to the group.

Apollonian: Immersed in "the search for self," this individual is wrapped up in the never-to-be-fulfilled process of "becoming." The important goal is the search, not the success of the search. The emphasis is on attempting to develop an identity and to achieve self-realization. It is necessary to make a difference in the world. Life is a drama and everything has a heightened sense of meaning. Relationships are of extreme importance. Because of a heightened sense of empathy, this person may appear to be whatever the beholder wants to see. Therefore, the charge that this individual is a social, political, and intellectual butterfly may appear to be justified.

Source: This material is summarized from David Keirsey and Marilyn Bates, *Please Understand Me: Character and Temperament Types* (Del Mar: Prometheus Nemesis Books, 1984).

of perceptions and proposed outcomes. Not only would each individual's approach to the problem be different, but the group's ability to communicate and empathize with one another would be severely restricted unless they were able to comprehend "where the other people were coming from."

To further clarify these theories, let us consider a hypothetical case—similar in many ways to some of the situations described during the interviews carried out for this research—in order to see how this kind of model, and the insight it gives us about significant others, can help in dealing with an ethical problem when it arises.

- After some self-analysis, you understand that you tend to operate in the Promethean mode—you tend to seek competence, knowing the facts and how they "fit into the big picture," and you believe in changing organizational rules and regulations so progress can be made toward achieving your vision of the bureau at some future point.
- It has come to your attention that a serious disservice is being done to the bureau's constituency because the environment in which you work has changed; however, the bureau is in a sensitive position where it needs general public support, there has been no change in the law authorizing the work of the agency, and there is—as of yet—no public outcry for change.
- It is clear to you that your superior tends to operate in an Epimethean manner. She accepts the bureau structure as it exists and makes an extreme effort to serve the bureau

and its current mission as she understands it. She is extremely proud of the heritage and tradition of the bureau.

- At the same time, your immediate subordinate is an Apollonian, interested in the search for self, and empathetic to the clients when talking to them about the problem faced— but also very deferential to you and your supervisor.
- What do you do? How can you make sure the information you have is acted on, and everyone will work together to solve the problem?

There is no easy answer, but an understanding of the personality characteristics of the actors may help resolve the problem because it allows one to find a way to deal with the differing perceptions and behavior patterns of all of the actors, *including yourself*. The inability to understand yourself and your immediate coworkers could lead to all sorts of complications. You might, for example, interpret the normal, expected responses of your two coworkers as an apparent lack of good faith by your subordinate and inexcusable intransigence by your boss, and this would be a misreading of both of them. Such a misreading could very easily lead to confrontations and ill will and destroy the possibility of any further cooperation in solving the problem. A knowledge of your and their perceptions, analytic styles, and behavior in and toward such a situation may be an essential step in allowing you to deal adequately with the ethical dilemma and reducing some of the trauma. There will often be enough trauma without making the situation worse because of needless misunderstandings.

Above all, however, these authors believe personal understanding is the essential key to success in perception of the problem and in working through it with others. It is essential to know: whether you perceive issues as clearly "black and white" or "in shades of gray"; whether you feel closely bound to tradition (especially regulations and the hierarchy of the organization) or you feel free to work for change in both; how you react to pressure; how you deal with the "humanity" of others—especially their lack of competence and failures; and how willing you are to recognize the need for, and the possibility of, compromise. While it is often possible to understand others—to realize "what makes them tick"—and you may use that understanding to try to influence their perceptions and choices, it is both impossible and improper to totally control their actions. The only factor you can have relatively total control over is yourself—your attitudes and how you act.

MORAL/ETHICAL MATURITY

Well-meaning people of good will often disagree dramatically about specific ethical situations. Their interpretation of, and their reaction to, a dilemma may be quite different. Personal backgrounds and personalities help to explain this phenomenon. However, another important factor in explaining this difference is what Lawrence Kohlberg calls "moral maturity." Kohlberg's model of moral maturity is somewhat controversial; however, it is an extension of other theories

Table 5
The Stages of Moral Maturity

Pre-Conventional

--An orientation to punishment and reward, and to physical and material power. Morality is defined by avoiding punishment or being rewarded.

--A hedonistic orientation with an instrumental view of human relations, and some sense of reciprocity and exchange of favors. Morality is meeting one's interests and living up to an agreement.

Conventional

--A "good person" orientation in which one seeks to maintain expectations and win approval from one's group. Morality is defined by individual ties and relationships.

--An orientation to authority, law, and duty. Morality is maintaining a fixed order, whether social or religious, which is assumed to be the primary value.

Principled or Post-Conventional

--An orientation to "the social contract." Morality is based on the protection of rational social utility--in the United States, the individual rights granted by the democratically established order.

--The acceptance of a morality based on self-chosen principles which are applied universally. Value is defined in terms of equal respect for all human personality. Likewise, principles of justice are based on the fundamental equal worth of individuals. The social contract, important in the fifth stage, is seen as deriving from, or establishing, such principles of justice.

Source: Paraphrased from Lawrence Kohlberg, "Children's Perceptions of Contemporary Values," in Nathan Talbot, ed., *Raising Children in Modern America: Problems and Perspective Solutions* (Boston: Little, Brown, 1976), pp. 98–118.

(John Dewey 1932; Jean Piaget 1932, 1960, 1972) of human intellectual and social development, and it paints a picture of another facet of the individual that is necessary to understand when analyzing ethical dilemmas faced by middle managers.

Central to Kohlberg's study of moral maturity, or as he sometimes refers to it, "moral psychology," is the belief in a set of universal human ethical values and principles. The key word, according to Kohlberg, is "principles" because a moral principle is not the same as a rule. People obey rules, but the rules are based on principles.

"Thou shalt not commit adultery" is a rule for specific behavior in specific situations, in a monogamous society. By contrast, the categorical imperative (act only as you would be willing that everyone should act in the same situation) is a principle—not a prescription for behavior, but a guide for choosing among behaviors. As such it is free from culturally defined content; it both transcends and subsumes particular social laws and hence has universal applicability. (1976, 100)

According to Kohlberg's research, individuals progress through six stages of moral judgement (see Table 5). Two important factors must be noted in using this categorization of moral development. First, people operate at different levels within this hierarchy at various phases of their lives, just as Erikson noted, at a more general level, that people developed through a series of stages. Stages one and two, described as "preconventional," are typical of children and delinquents, and are based on self-interest and material considerations. Obviously, some people never evolve beyond this stage. Our prisons are full of such individuals; many more, including, for example, some who work in corporate finance and our various stock and commodity markets, live by this rule but have not gone to prison for it.

Stages three and four, described as "conventional," are the ones at which most of the adult population operates. The fifth and sixth stages, described as "principled," are achieved by relatively few people. According to Kohlberg, these last two stages were "characteristic of about 10 to 20 percent of the adult population, with perhaps 5 percent arriving at Stage 6" (1976, 101). While there may be an implicit value judgement in Kohlberg's statement, no explicit claim is made for one level as "right" and the other "wrong" or of lesser value. He simply states a fact: People fall across this continuum, with most adults in the conventional stage.

Second, as one moves upward from stage one to stage six, each level represents a progressively more sophisticated view of the world and an ability on the part of the individual to recognize the complexity of both the problem faced and the available alternatives. If someone is only able to recognize and react to approval from one's group (stage three), there is no use attempting to present an ethical or moral argument to that person from the perspective of self-chosen universal principles based on the fundamental equal worth of individuals (stage six). Such an effort will be frustrating, and perhaps dangerous, because the effort will often be misinterpreted as wrong-headed and possibly subversive to values held dear by the individual being addressed. It is possible in such situations for one's keen interest in and devotion to the organization, albeit at a higher level of abstraction, to be misinterpreted as disloyalty. In the opposite direction, an argument from someone at a lower stage of moral development will probably be seen as simple-minded and not carry much weight with someone who has surpassed that level.

If these theories are applied to organizations, it can be seen that many arguments about ethical issues in organizations result in what appears to be an unresolvable impasse because of the different perceptions of individuals who are involved. This is not to say one is right because he is "morally superior" and the other wrong because she is operating at a lower moral stage. The point is that these individuals may (1) perceive the major issues as totally different factors, (2) interpret those issues using different values, and (3) talk past each other, with both imagining they are making telling arguments while neither is actually touching on points of importance to the other. Understanding the level of moral sophistication existent among those around you is exceedingly useful in such a case. Such knowledge can be critical in getting the feuding parties to resolve the dilemma they face or to achieve a mutually meaningful solution.

Wise management requires an understanding of the difficulties caused by the differences in the level of moral maturity. The perceptions and reactions of individuals involved in any ethical dilemma will determine much about the role a manager must play. Success in resolving the situation faced will require working through the problem by a combination of empathy with other people and translation of the problem to the appropriate level of sophistication for them.

By combining the self-analytic elements discussed above (personal background, personality, and moral maturity), the middle manager arrives at a deeper understanding of certain features of what is often blithely referred to as "management style." (Of course, there is much more to "management style" than the characteristics discussed here.) Not only does one end up better understanding one's self, but a whole new set of factors can now be used to develop an understanding of: (1) superiors, to whom one is accountable; (2) peers/colleagues, with whom one must cooperate; and (3) subordinates, for whom one must act as leader. Hopefully, this knowledge will help to create an environment of trust throughout the organization. Organizations without trust (belief in the ethical nature of coworkers is *one* central element of trust in the larger universe of public bureaucratic life) cannot function efficiently, effectively, and productively. As William Ouchi (1982) notes, trust is central to productivity (the goal of all organizations, public or private) because trust allows subtlety. *Subtlety* is the characteristic most important in working with people.

Relationships between people are always complex and changing. A [manager] who knows his workers well can pinpoint personalities, decide who works well with whom, and thus put together work teams of maximal effectiveness. These subleties can never be captured explicitly, and any bureaucratic rule will do violence to them. . . . Productivity, trust and subtlety are not isolated elements. Not only do trust and subtlety yield greater productivity through more effective coordination, trust and subtlety are inextricably linked to each other. . . . A decision made for subtle reasons is a decision that will not stand up to the crude scrutiny of an uninformed outsider (e.g., a higher-up manager, another agency or a union). . . . In [any] case, a lack of trust between parties will end up requiring that subtlety be thrown overboard in the face of the need for explicitly defensible decisions and actions. (Ouchi 1982, 6–7)

Subtlety goes with sensitivity, and sensitivity to ethical problems is easier to maintain when the presence of subtlety is recognized and valued. Even if others are not subtle in the sense Ouchi is discussing, it is important to attempt to maintain that capability in one's self, and sensitivity is possible only when we understand our own personal characteristics as they apply in the organizational context and with those whom we interact regularly.

THE IMPORTANCE OF SELF-UNDERSTANDING IN THE REAL WORLD

The theories discussed above help describe and explain the perceptions and actions of the public managers interviewed for this study. They were aware of and sensitive to the various factors mentioned although in many cases they had no formal training or analysis in some of the specific areas developed here. Let us consider each of the factors we have discussed.

Family and religious values were almost never mentioned in the initial description of the cases presented by the interviewed managers. Once asked about such influences most managers responded that these factors were undoubtedly present and influenced their perceptions; however, family and religious influences were far enough removed from the issues being considered that the managers were not cognizant of their impact. No one discounted the importance of such factors, however, because they realized it is often hard to recognize and measure such variables.

In one case, that of a black woman who was a professional employee in a program working with nutrition programs (see the case in Chapter 4), these two factors did play a more central role. She noted both her family and her religious training, which had continued through her undergraduate education (for she went to a college affiliated with her church), had created for her a very strong set of values especially related to the importance of helping powerless people develop themselves as part of society. Her professional training in nutrition also reinforced these values, and when she found her organization not upholding these values she felt compelled to fight to bring the program into compliance with the laws that emphasized help to these categories of people.

Once she had entered into the battle over her unserved clients she also recognized the importance of her religious values and her family ties in helping her survive through the protracted conflict that followed her questioning of agency policies. She noted that the ability to "retreat into the calmness, understanding, and reinforcement of both my family and my religious faith allowed me to recover from the tension and enervation that are natural to such a drawn-out confrontation."

Education was recognized as an important element in the recognition and solution of ethical problems. Graduate and professional education were the specific locations of training in ethics; several of the individuals interviewed noted that they had, within their graduate or professional education, taken courses related to ethics or been in an educational environment where ethics and values were stressed. Typical of these comments was one by a lawyer faced with a situation where her prime witness was being pressured, by his supervisor, to alter testimony in a regulatory case (see the case in Chapter 7). When trying to stop what was obviously illegal witness tampering in a way that would meet the needs of the case while also meeting the needs of the individual involved and of the regulatory organization, the lawyer said that she was inevitably drawn back to her course on the ethics of law and the legal profession to help her determine what to do.

Typical of comments by managers was that of an individual faced with figuring out what to do with an employee who had been promoted in the past although it was obvious she was not competent to do the work to which she was assigned (see the case in Chapter 5). This manager noted that,

Eighteen months before this situation arose, I had taken a course on ethics in graduate school. It helped immensely because it helped me to think through my responsibilities as a public manager and it forced me to consider my own personal values within the public context.

And he knew what drove him as an individual and understood his management style because he commented:

My own personal values informed me as I went along. My style was very open and driven by a pretty literal interpretation of the laws, rules, and regulations; however, I wanted to be recognized as fair, generous, honest.

Another individual who had attended a military academy and served in the armed services as an officer prior to becoming a civil servant commented that both the socialization of the academy and the formal education later received in graduate school influenced his actions:

I went to a military academy. Honor was stressed there, and it has become one of my central values. Further courses in graduate school have reinforced my understanding of that and other values by strengthening my intellectual understanding of their importance in addition to the informal inculcation that occurred at the academy.

In each case these individuals believed their education, especially in ethics, strengthened their ability to face ethical dilemmas and make appropriate decisions. Several other interviewees commented that their education, often through at least one graduate degree, had been valuable because it increased their level of sophistication when faced with such issues. They were able to spot the numerous, often not immediately recognizable, factors that had to be dealt with in these situations. (It should be noted also that most interviewees felt *experience*—having gone through a variety of situations in diverse environments—was of equal importance in dealing with ethical dilemmas. This is the "wisdom of experience.")

Somewhat surprisingly, none[4] of the individuals interviewed had ever had any training courses on ethics *within the government*. In a few cases ethics had been subsumed within some other more specific subject in which they had received training; however, they had participated in no formal training sponsored by the government specifically focusing on ethics.

Very few of the interviewees had participated in any formal kind of "personality analysis" (such as having taken the Myers-Briggs Test). Only three of the individuals involved in the cases presented throughout this book had participated in such self-analysis. Still these individuals demonstrated an understanding of "what made them tick." An amazing level of self-understanding was present, although responses to questions did not often elicit the jargon of the professional analysts. This can be best emphasized by presenting an example case.

Bob Fellows had been brought in as the "new broom to sweep clean" after the particular Air Force office in question had gone through successive very bad reviews. The previous civilian personnel officer had been fired and Bob was brought in to clean house. He had a reputation for being hardnosed. Bob recognized the validity of the description of one of his subordinates who said "Bob was firm but fair."

Things were beginning to fall into shape. Bob was able to start installing management systems, performance standards, and making other changes. Many of the staff had markedly improved their performance on the job. One GS 12 branch chief, however, was a problem. Wayne had been in that office since the operation had opened, and he was a good example of the Peter Principle in that he was a very earnest and conscientious person, but he did not have what it took to manage that particular operation. The handwriting was on the wall. As distasteful and difficult as the task was, Bob was going to have to start proceedings to fire Wayne.

Wayne also saw the handwriting; therefore, he came in one day and said, "Look Bob. I can see what is happening here. We are getting ready to act out the lines of a Greek tragedy. There is no way that I am going to be able to satisfy you, and what you are doing is apparently what your superiors want you to do. I had better make tracks. However, I know that unless I get a decent reference from you, I am not going to get a job elsewhere. Will you give me a good recommendation?"

Thus Bob faced a dilemma that often occurs for supervisors in the bureaucracy. Here was a chance to get rid of an employee whose work was unsatisfactory. All he had to do was give Wayne a good reference when some other organization offered him a job. The reference request from the prospective employer, however, would ask a number of detailed questions about this employee's performance. In its starkest terms, the dilemma was that if Bob gave Wayne an honest evaluation, that would be a bad reference which would kill his chances of getting the job. Thus Bob would still have Wayne to deal with, and it would mean creating a "federal case" to get rid of him. On the other hand, if Bob gave Wayne a favorable evaluation, even a generally favorable one, so he was likely to get the job he was seeking, Bob would have perpetuated the employment of an ineffective employee in the government.

A second problem also faced Bob as he decided what to do. If Bob damned Wayne's work with faint praise, he risked a backlash from Wayne, who under the freedom of information rules could find out what Bob had said. Wayne might very well come after Bob with a grievance or a complaint and make serious trouble for Bob and/or the organization. At best, the poor recommendation could only exacerbate the problem that currently existed by lowering Wayne's morale.

Finally, Wayne was well known around the installation—he had "been there forever"—and was well liked by his subordinates and the other employees. Any action that was seen as harsh or retributive against Wayne would undoubtedly have a spillover effect on the other employees, perhaps even to the extent of undoing some of the positive steps that had been taken to improve performance.

By this time Bob and Wayne had been through several iterations of Wayne's shortcomings and how he could overcome them. The two men had maintained a positive relationship in spite of the fact that Bob had been quite critical of Wayne's performance. This permitted them to be very candid and "put their cards on the table." Bob's comment was, "One thing was working here—he [Wayne] was a decent man. So I was looking for a way to treat the guy fairly without being open to subsequent criticism for not giving him an accurate evaluation."

After discussing the issue completely, and then thinking about the situation for some time, Bob worked out what he thought was an honorable compromise. He responded to Wayne's request by saying, "I have no problem in giving you a positive recommendation if you have demonstrated the competence to do the job for which you have applied. I will not lie on a reference, but if you are applying for a non-supervisory position—one that does not entail supervisory skills—then there is no reason why I have to volunteer any information about your deficiencies as a supervisor."

Wayne applied for a GS 11 non-supervisory job. Bob was able to give him a decent reference. (According to Bob, "My recommendation did not go off-scale, but I gave him above-average ratings.") Wayne got the job, and then in a couple of years he was promoted in the new agency to a supervisory position. Bob believed his action was quite rational and ethical. "I believe that it was an honorable compromise because it did not hurt Wayne's career. Pay setting practices being what they were, he did not lose any money. He was competent to do the job for which he was originally hired. And who knows, in later years maybe he learned a few things and deserved to be repromoted to supervisor." While some of the employees in the Air Force installation felt that Bob had mistreated Wayne, there was not enough reaction to have any negative impact on the operation, and the operation continued to steadily improve.

Both individuals in this case knew what drove Bob as supervisor, and how to describe his management style. As Bob Fellows described himself:

I had a reputation for being "hardnosed," but people agreed that I was hard on myself also. As one of my co-supervisors put it, "you are seen by your subordinates as firm but fair." In addition, I had to let the facts speak for themselves, although I was certainly open to broad interpretation of those facts and looked for creative ways to deal with what they told me.

In return Bob understood the personality and desires of Wayne. Therefore both individuals could communicate about this situation and deal with the thorny personal and organizational problems. And, above all, Bob was neither locked into a literal interpretation of the rules and regulations nor unwilling to arrive at a compromise that maintained the intent of the rules while recognizing a more universal set of values and principles.

Other managers frequently discussed their self-examination of personal views about loyalty to the organization and its mission, management duties, professionalism, self-fulfillment, regulation, and other issues included in personal feelings and personality characteristics. The interviewees often couched their self-analysis in terms of "management style." This was a language with which they felt comfortable, and they understood the basic personality characteristics as well as the organizational variations influencing their style of managing people. At the same time, they could apply those concepts to those above and below themselves, and when political actors got involved in the cases, they understood the political forces with which they had to deal. These managers were especially aware of the importance of subtlety in dealing with individuals and human problems. They often described their sense of frustration in not being able to deal with particular situations in subtle ways but instead being forced to use the much less satisfactory "formal" rules. The managers were often given the "formal" interpretation of the statutes or rules and then "informally" informed why those procedures would not work and how to try to resolve their problems through informal systems. In fact, many of the cases could not be solved effectively unless and until informal ways of dealing with them were uncovered. The interviews made it very clear that in most cases self-understanding existed at a relatively high level even though it was not based on academic or psychological theories.

Finally, none of the individuals thought about themselves, their moral maturity, or their ability to handle the dilemmas, in the formal theoretical way developed by Kohlberg; however, several of them were aware of the phenomenon described by Kohlberg and used language that was surprisingly similar to his in discussing themselves and the individuals with whom they were interacting. In other words, an understanding of moral maturity often existed although they were not cognizant of its existence as a formal theory.

The existence of such an hierarchy of moral sophistication became glaringly apparent as I talked to an increasing number of interviewees. I was able to locate individuals within Kohlberg's model, and that ability helped on more than one occasion to allow the interview to be productive. One particular interview brought this home, and it was essential to discuss this case in some detail in order to further elucidate Kohlberg's ideas.

One individual, let us call him Jim, upon being asked to describe his ethical dilemma presented a rather lengthy story. While working for an agency involved in recreation and historical preservation, he was asked to represent the agency in its request for special funds for bicentennial restoration and activities. This was a special chance for the agency to get additional money to carry out projects that had been on the drawing board for some time but for which no money had been available. With the emotional appeal of the bicentennial there was some possibility of getting funds that would otherwise never be available. Jim had to decide whether to present the budget request in the strongest light possible, as an "agency advocate," or to provide the information in a "professional and objective" manner that would gain for him the respect of the budget examiners from the Office of Management and Budget. To make a long story short, Jim decided to present the information in a manner that he hoped would accomplish both goals—trying to please both sides—and as a result the agency did not get much of the money it sought. Jim could not really tell if the presentation had anything to do with the budget decisions or if external factors, such as economic conditions and budget deficits, were the major causes of the failure to fund. However, he felt he had failed to operate ethically in this situation.

After listening to Jim's story, I was somewhat puzzled. I had not been able to clearly identify what Jim saw as the ethical dilemma being discussed. Therefore, I asked him to define for me, in one sentence, what he considered to be the ethical dilemma that he had faced in this situation. Jim's response was:

My ethical dilemma was whether to maintain complete agency loyalty, in which case I might be a hero in the agency, or to attempt to develop and maintain the respect of the individuals in the other agency who were fellow members of my profession.

At that point it became clear that Jim was operating at level three of Kohlberg's six stages of moral maturity. To Jim the ethical question was defined as choosing between ties to one's agency and one's profession. In either case, he wanted to win the approval from his peer group, only he could not decide which side contained his peer group and was, therefore, most important to him. My initial puzzlement in attempting to understand his ethical dilemma was related to the fact that I had been looking for something related to pressure being placed on him to break the law or his personal code—something related to a higher level of the model.

Jim was convinced that he had failed in this case because he won neither the accolades of his peers in the other department nor did he bring back to his organization any results that would win him esteem among his agency peers. When asked what lessons he had learned from the experience, Jim listed three:

1. Don't be too friendly with counterparts in adversarial agencies;
2. Maintain loyalty to one's self first, to the agency second, and to one's profession third; and
3. Present all self-prepared materials up the agency ladder for approval, so you will be sure you are saying what your boss wants you to say, especially if there is a chance those materials will go outside the agency.

The last question I asked everyone in my interview was what advice they might like to offer to others who faced situations similar to theirs. Jim was prepared for such a question and proceeded to give advice on a set of self-selected typical ethical issues regularly faced by bureaucrats.

• What should be one's goal when preparing policy papers for the agency? If you are faced with writing a position paper or helping to determine the policy direction of an agency, put down what you think those above you want. You are judged on your ability to get your memo signed by superiors, not on its contents.

• Should an individual apply for a carpool permit without having a valid number of riders—even though he or she knows that there is flagrant abuse of the carpool regulations and falsification of applications? Yes, it is okay to stretch the truth as long as you do not falsify records and you go no further than the other individuals.

• To what extent is it okay to use the government's telephone long distance WATS lines for personal calls? It is okay to make personal calls as long as you do not flagrantly abuse the privilege. Everyone else does it; however, you do not want to get caught, so deny misuse if you are ever challenged.

• What does an individual do as a member of an agency if he or she believes a contractor's compensation for services rendered is being unnecessarily delayed and the agency is not paying interest on the delayed payments as the law says should be done? You cannot carry your agency's water to the adversary, but you can help the adversary *find* the water. You confide off the record to the contractor's lawyer so that he will become aware of the law and take care of the contractor, but you stay out of the picture.

These answers appear incredibly cynical to individuals who operate at higher levels of moral maturity; however, they were volunteered as part of a sincere effort to help other civil servants, especially new ones who have not "learned the ropes," to cope with the ethical problems one regularly faces. Jim's answers were quite consistent. They were all driven by his desire to maintain the approval of superiors and peers.

Given this approach to ethical dilemmas it is obvious that the nature of Jim's supervision must be quite different than for those at higher levels of moral maturity. Once Jim knows what is wanted by his superiors he will do his best to achieve it; however, he cannot be turned loose to solve complex problems; he will not function well without guidance; and he will never challenge an order from above. Neither could he ever compromise on an issue in an intelligent way because he would not understand what the vital issues were within the problem being faced. When the general details of this case were presented to a retired top government official who had spent his entire career within the merit system, he responded by saying:

I have known several individuals like Jim in my time. They are almost useless to their superiors because that kind of individual always tries to give you what he thinks you want rather than dealing with the facts and giving you good objective analysis and advice. He will go to any length to endear himself to you, but what you need is someone who will help you to understand the world. These kinds of individuals get you into real hot water because they will not tell you that you are about to make a mistake; instead they will go so far in trying to do whatever you want that you end up in trouble with everybody—the president's office, Congress, constituents, other agencies—because no one is satisfied with the convoluted results of this mistaken effort to please.

Oh, by the way, as an aside, if this individual has risen to the highest level of middle-management (GS 15), usually he desperately wishes to become a member of the SES since he sees that as the ultimate symbol of acceptance. However, such individuals never make it because of this fatal flaw. They try so hard, fail, never understand why, and often become bitter.

Again, this manager did not use the language of Kohlberg, but he certainly understood that people operated at different levels of maturity and sophistication in both their general work and in facing ethical situations. He also understood the pitfalls presented in dealing with such individuals. The kinds of assignments given to individuals under him, and the way he supervised them, varied according to the qualities and abilities of the person involved. He wanted individuals working for him who represented the qualities described by Stephen Bailey at the beginning of this chapter. His response is typical of most managers interviewed in this research.

Self-understanding and self-control are elements vital to success. They are precious because, in addition to allowing you to carry out your mission successfully, they allow you to look in the mirror and like and respect the person you see. It is impossible to succeed in dealing with the constant flow of thorny, complex, and often long-lasting ethical issues that are faced in middle-management positions without the assurance that you have both a good understanding of the problem and a clear comprehension of your position in the matter.

Even when comfortable in your understanding of your personal characteristics, however, that knowledge must not lead to a sense of smugness or superiority. The only way to guarantee the proper use of that knowledge is to continue to question yourself and the stance you have taken in the ongoing situation—not with the sense that you might be "wrong" so much as with the sense of maintaining an open and receptive mind toward all of the external influences and information that may be essential in further understanding the circumstances faced and opening the door to any reasonable resolution of the dilemma. Security in the "rightness" of your cause, and your stance in that cause, creates an inability to recognize opportunity when it knocks at the door of your righteous citadel.

NOTES

1. Nonpolitical individuals view the world from a different perspective than do political activists. If an individual holds no religious beliefs, that is equally important to understand, although it says nothing about the presence or absence of an ethical nature.

2. In other societies, such as in the Moslem world, where there is no separation between church and state, the same problem might not exist, certainly not to the same degree.

3. The idea of personality analysis, as applied in this study, is to develop understanding, *not* to try to *change* people, although that may need to be done on occasion.

4. No attempt was made to discover and include any specific types of cases in the sample of interviews carried out for this research; therefore, no attempt to estimate the probable occurrence of any type of case in the larger universe is possible.

CHAPTER 4

ETHICS AND THE LAW

Abraham Lincoln was probably neither the first nor last, but he was certainly the best known person to ever note that we "have a government of laws, not of men." The "law" is society's attempt to present, for all to see, what is its will toward specific issues of public concern. It is a statement of what is in the public's interest and how that goal is to be achieved. The substantive goal of any statute is stated within its body, often within its preamble. In addition, the Constitution, the basic law of the land, states that all individuals are to be treated equally before the law; therefore, substantive goals are to be achieved while guaranteeing this democratic concept of equality.

Public managers live in a legal world, and are always cognizant of the impact of the law on all of their actions. Governmental decisions and actions come about in response to laws that establish certain rights and responsibilities; the bureaucracy is the resulting organization established to ensure that the laws are carried out in a reasonable and effective manner. Since the law is the foundation or the starting place, and carrying out the law is the raison d'etre for public bureaucracies, the public servant must comprehend the laws that influence the decisions, the legal system within which those laws operate, and the political system which establishes the laws and the legal system. Two kinds of laws influence bureaucratic decisions—substantive laws dealing with the program goals and policies central to the situation at hand, and procedural law dealing with the method of decision making. Only after both types of laws are completely understood can one come to a valid conclusion.

After having made this strong general statement about the centrality of the law in the public bureaucracy, a caveat should be added. The legal context of ethical problems is seldom the only or most important aspect of any ethical dilemma faced by public managers; we must remember that ethical dilemmas involve conflicting *values*. However, it is often impossible to make an ethical judgment until one is thoroughly familiar with the legal foundation of the problem being faced. It is true that the law[1] forms "an authoritative force, or combination of forces, that recognizes, creates, and enforces rights and duties" (Zelermyer 1960, 105). The problem with any such statement is that the law, or a specific statute, serves a multiplicity of purposes. For example, every time the rights and liberties of an individual are protected there is a limit placed on someone else's freedom of action, creating two differing results from one law. Therefore, the acceptability of any limitation depends upon its justifiability, and when an adequate justification is not forthcoming, the law can easily become an instrument of oppression (Beauchamp and Pinkard 1983). It is often the public bureaucrat who ultimately determines whether the limitation is justifiable, because, as the responsible government official, s/he must initiate the actions to see that the law is applied. This is known as "defining the law through action." The bureaucrat usually has some choice of action, since in almost every case the legislature leaves an area of discretion to the administrator—even when this is not the intent of the legislators. After all, no statute can deal with every twist and turn taken by human affairs. Numerous borderline cases arise that can be decided either way with equal rationality or irrationality.

The fact that many troublesome issues are not, indeed cannot be, resolved by the legislature, but are decided during implementation, is at the foundation of the ethical dilemma (usually macro-ethical) of the public administrator at the top of the bureaucracy. Ethical guidelines, however, are often couched in terms created by the civil service reform mentality; this has limited ethical discussion to what should *not* be done, issues such as avoiding conflict of interest and partisanship. These issues are important, but they only begin to deal with the larger ethical matters that must be faced by decision makers (Rohr 1978). Many times the problem relates to how something should be done rather than what one should not do; therefore, public administrators in policy-level positions must move beyond the more limited debate of the past and deal with both the positive and negative sides of ethics. They must also use all of the analytic tools available in such debate. Rohr, for example, argues that the best way for bureaucrats to understand the enduring values of society, and how they mutate or evolve, is to examine the debates that occur in the Supreme Court. This allows individuals to see the dynamics of the debate as it applies to real-world issues, to understand what the major pro and con arguments are at any moment, and perhaps to recognize shifts in values within society.

Even though public administrators at lower levels of the bureaucracy seldom make major policy decisions, they may have ample opportunity to have input into the policy process in a variety of ways; however, they must often move beyond the more limited considerations of the traditional civil service mentality. The decisions made by the civil servants interviewed for this research, even though the incidents occurred in what we would call managerial (non-policy-making or micro-ethical) levels, generally contained questions that went far beyond mere adherence to a set of rules or guidelines for civil servants. The impact of their decisions regularly played a major role in the *efficient and/or effective operation* of the organizations within which they functioned, and there was often a "spillover" into policies and practices not directly related to the specific issue at hand.

In these situations, a variety of questions related to the law always had to be answered. Even though these questions were usually not the central issue in the cases, they had to be clarified before the managers could move on to the other involved factors. The legal questions were the base from which other actions could then be planned or carried out.

LEGAL ANALYSIS AND ETHICAL ISSUES

The act of legal analysis requires well-honed skills acquired only by practice. The legal interpreter's act is *not* unrestrained, it is not freely creative, but is tied to the legislative text as well as other facets of the legal system. As interpretations of a statute are made, it is necessary to multiply the legal possibilities and then resolve them as much as possible by carrying them to their logical ends. The analyst must remember that the goal of the analytic process is to accomplish something constructive, not merely to analyze situations in legal terms. Because legal shoals will appear often, this goal requires the analyst to adopt a safe course (as far as interpretation of a statute is concerned), coming no closer to legal problems than is necessary (Shartel 1951).

With an understanding of these few basic rules of analysis, we can focus on the process of applying the law to an ethical decision. The appropriate place to start the analysis is with the specific statute pertinent to the situation at hand, not only the statute but its legislative history. Two further tools of analysis are also discussed; the rules and regulations explaining the statute and the court rulings that have been handed down concerning it. All of this information allows us to examine the role of law and the legal system in society, so both the specific statute is made clearer and the role of the bureaucrat within the system can be understood.

The statute provides "two important sets of materials to work with: (1) the language which the legislature has used; and (2) the context in which the language is used" (Shartel 1951, 329). A statute usually asserts, in a straightforward way, that "this is forbidden, this is required, this is authorized." Legislation is passed to control the actions of citizens, so legislators are communicating a message to the public. If that message is to be understood, legislators must write statutes in a manner that can be reasonably interpreted, if not by all citizens, at least by their lawyers. Therefore, when reading the statute it is not the reader's job to figure out what the legislature meant to say, but what it succeeded in saying. It is usually necessary to go beyond a "face value" interpretation of a statute;

nonetheless, all further analysis must be based on this foundation. In fact some legal scholars argue that this type of analysis is the only rational way to study the law, because it is concerned strictly with the established meaning of the language which the lawmaker has used, giving this approach "the advantage of frankly converting the process of interpretation into an inquiry based on objective materials" (Shartel 1951, 325). One is investigating the proper meaning of words, not someone's motivations or intentions.[2]

Legislation is composed of three basic parts—preamble, definitions, and body—and each part serves a special role in the process of analysis. Central to the literal interpretations of statutes are the latter two parts. The definitions of special terms (for example, "The term 'Secretary' refers to the Secretary of Commerce") are included in order to guarantee that everyone who reads the statute will share a common understanding of its key elements. The inclusion of the definition section certainly lends credence to the literal interpretation approach to a statute: There would be no reason for the legislature to define terms if the literal interpretation of the statute was not important.

Once a firm grasp on the definitions is achieved, it is possible to move into the body of an enactment and grapple with the do's and don'ts. This is the heart of the analysis. It may take numerous readings to make heads or tails of most statutes; in spite of the fact that they are meant for public consumption, they do not read like a soap opera script. Some cynics argue that laws are complex because lawyers, the largest single group in most legislatures, write statutes for other lawyers, thus guaranteeing the legal profession plenty of work. Although this explanation may have a breath of truth in it, the major reason for the complexity of statutes can be traced directly to the complexity of society and the individuals who are supposed to be controlled by the law. Also, the attempt to guarantee as much explicitness as possible requires intricacy of language, and lawyers are often the best qualified to develop the proper level of explicitness versus generality; thus, "the enactment drafted by an experienced lawyer is . . . less likely to be plagued by the problem of the unforeseen case than is one drafted by a layman" (Fuller 1968, 13).

It does not matter how carefully a piece of legislation is drafted, some points will be left unclear. These questions can often be answered by looking at the context in which language is used. This idea begins to move toward the second major type of analysis (legal intent); nevertheless, when considering context the focus is still on the statute as written. To focus on the contextual definition of an enactment is to define the terms and phrases according to its overall thrust. When a term is vague or has multiple meanings, it is often possible to arrive at a clear and unique definition through the process of elimination because only one definition, precisely interpreted, fits with the rest of the statute.

As we noted above, much legislation has an introductory statement, the preamble. The most famous of these preambles (We the people, in order to form a more perfect union . . .) served exactly the same purpose, although on a grander scale, as that served by the preamble to a parking ordinance in Parkersburg,

Pennsylvania. The preamble to a statute serves to describe the evil it is intended to avoid or the good it is meant to promote. On the other hand, sometimes it is suspected that the preamble helps to cover up poor draftsmanship. For example, "The legislature says, in effect, 'We may not have expressed very well just *what* we want, but you can figure this out for yourself by reading the preamble which tells you *why* we want it'' (Fuller 1968, 90).[3] For whatever reason the preamble exists, it helps to establish a contextual definition of terms and phrases in a law.

One other type of contextual factor must be considered as the text of a statute is analyzed; the context of a statute stretches far beyond its own content. Many terms in a specific enactment may seem vague or appear to have multiple meanings, when in fact they are quite clear to those who are well versed in the law and the legal system. These terms are commonly used and, therefore, assumed to be common knowledge. Likewise, in relation to provisions for official actions,

only if the lawmaker wants to make some special provision relative to the way in which the new legislation is to be applied, enforced, or interpreted, does he take the trouble to refer explicitly to general functions and techniques of officials. (Shartel 1951, 339)

In order to comprehend fully a law and use it in deciding what to do when faced with an ethical dilemma, one must understand this broader statutory context. Included in the broader context are such factors as the history of "the law" and the written commentary of legal experts in addition to the constitution and existing statutes with which an enactment must be in consonance. Even when understood in the broader context, however, problems are still likely to exist. Laws are composed of words, and regardless of their arrangement, they cannot express every deep idea adequately; hence, legislation may ultimately end up being ambiguous, contradictory, inconsistent, or incomplete.

This continued lack of clarity may occur for several reasons. First, legislation is written in general terms, and it is impossible to gain unanimity of meaning since many terms in our language are relationally defined (defined in relation to experiences and perceptions of the world). These experiences and perceptions vary in the separate parts of the country and in the different socioeconomic groups.

Second, laws are written in the face of an uncertain future. Statutes mean something new to each ensuing generation; however, the problem of definitional change occurs more rapidly than that, hence, laws must be written so that they maintain their relevance in spite of new social movements or technological innovations. It is impossible to foresee exactly when a new economic development, computer or information technology breakthrough, or civil rights movement will occur, but it is certain that these types of situations will arise; therefore, lawmakers attempt to write their statutes broadly enough to envelope the new situations. Anything written in such broad language is bound to create problems in interpretation and understanding.

Third, legislators often have to work out compromises in wording so that legislation can be passed. In such situations it is not uncommon for purposely ambiguous language to be included relating to important matters. At the outset these clauses may seem hopelessly ambiguous, but it is hoped that they will acquire explicitness of meaning as actions related to the statute are carried out over a period of time (Lindblom 1959). This is done because lawmakers' constituencies often have conflicting interests, and the lawmakers cannot foresee what kind of accommodation best serves their respective interests. The best accommodation that can be reached is the development of means and, often, ends as the situation evolves in the future. Hopefully, at that time current deadlocks can be settled, because it is often easier to settle such disputes when they move from the philosophical level to concrete situations requiring action.

Finally, legislation is often unclear because the lawmakers do not know how to state their ideas precisely. There are limits to the descriptive and expressive power of words.

LOOKING BEYOND THE STATUTE

Beyond the statute are "extrinsic aids" that help one to discover "legislative intent" (Shartel 1951). These aids are contextual, still within the sphere of the legislative process as it acts to pass the bill, and are not limited to, but include: the occasion for enactment; the legislative history of the bill—embracing all changes in its wording from introduction to final approval; any reports by legislative committees, official agencies, or outside groups involved in preparing the considered draft; and statements made by persons charged with steering the bill through the legislative processes.[4]

During the procedure of introduction, hearings, and adjustment, which may extend over a number of years, the legislators and the various interests have a chance to state their cases as eloquently and factually (the two need not coincide) as possible. Most important legislation goes through a long period of gestation; during this time a combination of honing the bill and developing support through coalition building and "education" by advocates leads to the utlimate passage of a law. As the bill evolves, the meaning desired by legislators is clarified, because they move *away* from some possible constructions and *toward* others.

The legislative history, including the statements of the lawmakers concerning the issue on which they are voting, may be exactly what is needed to clarify the ethical question. On the other hand, it must be remembered that a political game is being presented through inanimate letters on a page; therefore, it is not possible to comprehend all of the innuendo and strategy that exists during the actual struggle for minds and votes. Just the inflection of a speaker's voice may totally change the meaning of a word or a phrase, and no one has yet invented a way of portraying such factors through the printed word. In addition, there may be no reference to the issue for which clarification is being sought because the situation being considered may have never entered anyone's mind as the bill was enacted. Therefore, this type of analysis may or may not help develop a proper understanding of a statute. Even if it accomplishes that task, of course, understanding the legislative history of a law can never be accepted as adequate justification, in or of itself, for a decision.

There are two additional sources where one can look beyond the specific statute for guidance. First, when further information is needed about the legality of decisions and actions, formally established rules and regulations offer procedural interpretations of the law or statements of how the agency involved in administering the program proposes to interpret and apply the statutes creating and enabling the program.

The main purposes of the regulations are to define general and ambiguous language in the decree, to specify what actions are covered, and to spell out specific procedures to be followed in order to meet the requirements in the statute. Here specific, substantive meat is being applied to the skeleton established by the statute, and as the flesh is developed it is possible to see how strong or weak that body is, exactly how the muscles are designed to work, and which bodily functions will perform best.

Regulations often have a history just as does a law, and by observing their development as they are (1) initially proposed, (2) responded to by interested parties, (3) amended, (4) commented on again, and (5) released as official regulations, it is possible to gain an understanding of the way a law is officially interpreted. From all of this discussion between the administering agency and outside interests, including other government agencies, regulated industries, labor organizations, environmental and consumer groups, and individuals, it is possible to pinpoint areas of controversy and to note the agency's official stance. Just as with the original statute, it is also possible to note the tenor and direction of amendments to the regulations so that a philosophical and political stance becomes more concrete.

A second place to look for explanation and edification of a statute, especially if it has been in existence for some time, is in court decisions, either administrative or general civil courts, that have been handed down concerning it; while legislation lays down general rules in anticipation of future events, courts interpret those enactments as they apply to specific controversies between people in society. Courts of common law do not decide which cases should be brought before them, they must wait for the litigants to bring issues before the bench. This means that the shape taken by legal doctrine in a particular jurisdiction may be influenced by the accidents of history; however, controversial and important issues will inevitably make it before the courts. Once the issue gets to court, the eminent jurist, Roscoe Pound notes:

Three steps are involved in the adjudication of a controversy according to law: (1) Finding the law, ascertaining which of the many rules in the legal system is to be applied, or, if none is applicable, reaching a rule for the case (which may or may not stand as a rule in subsequent cases) on the basis of given materials in some way which the legal system points out; (2) interpreting the rule so chosen or ascertained, that is, determining its meaning as it was framed and with respect to its intended scope; (3) applying to the case in hand the rule so found and interpreted. (1954, 48)

As a result of these three steps, the court hands down an extremely useful decision to anyone pondering the pros and cons of that or a similar issue (Rohr 1978). In the decision the facts of the case are set forth in considerable detail. Given those facts, the rule that is applied, and the reasons justifying the use of that rule, it is possible to examine the intellectual process used by the judge or judges from the time they start with a law, and an incident concerning that law, to the point where they bring the two together in a judicial decision. Throughout this process, judges are always ready to look behind the words of a law, or a precedent established in a prior case, to see what the legislature or court was trying to say. In a similar vein, the judges consider the case in light of the overall legal/social system. The information converges in a manner that allows the analytical spotlight to examine every bit of the case, and all of the attention helps to clarify ideas about an ethical dilemma whenever the case can be applied.

Nor will the ideas and arguments made available always show only one side of the issue. It is common for important cases to bring out disagreement among the judges, with dissenting or concurring opinions being prepared to present views that have not currently carried the day. Dissenting opinions of Supreme Court justices have, on occasion, become the majority opinions in later years; even when such has not occurred, the dissents are given great weight, so much so that in a few cases the Supreme Court has delayed ruling on a profound issue until there was a unanimous court, thus denying die-hard opponents to a Constitutional interpretation a dissent on which to build their resistance.[5] However, the importance of dissent is that the debate helps to illuminate the most telling arguments against a particular decision, and, therefore, to present the issue in all of its complexity. This ability to examine impassionately and carefully all facets of a situation where generality must be applied to human reality is the skill applied by successful judges, and that is the skill that administrators must develop when dealing with ethical issues. Such an ability does not create unanimity. Dissent will always exist. In many cases there is no one *right* interpretation of a law. However, the judicial process does guarantee, insofar as possible, that justice will be achieved.

Through an in-depth analysis of the law, involving at least all of the steps noted above, public administrators can be sure that they know the law and understand the legal basis from which any decisions or actions must proceed. This is the first step often proposed for achieving an ethical administration; but does the role of the law translate into the central ethical issue portrayed by this argument, and does this kind of analysis occur among public managers? Let us examine the experience of our real-life managers.

PUBLIC MANAGERS AND THE LAW IN EVERYDAY LIFE

An emphasis on analysis of the law as a first step in making ethical decisions undoubtedly plays a major role for public administrators at the policy levels of the hierarchy and for people who are involved in the initiation of a new program. At this point new and often macro-ethical issues are usually involved. Such issues require special attention.

The importance of legal analysis to the public servants interviewed in this research depended on the particular situation they faced and the role they saw for themselves in that case. The majority of those interviewed saw themselves as *managers* in the bureaucracy, and for them the law played a very specific and clearly defined role in their lives. Little time was spent in the kind of in-depth analysis of the law presented above. For these people and the programs they were running, most if not all of the legal analysis had been done by someone else, now they were simply trying to live within the confines of the law as established for them while getting their jobs done. As noted by one interviewee:

It is important to separate the ideas of legality and ethicality. It [a legal conflict] cannot be an ethical conflict because in case of any legal question you can get some legal advice or ruling on what you are required to do. You are expected to obey the law, you are told what the law means, and if you do not follow the law you are performing an illegal act. Of course, whether or not it is an ethical act is another question.

The law does play a central role for the manager, however, because it creates the boundaries within which action must take place. All of the public managers regularly mentioned the law—usually referring to statutes, rules, or regulations—as they described the ethical situations they faced and the actions taken. In most cases they thought in terms of the rules and regulations that applied to their office and program, not in the more general sense of the statutes that established the program or "the law." Nevertheless, their understanding of "the law" and its interpretation of social goals was usually in the back of their minds, and any probing brought from them a recognition that they were attempting to deal with this concept.

It would be hypothetically possible to get a response from individuals that "there was no law applicable to my case." Such did not occur. Given the number of laws in existence and the breadth of issues they cover, this result should not be surprising. There are undoubtedly situations where no specific statute is applicable, and in this case we often refer to the fact that an issue or client "falls between the cracks." Any attempt to figure out how often managers face such situations is speculative. Since the focus is on everyday operation within the public bureaucracy such cases are rare.

In all but one case the legal background of the case being discussed was clear in the minds of the interviewees. (In one case, the law was not mentioned. This unique case, involving "Jim," was discussed in Chapter 3.) The managers understood the law or they were able to get advice from experts. Instead they generally faced one or more of three problems: (1) The law served as a delimiter—managers had to deal with ethical situations where the law was a limiting factor—they wanted to accomplish their goal *and* stay within the rules and regulations; (2) the law served as protection and support—mangers were pressured to do things that they felt were not appropriate or within the strict interpretation of the law as it applied to that case; and/or (3) the law served as the focal point of contention—managers had to deal with a problem where others were misinterpreting, misapplying, or ignoring the law. We shall look briefly at the role of the law in each of these cases as faced by mid-level managers.

Finally, in one case the manager felt that the law was wrong; he arrived at the decision that one specific statute had to be broken in order to achieve the public interest as it was stated in other overriding legislation (including treaties with other nations). We shall discuss, after covering our three major categories, how that situation arose and how it was resolved.

Law as Delimiter

In many cases the problems faced by managers are *not* caused by external pressures or by someone's misuse of the law; instead the ethical dilemmas are created by the fact that the managers feel pressure, internal or external, to achieve reasonable goals, and at the same time they are expected to stay within the rules and regulations that govern their management activity. Many alternatives, in some cases the easiest ones, are ruled out because they fall outside the limits of legal action. This ideal of staying within clearly and stringently defined legal boundaries is sometimes a self-assigned limitation, but that only increases its importance to the practice of public management as a public trust because such self-direction and control is necessary for the bureaucracy to function satisfactorily.

This type of situation is exemplified by Robert Fellows, in the case presented in the prior chapter, when he faced a problem regularly occurring for managers. "What do I do with a problem employee, one who cannot fulfill his responsibilities?" A common approach to this problem is to dump the problem individual through inappropriate personnel action, with the understanding "that the employee is then the next manager's problem, not mine." In other words, give the problem employee a good rating and get rid of him or her: Let the next supervisor worry about the problem.

Common practice may very well not be legal practice. Dumping an employee by falsifying recommendations is clearly against the personnel rules of any organization. Robert Fellows was able to resolve the problem in an acceptable way because the individual he had to help move from the organization was placeable and reasonable in his expectations. It is not uncommon, however, for managers to be working under pressure, both from the subordinate and superiors, to ignore the rules.

In another case (presented in Chapter 6), the manager was asked to resolve a situation where entrance exams had been stolen and used by internal applicants for entry-level professional positions in the agency. Since the case had been "hanging around" for a long time, the only pressure on this individual was to "resolve the case once and for all." All statutory requirements had been met, yet top management did not "feel right" about the situation. Any consideration given the alleged culprits was above and beyond that required by personnel rules and regulations.

In this case the final delimiter was "the law" in its larger sense. The manager's alternatives were limited by her sensitivity to democratic values; she felt compelled to go beyond the rules and procedures of the agency and to guarantee that equal protection was granted to everyone involved in the case. Since she was not a personnel specialist, she reviewed these rules and procedures carefully with all of the appropriate individuals in the legal office and the personnel office before making a final decision. In other words, other experts could help her with the interpretation of the law, but she had to then apply it to the specific case at issue. And she wanted to make sure that her final decision took into account the individual rights and dignity of those involved in the case even though they were allegedly guilty of breaking important agency rules. When she felt comfortable that all rights had been protected she felt that the case had been properly handled, and, not surprisingly, her resolution cleared the air for everyone at all levels.

Law as Support

Occasionally managers are pressured to take inappropriate actions. George Anderson, another manager interviewed, was faced with a serious ethical problem when he found that a handicapped employee who was not competent had been foisted off on him. (This case is presented in detail in Chapter 5). He was told to "not make waves" when he suggested that he had a serious problem with the young lady who had been placed in his office. No one specifically said, "Break the rules and regulations, but don't tell us, and don't let your action cause us any trouble." A relatively common thread throughout the cases is the tacit or overt request by superiors or special interests for individuals to "shave the rules for us."

Not only are such requests common, but the necessity of doing exactly such a thing sometimes occurs. Before any decision can be made about such action, however, it is necessary to have carried out at least a minimal analysis of the statutes, rules, and regulations that are involved in the particular case *and* to understand what the greater intent of "the law" is in relation to the issues at hand. Only with such knowledge can intelligent decisions be made about the situation and whether or not serious consideration should be given to a request to bend the rules. And only with a clear knowledge of rules and regulations can one understand the possible impacts of such action on larger questions of agency mission and the public trust. As one contract administrator noted, "Before I can decide to bend the rules, I must know them intimately so that I know I am not breaking them.''

George Anderson, in deciding what to do with his new problem employee, turned to the personnel office for advice, and found that what he was asked to do was against the rules; the personnel officers, as neutral advisors, argued such actions were detrimental to the overall health of the organization. After careful examination, George felt that the rules and regulations supported his decision to take action against the employee (but in a way that he felt was humane to the individual involved and forced his superiors to face the problem they had created for him). He refused to approve her promotion and gave her an evaluation based on a lower GS level than she currently filled. The evaluation, still not satisfactory, did not force her out of the organization but clearly pointed out her problems. The clear understanding that he was bending the letter of the law (by evaluating her for a lower position than she held) but obeying its intent regarding handi-capped employees gave him the support and strength he needed to make the "right" decision.

Law as Focal Point of Contention

A closely related problem is that of being placed in a situation where one discovers others are misinterpreting, misapplying, or ignoring the law. In such a case the expected response is to attempt to correct the situation, and if it can be corrected there is probably no ethical dilemma. However, in many cases, rather than being able to correct the situation, the individuals who become aware of such problems are faced with threats, intimidation, or active efforts to guar-antee that nothing changes and that they keep their mouths shut. A classic example of such a situation, with racial overtones, occurred in one of the cases presented to me during my interviews.[6]

Dr. Valerie Franklin was the first black nutritionist to work for a federal agency that had for years been delivering a variety of services related to nutrition across the United States, Puerto Rico, and the Virgin Islands. She was secure in her professional accomplishments, proud of the advancements that had been made in her field, pleased with the mission of the agency, and happy to serve everyone who came to her for assistance. She was able to fit into the organization rather rapidly as a national program leader and technical expert in a program that served low-income families. This program was designed to provide nutrition education to low-income families through the use of paraprofessionals chosen from the communities where they provided services. This program, although delivered at the county level, was monitored and administered by the respective state land grant universities in conjunction with the federal agency.

When Dr. Franklin was hired, she was brought on board two steps below the entry level for which she was qualified and at which the job was advertised; this happened even though she was the number one person on the list of eligibles on the basis of her education and prior experience. When she questioned the grade level, there was much initial resistance; however, two months later she was upgraded one level, and she quickly forgot about the matter and went about her job.

Dr. Franklin became more and more familiar with a very complex structure. There were many unwritten rules and regulations. In many situations the rules and regulations were written down but not followed as written; instead they were followed "as understood by the old timers."

Several months went by, and Dr. Franklin, as part of the staff, was asked to participate in the rating of proposals for funding from the state land grant universities. In rating the proposals as a staff, it became apparent that none of the historically black land grant universities submitting proposals received favorable ratings. Therefore, none of them received federal funds for special nutrition projects.

In order to understand the situation, it is necessary to look briefly at the history of these institutions. State land grant colleges and universities came into being in 1862; however, there are two different groups—originally white-only institutions were established, but it was not until 1890 (under the separate-but-equal doctrine) that black land grant colleges were created. Thus two groups of colleges—the 1862 and the 1890 institutions—existed, and those dates are still used to designate the origin of the two sets of schools.

While several of the nutrition proposals were from the 1890 colleges, none received a grant. Dr. Franklin did two things: she made the observation to her supervisor that none of the 1890 colleges were among the top-rated proposals, and she also offered—on her own time—to help the professionals at the 1890 institutions improve their proposals for the next round of grants. A key responsibility of her job was to assist professionals at all 1862 and 1890 institutions. It appeared that no one had either the interest or the expertise to specifically address the problems faced in the black land grant colleges. In response, she was asked to rank the top three grant proposals from the 1890 institutions. She did so but heard nothing more about the issue.

In the meantime, Dr. Franklin had let the professionals at both the 1862 and 1890 institutions know that she would be willing to help them with their proposals. She began to be contacted by several of them for technical assistance. Whenever she took a professional trip to an 1862 institution, she would arrange time for technical assistance to the 1890 college in that state. This technical assistance was used for such activities as consultation and training sessions to provide state-of-the-art nutritional science information to nutritionists, home economists, and other interested individuals from the 1890 schools. This tended to improve both their service delivery and their ability to write grant proposals. As her reputation grew she was also asked by professionals working for the District of Columbia government to help them with some nutrition projects.

After a short time, she began to experience increasing difficulties in arranging her trips to 1890 universities or other black organizations, and she was questioned about the time she was using for technical assistance to the 1890 institutions. At her following annual review of travel, she was told that she could make only one professional trip during the year to a black institution or organization. When she questioned this ruling and observed that it appeared to be specifically aimed at limiting her ability to work with the 1890 institutions, her supervisor suggested that she was upsetting the normal operating procedures that had developed over the years. She was told by her supervisor, "They [the 1890 institutions] are black, you are black, and I want to bring them into the mainstream." It was suggested that a black person should not be encouraging them to seek consultation. The supervisor continued by saying that "the 1890s [black universities] should go to the 1862s [white universities] for help, and the 1862s come to us at the federal level. This way everybody gets served."

But the agency's formal policy stated that both the 1862 and the 1890 institutions had equal access to consultation at the federal level. At this point it was obvious to Dr. Franklin that she was caught up in a situation with racial overtones. Stereotyping was creating a situation of permanent second-class constituency. The law made no distinction between categories of schools. All were to be served equally. She began to feel very uncomfortable because her professional and personal values and the demands being put upon her within the organization were completely out of sequence. She could not accept what was going on but wanted to find some constructive way to deal with it.

It became obvious that her supervisor would not voluntarily change the current unwritten procedures, which denied the minority land grant colleges receipt of service and funds. Therefore, after some thought, Dr. Franklin decided to speak with an agency counselor to help resolve the issue informally. It quickly became obvious that she had touched a raw nerve because, immediately after she met with the agency counselor, her supervisor started action to fire her on the basis of alleged misuse of travel funds, mismanagement, and failure to follow established procedures in the agency.

Dr. Franklin became aware that racial epithets were used by white coworkers in the presence of her supervisor in describing her and her efforts, and no action was taken to stop those epithets. The situation had obviously escalated. The case had moved beyond one with racial overtones, where mistaken stereotypes were involved; the new information made it obvious that Dr. Franklin's superior had a racial ideology (in other words there seemed to be an obsession to make those stereotypes true and to keep anything from happening that would allow those stereotypes to be broken or overcome).

After trying to resolve issues informally and instead suffering retaliation, Dr. Franklin filed a formal complaint of discrimination with her federal agency. She also hired an attorney because of the charges made against her in the action to fire her. For several months there was a lot of tension around the office, and she was not allowed to carry out her usual functions because of limitations placed upon her freedom to perform her official duties. Initially Dr. Franklin's superior was able to gain the active support of individuals in the agency's personnel office. The personnel office worked with the supervisor in auditing all of Dr. Franklin's travel and in moving forward with the actions that limited her ability to carry out her job. After several months of exhausting the internal appeal routes, she received notice that she was fired. But just before the firing action took place the agency's personnel director called her attorney to rescind the firing order.

The personnel director, after rescinding Dr. Franklin's firing, informed her attorney that she had not been provided adequate time to prepare her response to her supervisor's allegations. After a public hearing and submission of Dr. Franklin's written response to the allegations, it became obvious that all charges were false, and Dr. Franklin was reinstated to her position. The agency was also ordered to expunge her personnel record of all information related to the issue. Over a six year period of agonizing personal crisis, she had cleared her own name, but nothing had officially been done about her original charge that there had been discrimination in the distribution of services and grant funds.

At this point, Dr. Franklin's attorney was told that the secretary of the agency wanted to resolve the issues raised by her complaint of discrimination. Two significant steps were taken. First, a memorandum was sent to all employees in the agency, both management and staff, stating that discrimination would not be tolerated. Second, Dr. Franklin was offered the opportunity to arrange an Intergovernmental Personnel Act transfer (the government would pay her salary but she could work with a state or local government organization) for two years. This would allow her to carry on work in her field, and it would also allow the environment in her agency to "cool off" as the issue became distant in time. With this resolution, the matter was considered officially closed.

In such a situation the first action of the individual is to carefully check to make sure s/he is interpreting the law properly. Only after being sure you are correct in your understanding of the law can you act. In most cases recognizing and clarifying what is proper interpretation of the law does not require much effort; the law involved is relatively clear. As in Dr. Valerie Franklin's case, however, it may become apparent only over time that the law is being ignored. Dr. Franklin, through repeated incidents, became convinced the program was not meeting its stated purpose and that the law, in which the purpose was recognized, was being ignored. The misapplication was the result of the desire of her superior to continue carrying on activities in the usual way, which meant black land grant universities would remain "second-class citizens" and would not receive the service due them.

When her supervisor made it clear he did not wish to change, Dr. Franklin's value system dictated that any actions she took should be sanctioned by the law. At the same time she, out of a sense of fairness and adherence to non-discriminatory delivery of program services, attempted to carry out her responsibilities in spite of the odds. Even so *she*, rather than the wrongful procedures of the agency, became the focus of contention. When she tried to help create change in the organization's philosophy and interpretation of the law, or more specifically in this case, the habits that had developed around the implementation of the law, she was attacked and nearly fired. Had she gone along with the current practices she would not have had these problems; however, her understanding of, and commitment to, the law and the statutes that spelled out its intent for the mission of her agency would not allow her to accept the status quo. In her situation Dr. Franklin had to be sure she was interpreting the law correctly. In order to understand "the law" she had to look not only at the statutes directly relevant to her agency, but she had to examine and apply statutes dealing with civil rights and equal opportunity; as a whole all of these statutes clearly stated what was proper procedure.

A similar case clearly dealing with ignoring the law was faced by David Weathers. A contractor had acquired access to data bases that were supposed to be top secret, and while no one told him to overlook the situation, it was abundantly obvious from other occurrences within his office that he could not expect support from his superiors in his attempt to correct the situation. In this case, not only did Dave have to carefully analyze the specific statute related to the national energy study with which he was involved, but he had to look at the larger set of statutes, rules, and regulations that covered federal procedures for the awarding of contracts. It was only when he moved to this second level of rules that he discovered a way to resolve his dilemma.

If the pressure for misapplication of the law was traceable to forces outside the immediate group, or even outside the organization, it was easier to deal with the issue. Fellow bureaucrats usually share at least a minimal level of loyalty to their group and/or organization, and they attempt to protect themselves and the organization from such a perceived threat. As noted by a manager who faced pressure from an outside interest group to reinterpret a law negatively affecting them, "Few people wish to work in a situation that cannot be controlled, and it was obvious to everyone around me that if outside groups could apply such pressures we had lost control of our own fate." Once the threat is dissipated, however, most other individuals immediately lose interest in the issue. They have their own problems to deal with. In none of the cases studied was the manager who faced the ethical dilemma able to garner support for an effort to change the law to protect the agency from such threats in the future. Those kinds of pressures were taken for granted in the political world of the public bureaucrat.

Law as Problem

What if, after careful analysis, the directly applicable statute appears to be wrong? There is no void, no vagueness. Strict adherence to rules and regulations will lead to a wrong result. There is no way to apply the statute and to arrive at an ethical resolution of the problem. What process can be followed in this situation?

The first step usually taken is to try to stop the process, to delay action. However, this is not always possible, for to stop the bureaucratic wheels from turning is extremely difficult and cannot be accomplished instantaneously.

If action cannot be stopped, it may be possible to encourage the individuals who are adversely affected by the law to seek relief from the courts. There have been occasions where public administrators have welcomed "friendly suits" filed in order to gain clarification of, or to overturn, a law that caused special problems for everyone concerned.

There is also the chance, of course, that the law has the opposite effect; action desperately needed cannot be taken. Indeed, this was the problem faced in the one case presented during this research where a public servant decided the law should not be followed because there was a hierarchy of law in effect, and other more general laws took precedence over the specific one ultimately broken.

While it is inappropriate for me to go into great detail, the case involved spending money to repair a major weapons system that was rendered totally inoperable because of a computer program malfunction. The presence of this weapons system in operational form was specifically called for in several bilateral and multilateral treaties. All units of the system around the world were affected. It was believed public knowledge of the weapons failure would have numerous, serious, negative impacts. However, the problem could be corrected at relatively low cost by Department of Defense standards.

The difficulty was that money was unavailable from that year's budget (defense budgets are complex, and repair money is a special category of fund allocated by year), but money was available in the repair category from a contiguous year.

Rather than going back to Congress for a supplementary allotment, which would have forced disclosure of the weapons system failure and would have taken a considerable amount of time during which the weapons system would have remained incapacitated, the decision was made to "cook the books" in order to obtain the few million dollars needed to make the adjustments to the computer program at the various locations of the weapons system.

There was a clear recognition that the rules established in the budgetary statutes were being broken in this case, and there was agreement with Peter Singer (1974) that the reasons for disobeying a legitimate, democratically arrived at law have to be overwhelming. Therefore, the decision was taken only after carefully reviewing all of the laws related to the transaction and comparing the results of breaking them against the consequences of delaying the reactivation of the weapons system.

Neither was this decision taken by the single individual relating the case. A small group of people at immediately contiguous levels within the budget office hierarchy were involved in making the decision. The basis for their final decision was the belief that the public interest (as determined by personal and group understanding of the concept and a quick but intensive survey of statutes as they applied to the particular case and as they compared to the other levels of relevant law—including the affected treaties) was best served by carrying out their chosen action.

It was stressed by the individual relating this case that when he came to the conclusion that the specific statute failed to deal with the current problem, he felt it was necessary to involve his immediate peers and superiors in the case. He was convinced that their involvement helped put a proper check on his decision. He not only needed their insight and experience to draw on, but also their support for any action that would ultimately be taken because any decision made carried with it serious implications. If the members of the bureaucracy agreed that the law was wrong, that it could not be applied to the case at issue in a way that was just and equitable, then it would perhaps be possible to develop a combined strategy that maximized the possibility of doing the right thing. The administrator needed the added assurance that other interested people agreed with his conclusion and that all group members would act and speak as a single voice. If it had been impossible to gain unanimity in interpretation and action, the case would have been harder to resolve. Countervailing arguments that remained strong would have created a sense of distrust of their logic on the part of the decision makers, and the inability to get everyone to work together would have made it impossible to act because of the high likelihood of someone blowing the whistle. In case of inability to resolve the issue clearly and firmly internally it would have been necessary to seek help outside the organization, and at this point the effort to act quickly would have been moot.

The decision made, and the actions taken, by the group are debatable. Undoubtedly other individuals looking at their decision from other perspectives would disagree with their choice, and some people might call the process used by the administrator "dragging others into his illegal act through collusion." This was recognized by the participants, and with this in mind the relator commented, "No one acting in this case felt especially righteous about our choice or triumphant because we were able to accomplish our goal. We did, however, feel that our decision best fulfilled our mission of serving the public trust. It [making that kind of decision] is not something I ever look forward to doing again."

Should one try to change the law if it is wrong or inappropriate to the situation? Once past the question of how to deal with the immediate case, theoretically it is appropriate to attack the cause of the problem. The easiest way to deal with the offending law is to amend it so it appropriately deals with the type of situation that caused the crisis. If amending does not appear to be a viable alternative, then the other courses of totally rewriting the law, writing a new law that solves the problem (and working to get it passed), or trying to get the offending law repealed must be considered, and the course most likely to bring success must be followed.

Realistically, in most ethical cases faced by public managers there was little consideration of such activity. The issues were usually not related to the non-existence of law or the existence of bad law, but were instead the result of other pressures within the bureaucracy. In the one case just mentioned, where the law was contrary to what they saw as the best solution of the situation at hand, the individuals involved were convinced any attempt to change the law would have side effects that would actually keep them from fulfilling their greater goal. Given the decision they made, it was impossible to suggest the law be changed because that would have raised questions about why they were making such suggestions. Pushing for change would have probably brought to light the action they had taken.

Obviously, the precise response to an ethical problem fraught with legal issues cannot be given in advance; anyone who can always give immediate and simple answers to such situations is almost certainly a charlatan. However, it is more often than not true that the legal aspect of an ethical problem makes up only a minor element in the total dilemma. To the extent the law plays a part in an ethical problem, we can usually categorize the law as playing the role of (1) delimiter for the manager, (2) supporter of the manager in his or her action, and (3) the focal point of contention because it is being misinterpreted, misapplied, or ignored, or because it is inappropriate to the situation at hand.

By analyzing the legal facets of the problem thoroughly and asking the appropriate questions regarding the law and its relevance and application to the dilemma being faced, it is possible to greatly increase one's knowledge about the issue—and information plus knowledge equals power. Hopefully, anyone interested enough in ethics to do this much analysis will use the power gained from that work to the benefit of mankind. Once that knowledge is gained, however, it is probable that other elements of the environment are important to the case, so our analysis is not yet done.

NOTES

1. When I refer to "the law," the term includes the complete system of common and statutory law, and may encompass the legal system as well; the term "statute" refers to a particular piece of passed legislation.

2. According to Fuller:

A statute derives from a determinate human source. It is enacted by the decision of a legislator or a legislative body. It comes into being at a determinate time. . . . Its terms are to be found in the words of the statute itself. If we want to know what these words mean, we look first at the words themselves and not at some expression of a more or less equivalent thought to be found somewhere else in the literature of the law. (Fuller 1968, 44)

3. Fuller continues this discussion by saying:

[I]t is significant that the countries of the Communist bloc made a free use of the statutory preamble, even the most insignificant ordinance commonly being preceded by an elaborate explanation of the evils intended to correct, a statement that it owes enactment to the continued influence of reactionary forces in the management of industry, etc. In such cases it is evident that the legislator intends not only to impose on the citizen obligations to act or forbear in certain ways, but to give direction to his thinking as well. (1968, 90–91)

4. Public administrators at the state and especially the local level, often find it difficult to discover the history of legislation because of the lack of written documentation except in newspapers (oral history in such cases is highly suspect) and the rapid turnover of actors in the political process.

5. On the inflammatory issue of school segregation, the Supreme Court avoided reversing *Plessy vs. Ferguson* until there was a unanimous court. It was believed that if any justice had dissented, the segregationists would have used his argument as a major element of their defiance of the Court's order to desegregate, and since the Court had no power other than moral force to gain compliance with their decisions, they needed the added weight of unanimity to add authority to their decision.

6. Upon reading this case, several individuals commented that it was surely dated because of the nature of the racism it described. Not so. This case occurred totally within the 1980s. We have not moved beyond the point where this kind of blatant racism can no longer occur.

CHAPTER 5

LOOKING AT THE DEEPER QUESTIONS: CULTURE AND VALUES

It may seem somewhat esoteric and removed from reality to argue that great thinkers from the past have anything to say about current ethical crises, but their impact and influence on our thoughts and actions is far greater than we may imagine. In fact, those who created our philosophical, political, and religious ideas have helped to create the bounds of our imagination. The impact of prior thinkers becomes especially apparent when we begin to compare our perceptions of the world and the way we think about it with the perceptions of individuals from other cultures and how they carry out the same tasks. Western culture, based to a great extent on philosophy rooted in the Greco-Roman societies and religion based on the Judeo-Christian tradition, holds and operates by a different set of values than do societies in other parts of the world. The difference in values within cultures was brought startlingly into focus by the contrasting reactions within Western/democratic societies and Middle-Eastern/Islamic societies over the publication in 1989 of Salmon Rushdie's book, *Satanic Verses*. Still other societies, with their values rooted in the teachings of additional philosophers or religious teachers such as Confucius or Buddha, have developed their own distinct cultures. Obviously other environmental factors have also influenced the differences between societies; but, hopefully, the point is made that no part of the world is free from such influences.

When dealing with ethical problems in the United States, we must understand our background; if dealing with ethical problems involving other cultures, we must be aware of their backgrounds and values. Culture, which includes an almost infinite number of factors, plays a major role in deciding how and what we value, so we must include a consideration of these issues in our understanding of bureaucrats and how they face and deal with ethical problems. It also means that the kinds of problems faced by bureaucrats within a society (e.g., in the Washington offices of the General Accounting Office or the Department of Agriculture) will be different than those faced by bureaucrats who work in positions crossing cultures (e.g., in the Agency for International Development or the State Department). Differences in values between Washington bureaucrats and local government workers often cause tension over health, housing, or highway programs. Failure to recognize these differences in values or culture between parts of the country, or between countries, will guarantee failure to resolve ethical problems in a meaningful way.

Even though bureaucrats ensconced within the federal bureaucracy of the United States are removed from direct contact with the external forces playing in the political arena—this is one of the major functions of the bureaucracy in general and the merit system in particular—they are still influenced by and react to the culture, ideals, and values of American society. The issues discussed in this chapter often seem relatively far removed from the public managers' immediate problems, and that is natural. The ideas developed by philosophers, religious leaders, and other great thinkers who have influenced society over a long period of time, are necessarily broad and require at least a minimal amount of interpretation in order to apply them to any current, specific situation; nonetheless, they influence the basic tenets of society, government, and personal conduct we take for granted. The ideas of ancient and recent philosophers, and the beliefs of those who founded the nation, have helped to create the values we hold dear and the current governmental structure and procedures within which we operate. Therefore, even though this is an area that does not impinge directly on our minds as we struggle with an ethical crisis that must be resolved immediately, we need to understand and to feel comfortable with the social and political milieu in order to guarantee our actions will remain within acceptable boundaries, as spelled out by our society's basic beliefs and values.

Since ethical dilemmas always involve conflicting values, we need to be familiar with existing values within our society and ourselves. These are encompassed within the subject of culture broadly defined; however, in order to limit the parameters of this discussion we shall focus on three segments of culture. First, our social values, structures, and processes (speaking from the perspective of Western democracies in general and the United States in particular) are heavily influenced by the thoughts of Western philosophers who can be traced back to Socrates (actually beyond the Greeks to earlier cultures). Second, the United States was established on a specific set of political values that, while it has evolved in interpretation over the years, still remains the underpinning of the governmental and political system. Finally, religious or theological tenets are central to our social system—even the fact that there is sometimes near-violent debate over what the role of religion should be further verifies the point that it plays an important part in society.

These three elements of thought are central to determining what we consider acceptable or permissible values, beliefs, and/or activities in society. Therefore, some knowledge of these three elements in our social and political background is useful, especially in helping us to phrase the questions that we need to ask when attempting to deal with ethical problems in a way that serves the public interest (the ultimate goal of public administration). After looking at these major elements in deciding our political culture, we shall examine the values and actions of our sample set of middle managers to see how these factors influenced them in the ethical dilemmas they faced in their everyday administrative world.

WESTERN POLITICAL PHILOSOPHY

The usual point of departure in a discussion of Western thought is with the Greek philosophers, followed by a chain of ideas moving forward to the present day. We accept these ideas, and build our world on the concepts and categories therein, because they help us to draw connections between varying phenomena. In this way we impart some order to what would otherwise appear anarchic, a hopeless chaos of activities. Especially in the political world we are examining here, these ideas, concepts, and categories mediate between us and the political world we seek to render intelligible. Without having to spend much time coming up with an order for the world, these ideas "create an area of determinate awareness and thus help to separate the relevant phenomena from the irrelevant" (Wolin 1960, 6).

Of course, in politics as in other parts of our lives, all of this happens without our necessarily being aware of it. Only if we stop to think specifically about our definition of "reality," and the impact of that definition on our perceptions and ideas, do we begin to recognize the influence prior thinkers have on our current life. Anyone who studies ethics should have at least a rudimentary knowledge of political philosophy because it impinges on the way we define the ethical problems we face and the types of decisions and actions we take.

Central to all of this is the fact that public administrative ethical situations occur within the political sphere. According to Sheldon Wolin, the definition of "politics" must include at least:

(a) a form of activity centering around the quest for competitive advantage between groups, individuals, or societies; (b) a form of activity conditioned by the fact that it occurs within a situation of change and relative scarcity; (c) a form of activity in which the pursuit of advantage produces consequences of such a magnitude that they affect in a significant way the whole society or a substantial portion of it. [Given the nature of "politics"], the subject matter of political philosophy has consisted in large measure of the attempt to render politics compatible with the requirements of order. (1960, 10–11)

Because the dilemma faced by the public administrator appears to be personal or removed from the larger aspects of the definition just given, it may seem not to be political in its essence. However, a public manager's decision is made

within a political environment and must fit within the parameters established by
the values of the system. Otherwise, as noted in the first chapter, the cumulative
effects of many decisions may have a negative impact on citizens and their faith
in government; and the citizens must maintain their faith in the integrity and
fairness of the total political system or it will begin to falter and perhaps ultimately
fail. Legislators and chief executives are not the only actors to have an impact
on trust in the political system.

What are the parameters established by the social/political system? At the
broadest level, discussed in political philosophy, the parameters within any
particular system try to allow adjustment within society while maintaining some
semblance of order—however order is defined. Maintaining basic order while
allowing constructive conflict is central to the debate because politics is a system
that controls conflict and allows it to be resolved in a way that maintains the
identity and commitment of the people to the political and social system. Political
activities are a response to fundamental changes taking place in society, while
at the same time the activities are the source of conflict because they represent
the struggle of individuals and groups to "stabilize a situation in a way congenial
to their aspirations and needs" (Wolin 1960, 11). Individuals and groups are
contesting over both values *and* material benefits, with the vigor of the conflict
often unrelated to the nature of the rewards to be won. In fact, differences over
values may be harder to resolve, for many reasons, than conflict over concrete
issues or material benefits.

Public administrators do not usually have the time or inclination to become
experts in political philosophy (Rohr 1978); however, that is no excuse for
ignorance in the area of the basic tenets of Western political thought. Current
students of philosophy rightly claim it is important to understand the set of basic
questions the major political philosophers were attempting to address. These
questions from the past are useful in two ways. First, we must remember the
fundamental values, raised by these philosophers, that are the basis of society
and must be maintained. Second, it is important to remember that in most ethical
dilemmas there is no agreed-upon right answer or perfect way to respond. What
is most useful in many such cases is an ability to ask the right questions so all
significant factors related to the problems are addressed as fully as possible.

These philosophical questions are extremely relevant to the analysis that may
be necessary when an individual tries to consider the impact of his or her action
within the larger governmental and political system. While some minimal understanding of the larger milieu within which the philosophers asked their questions is useful, it is not necessary to be intimately familiar with the background
or the intricacies of their argument in order to comprehend the basic questions
they were addressing and try to apply those questions to one's current situation.
These questions have been condensed and abstracted by several current writers
(Wolin's book is one excellent example) with the idea in mind that these efforts
might help non-experts in the field to benefit from the wisdom of the ages.

One of the best summaries of the critical questions asked within the various systems of ethics has been presented by Wayne A. R. Leys, in his book entitled *Ethics for Policy Decisions* ([1952] 1968). Leys gives a short review of each major school of philosophy, and he also lists in summary form the major questions being addressed by the thinkers/writers in that school. These questions are presented in Table 6. Upon examining the list it becomes clear that questions raised by political thinkers of the past are the same questions public administrators must deal with every day, only in a more specific form related to a real-life situation. It is also obvious that most of the questions we must face—at least as they relate to the political world—have been recognized for a long time as central to the human condition. We are reminded once again that there is little new under the sun.

Obviously, all of these questions are not appropriate in every situation. In fact, any individual who has carefully thought through his or her personal political philosophy may reject some of these questions as wrong in all cases. For example, the ultimate necessity and inevitability of a class war may not be accepted by many, if not most, individuals in democratic systems. Still, when basic philosophical issues must be faced in any situation, the checklist of questions presented by Leys closely resembles the panoply of issues that are addressed by politicians and public servants in Western democracies. There are few ethical dilemmas that cannot be at least clarified, if not resolved, once the relevant questions are answered. It is on this basis that current scholars argue for knowledge about and sensitivity to the basic ideas of Western philosophy. The general understanding gained from this analysis, however, must then be applied to the specific political system operant in the United States of America.

DEMOCRATIC TENETS AND AMERICAN POLITICAL VALUES

While there may be a "chicken and egg" problem (does the political system represent the values of the populace or are the desires and values of the populace formed by the political system?) in examining the basic tenets and values of any government, it is still important to understand the assumptions made by those creating the government and to have a general idea how those assumptions have changed over the years. Likewise, it is essential to understand the values of the citizenry of a state, and whether or not those values are matched by the actions of the political system. In fact, there is always some variance between the values of the citizenry and the actions in the system. The tension generated by this variance is healthy unless and until it becomes too strong, at which time it can lead to unrest and destabilization of the political system as a whole.

In the United States, one of the problems faced by public officials and administrators is developing an understanding of the most basic assumptions made by those who created our rather unique system of government, and the limits and opportunities that are generated by those assumptions. There is also a vociferous debate about the values of the American people and the ability or

Table 6
Critical Questions Developed in the Various Systems of Ethics

<u>Utilitarianism</u> (Bentham)

1. What are the probable consequences of alternative proposals?
2. Which policy will result in the greatest possible happiness of the greatest number?
3. How do the alternatives compare in the intensity, duration, certainty, propinquity, fecundity, purity, and extent of pleasures and pains?
4. What proposed actions are protected from a scrutiny of probable consequences by sacrosanct phrases?
5. What is the factual evidence for assertions about benefits and disadvantages?

<u>Casuistry</u> (Legal Reasoning)

1. What are the authoritative rules and precedents, the agreements and accepted practices? What would be _____'s attitude?
2. Which citations are irrelevant to the case in hand? Which are irrelevant: because they were not intended to apply; because they were not intended literally; because of expressed or unexpressed qualifications; because they were counsels rather than commands; because their meaning can be distinguished from the case at hand; because an application to the present case would not serve the original purpose of the authoritative rule?

<u>Moral Idealism</u> (Plato and Kant)

1. Can you define what you approve? Can you bring various approved practices under a general rule? Does the definition or generalization state what you always approve? Does it cover only those practices that you approve?
2. If there is a conflict of principles, can you find a more abstract statement, a "third principle," which will reconcile the conflicting principles?
3. What is your scale of values? Are you putting first things first?
4. What would you approve in an ideal community?
5. How can you be worthy of happiness?
6. Can you will that the maxim of your action should become the universal law?
7. Are you treating humanity as an end and not merely as a means?
8. Are you legislating for yourself, that is, laying down a rule that you recognize as right?

<u>Stoicism</u> (Epictetus and Spinoza)

1. What is not within our power?
2. What must be accepted as external conditions and what is intolerable because it destroys personal integrity?
3. To what must we be resigned in order to preserve our rationality and self-respect?

<u>Aristotle's Golden Mean</u>

1. What are the undesirable extremes in human disposition?
2. What is the golden mean that secures the highest good attainable under the circumstances?

<u>The Ethics of Psychologists</u> (Hobbes and Butler)

1. What is the nature of human nature? What controlling motives have been overlooked in your deliberations? Has sufficient consideration been given to the disguised selfish interests?
2. Are the motives that are being considered influenced or influenceable by cool reflection?
3. For what purpose do you reckon with the motives of other people?--for the purpose merely of protecting yourself?--with a view to manipulating other people to obtain some desired result?--to calm your own worries and secure peace of mind?--to conform as far as possible to the deliberate wishes of others?--to encourage the restraint of passions?

Table 6 (Continued)

The Historical "Logic" of Hegel

1. What are the main historical trends of institutions? What is the direction of national development?
2. How are our partisan causes related to this larger picture? How may my interests and ideas be reconciled with the interests and ideas of the opposition in the historical evolution of the nation? What is my station and its duties? To what can we all be loyal? In what can we all participate?
3. What synthesis has overcome the opposition of thesis and antithesis?

The Historical "Logic" of Marx

1. What are the fundamental changes in the mode of economic production? What economic classes are created by these changes?
2. How are all issues related to the class conflict? How do class interests determine ideology?
3. What action in the immediate situation will hasten the final show-down in the class war, regardless of the interests of the individuals immediately involved?

Dewey's Instrumental Thinking

1. What is the problematic situation that gave rise to deliberation?
2. What will satisfactorily terminate deliberation, that is, relieve the conflicts and tensions of the situation? Does the proposed solution anticipate consequences in the larger environment as well as the immediate situation?
3. Are our ends changing as well as the means of achieving ends? Does this evolution of ends and interests affect the merits of proposed solutions?

Semantic Analysis

1. Is your knowledge of fact confused by emotional language?
2. Does the language that you use prejudge the issues? Can you translate your description of fact into an expression that has a less or a different emotional meaning?
3. In choosing your course of action, do you select words (as a part of your action) to which other people will respond rationally? Are you engaging in unimportant verbal quibbles? Are you expecting words to do things that words cannot do? Are you failing to engage in verbal ceremonials that are required by other people? Should you engage in verbal trickery in dealing with irrational or preoccupied individuals and groups?

Source: Wayne A. R. Leys, *Ethics for Policy Decisions* (Englewood Cliffs, N.J.: Prentice-Hall, 1952), pp. 189–191.

willingness of the political system to address those values. Scholars of American government, therefore, regularly address the "intent" of the framers of the Constitution and the "values" of society and whether or not either of these elements is adequately addressed by the current political system.

American democracy was the first serious attempt to apply this new idea of participatory democracy, even though in a republican form, when it was established, and it has continued to be unique as it has developed over the years. This is not surprising because the government was established in 1787 to meet the specific problems faced by the thirteen states recently independent from British rule; however, there was at the same time an attempt on the part of the framers of the Constitution to think about the long-term needs of the country and to frame a basic law that would be adaptable as the years passed. They were surprisingly successful. The success came about, in part, because many of the values expressed at that time are still central to our way of governing; we should be aware of those values at all times as we perform our public duties.

What were the general assumptions about government and politics forming the basis on which the framers of the Constitution operated? What ideas led the framers to create specific structures, powers, and limits on the powers of government? Perhaps the best place to look for these ideas is in *The Federalist Papers*, the set of arguments presented by Alexander Hamilton, James Madison, and John Jay (1961) as they tried to convince the citizenry of the Confederation that the new Constitution was essential to governing the thirteen states. While many values, and ideas on structuring government to achieve those values, can be identified and presented from this set of essays, and it is worthwhile to review these invaluable documents every so often, here we look briefly at only three tenets.[1]

First, human nature requires government. *Self-interest* is the most powerful force within the individual, and the government established by the Constitution helps us to overcome this primeval force through the system of checks and balances. Each individual in government serves as a check on all others even as s/he focuses on his or her self-interest. Likewise, each part of the governmental system, in protecting its own powers, limits the powers of all other parts. Self-interest is turned into a force for control of self-interest.

Government must always think of the public good. That requires a method by which the public good can be discovered. Discovery can only be accomplished if the process by which debate and decision occurs remains democratic, or open to the citizens of the country. Thus the second factor comes into play—*process* is as important as substance in determining public policy: While we want to discover the best possible answer to public problems, minorities and individuals must be protected from "the tyranny of the majority." However, and third, once this has been guaranteed, and once we have discovered an acceptable policy, there must be *strength in government*; it must be able to act and fulfill the desires of society. The Constitution was the result of an attempt to balance these three needs: limiting self-interest in public sector decisions, procedurally guaranteeing minority and individual rights, and granting adequate (but no more) power to government to accomplish its goals.

In implementing public policy, the task of public administrators, it is essential to remember that both substance and process are central to proper decisions and actions. The democratic state is founded on the idea of the inherent value of each individual; therefore, public policy must take into consideration the final objective of any action *and* the effect of that action on each citizen as the objective is being attained (Gortner 1981).

A failure to remember this fact lies at the heart of the Iran/Contra scandal. Had Lt. Col. Oliver North remembered he not only wanted to fulfill the president's desires in relation to supporting the Nicaraguan Contras, but that our society and political system expected any such actions to be taken within carefully circumscribed limits, he might have avoided getting into the morass that ultimately led to removal from his job and a long period of debate and hearings trying to clarify what happened and how it could be kept from happening again. It is possible to debate whether or not the substantive goals he sought to accomplish were appropriate or "good," but there is little disagreement that the procedures used were inappropriate in our democratic society.

The central task for students and practitioners of government is to understand these most dear values of the Constitution and how they are interpreted by current society. Obviously, the first place to look is at the Constitution itself, and then to be aware of the evolution of the fundamental tenets of that document as its interpretation has shifted to keep up with the fundamental values of society. The question all public administrators must ask themselves occasionally is, "How does the Constitution (and its foremost interpreters—usually the Supreme Court) address the issues that are central to the ethical dilemma I face?" John Rohr (1978) makes a convincing argument that an ideal way to keep up with the changes in basic societal values is to watch the ongoing debate of the Supreme Court, where the ultimate meaning of concepts, phrases, and clauses of the Constitution are hammered out in the crucible of judicial argument about real-world situations.

The concepts in the Constitution have remained relatively steadfast, but in many cases they have been slowly but surely broadened in their meaning and in the context they are interpreted to cover. Basic values such as those guaranteed in the Bill of Rights and the Fourteenth Amendment have been applied to more people and reinterpreted to cover a wider range of aspects of personal life. It is essential to be aware of changes in individual rights, not only to keep from making grievous errors when faced with an ethical problem, but also to understand the historical movement of interpretations because such information can be used to project continuing societal changes in the future.

In a way the Supreme Court is a barometer of changing values in society. Rights are the external representation of the values held in society, and the Supreme Court is the ultimate guardian and interpreter of those rights, sometimes following public opinion and in other instances leading it. The rights get reinterpreted because of the shifting balance between the contending parts of our value system, which in turn is influenced, at least in part, by the changing economic, political, and social conditions in and around society.

Students of politics attempt to assess the current values held in American society, and to measure change occurring over time. Individuals involved in this activity argue it is impossible to serve the public unless you have an understanding of the public's basic values and political mood; however, understanding the public's attitudes toward government and politics is not easy. What those who examine such issues usually find, as evidenced by the work of Abraham Kaplan ([1963] 1980) and H. Mark Roelofs (1976), is a constant conflict between competing values, with both or all sets of values operant within society at the same time.

Abraham Kaplan, in the more optimistic of the two studies, argues there are several political ideals existent in America, and premier among those ideals are *liberty* (the rights primarily guaranteed in the Bill of Rights and the Fourteenth Amendment to the Constitution), *equality* (especially equal opportunity), and *fraternity* (kindness, human fellowship, and mutual help owed person to person).[2]

At the same time there are other values in society that compete with these three idealistic concepts. Freedom to search for the good life, closely related to all three of the principle values, was often transmuted into materialism. Liberty to think what one wishes, which recognizes contextualism in thought and values, often becomes moral absolutism. And the diversity promised by freedom is often overcome by demands for conformity on the part of the majority.

While he addresses everyone in society, the message of Kaplan is especially important to public servants. He argues that the way to resolve the conflicts created by these competing values, and the "vulgarization" of them, is to set public policy, make public decisions, and operate the political system and government according to moral bases. At the same time we must shun "the desire for absolutes and the pretense of certitude [which] are a constitutional weakness of democracy where everything turns on popular support" ([1963] 1980, 93).

Achieving this goal is not easy, but it is essential. Morality is not simply a matter of applying an agreed-upon principle to a case naturally falling within its scope. In the real world there *are* conflicting principles to weigh, and there *are not* easy, quantifiable results to be calculated for choosing any one principle to the exclusion of others. Instead, several conflicting principles often must be considered at once, and the answer arrived at, or the action taken, based on "a balance of probabilities on behalf of the preponderant values."

[I]n politics the straight line is the shortest distance to perdition. To move unswervingly toward predetermined objectives is inevitably to bypass morality. Circumstances alter cases, and whatever be true of abstract principles, concrete moral values are nothing if not circumstantial. God himself repented His creation when confronted by the generation of Noah. In a democracy, at any rate, policy must reconcile conflicting values, especially conflicting judgements of value, among the makers of policy. (Kaplan [1963] 1980, 91)

We generally operate as if the "government" and "the people" are unitary in nature and always operate singlemindedly, or agree on a common definition of the problem, available alternatives, and values related to choice. Or to quote another writer of the time, Charles Lindblom (1959), on decisions in the public policy process, we act as if decisions are made according to a rational model. Both Lindblom and Kaplan argue that such a model does not portray reality. Instead, an incremental model—with its existing multiple definitions, widely varied ideas about possible alternatives, and divergent values on the part of the actors—describes what happens. In this case, moral issues may be rampant, and they must be solved in the political or governmental arena.

For government, the locus of moral issues is in such encounters as that of a secretary of state facing a senatorial hearing. For the people, it is in the encounter, not only among a multiplicity of overlapping groups but also within the individual, among the fragmentary selves whose integration is the achievement of moral maturity. (Kaplan [1963] 1980, 92)

Kaplan believes that a recognition of the inevitable interaction of morality and power in achieving the public interest will help to guarantee the continuation of the best American values. He also believes that a major role in accomplishing that goal is in the hands of the public servant. Fulfilling that role will not be easy, but it can be accomplished.

Roelofs agrees with Kaplan that there is competition between values; however, he refers to this phenomenon in American society as a conflict between *ideology*—"the framework of political consciousness, the set of ideas, by which a people, or at least its dominant, governing element, organizes itself for political action"—and *myth*—the "framework of political consciousness by which a people becomes aware of itself as a people, as having an identity in history, and by which it is also prepared to recognize some governing regime within its community as legitimate" (1976, 4).

There is always, in every society, a fundamental and ongoing conflict between these disparate frameworks of political consciousness. Since myth is oriented toward national identification and aspiration (the dreams of society), and ideology attempts to explain the real-world patterns of operative behavior, it is almost impossible in organized societies to avoid discrepancies between ideologies and myths.

Both are fundamentally concerned with human memory, human action, and human aspiration. Both, in the jargon of scholars, are norm and value laden. But ideology is the thought pattern of persons whose work must be done day by day. Myth is the ancient memory and the generational hope of the whole people, its "civil religion." (Roelofs 1976, 4)

According to Roelofs, those in power in the United States operate under a set of rules he calls "bourgeois ideology," based on materialism and self-aggrandizement, while society at large accepts a "Protestant myth," based on the concepts of love and piety. Herein lies the conflict. Self-interest is at the center of bourgeois ideology and is the basis for political action[3], and it is on this basis the interior logic of the governmental engine was designed by Madison and his compatriots. However, the preaching and exhortation of a steady stream of religious leaders, populist politicians, and self-appointed protectors of the American political conscience have created "the most thoroughly moralistic and pietistic of modern countries" (Roelofs 1976, 75).

Three democratic myths are held dear by the public: egalitarianism, popular government, and presidential greatness. First, there is a common belief among the public that all people are equal, even though what "equal" means may vary greatly across the society. Second, it is believed the people are sovereign—they control government through popular elections—and therefore we have a "gov-

ernment of laws not of men," thus helping to guarantee the egalitarianism
perceived in the first axiom. Third, it is commonly accepted that the presidency,
to quote Clinton Rossiter is "one of the few truly successful institutions created
by men in their endless quest for the blessings of free government" (1962, 13).
The president is seen as omniscient and omnipotent, or as nearly so as man in
man-made office can be.

Against these myths Roelofs contrasts what he sees as the results of bourgeois
ideology in everyday life. The truth is: All people are not equal, in fact, a group
of "Barons" runs the most important parts of the country; government is not
controlled by the public, but by a privileged minority; and presidents are limited
in their knowledge and power. The conflict within society arises in the contrast
between belief and reality, and this is where the constant tension is created.

It is in the governmental bureaucracy that this conflict is faced and an attempt
is made to resolve it, although Roelofs seems to believe the attempt is futile.[4]
In the attempt to do the work of government with some regard to the public
interest, the public bureaucracy has adopted a "rational/professional" mind set.
The rational/professional mentality is not related to the other two frameworks
of political consciousness (myth and ideology), nor does it contain the schizo-
phrenic tendencies created by the conflict they suffer. Bureaucrats gain their
identity through demonstrable, acknowledged professional competence in a specific skill or position, and "they see themselves summoned to serve neither this
person nor that one, and certainly not themselves, but society generally" (Roelofs
1976, 205).

While bureaucrats, the rational/professional servants within the political system, are essential to the functioning of government, they fit neither the bourgeois
ideology nor the Protestant myth; therefore, the bureaucracy works in its own
set of confusions and strains. The bureaucracy, with its rational/professional
mind set, "while it strives nobly and competently to go about its work, finds
its motives as often frustrated as encouraged and its efforts harassed as often as
harnessed" (Roelofs 1976, 201). The political system gives these public servants
neither sufficient direction nor long-term discipline, so they try to do the public's
work in a frustrating and ambiguous environment. The political system gives
bureaucratic actors little help in facing any decisions, but especially ethical ones.
Yet those same actors are expected to maintain high ethical standards and they
must operate in the fishbowl of public scrutiny by individuals representing the
competing sets of values.

While Kaplan and Roelofs offer no specific guidance in resolving the problem
of conflicting values, they help to clarify our ideas about values and their importance in dealing with ethical issues in the political milieu faced by public
servants. In fact, in discussing this issue with students in a course dealing with
the ethical dimensions of public administration, it has become increasingly clear
that there are three major sets of values playing an important role in the decision
process of the public bureaucrat: democratic, bureaucratic, and personal values.
While there is some overlap in the three sets of values, there is also a significant

divergence in them, and that divergence creates frequent conflicts that define many ethical conflicts. Understanding this fact does not resolve the conflicts; however, it certainly helps to clarify the source and nature of them and allows public servants to make more intelligent decisions. This appears to be the best situation that we can hope to achieve in the human art of politics and government.

INSIGHTS FROM RELIGIOUS TEACHINGS

A third area where scholars argue much can be learned about the values held dear in society is the religious thought of the people. Religious teachings tell us much about society *and* ourselves. The personal aspect of religion was mentioned briefly in Chapter 3, where knowledge of individual characteristics is discussed. Here we focus on the "macro" elements of religious life and belief in society.

While we in the United States argue for total religious freedom, there is a common thread of religious teaching running through our social and political history. Although we argue for the separation of church and state, we certainly disagree about what constitutes minimal and proper separation; in fact, it can be argued that "separation of *church* and state" is quite different from "separation of *religion* and state," and this may be at the center of our ongoing debate about issues such as state support for religious education. However, it is indisputable that many values in the United States can be traced directly to society's religious background—the Judeo-Christian ethic—although it is important to note that these values have been enriched, in later years, by a mixture of other religions as individuals from other parts of the world have increasingly immigrated to our country.

The importance of religious teachings to our particular examination of ethical dilemmas is related to the basis of religion and its meaning. All religions attempt to help individuals deal with questions about personal existence, the value of the individual within the larger scheme of things, and the relative importance, value, and/or worth of concrete goods and abstract concepts—therefore, ideas worthy of personal commitment and sacrifice. These issues relate to the ethical questions with which we must deal. Obviously, many people participate in a religion at a very superficial level without ever addressing these basic questions; thus we can argue that people operate at different levels of religious commitment just as we can argue that individuals operate at different levels of moral maturity.

At the individual level, the religious background of any person helps to create the perspective that s/he has of what is or is not an ethical problem, how that problem should be defined, and how ethical questions in general are framed and analyzed. Therefore, it is important to be aware of this influence and to recognize the limitations this might place on individuals or groups as a dilemma is examined. This is especially true if groups involved in the situation are from different religious backgrounds. (Of course religious background is only one of a number of factors—for example, ethnicity, social class, etc.—that would influence any decision or action, but when combined with those other factors they can have a tremendous cumulative influence on the perceptions and actions of individuals.) A black Protestant bureaucrat in New York City who has to resolve a conflict involving Hasidic Jews and Hispanic Catholics must be aware of the impact of religion (and culture in its broader terms) on the way these individuals will interpret reality and define acceptable alternative solutions.

Even if one does not accept a particular theology, it is often true that useful insights about society as a whole, and about individuals in society, can be learned from its teachings. One cannot understand Israel, or the way an Israeli may think about political problems, without having some knowledge about the Jewish religion. Likewise, one cannot operate effectively in Moslem countries without understanding Islam, nor in countries in Latin America without understanding the role of the Catholic church in society. The fact that we have a mixture of national backgrounds as well as adherents to Protestant, Catholic, Jewish, and other religious faiths in the United States immediately says something about our country and the problems we face as we deal with sensitive issues where these religions and cultures intersect.

A special problem exists here. In some fundamental ways individual/religious values and societal/political values do not precisely correspond, and we must be aware of these divergences. Perhaps the most fundamental example of noncongruence has been noted by Reinhold Niebuhr ([1932] 1960) in his book, *Moral Man and Immoral Society*, when he comments:

From the perspective of society the highest moral ideal is justice. From the perspective of the individual the highest ideal is unselfishness. Society must strive for justice even if it is forced to use means, such as self-assertion, resistance, coercion and perhaps resentment, which cannot gain the moral sanction of the most sensitive moral spirit. The individual must strive to realise his life by losing and finding himself in something greater than himself. . . . (p. 257)

[A] high type of unselfishness, even if it brings ultimate rewards, demands immediate sacrifices. An individual may sacrifice his own interests, either without hope of reward or in the hope of an ultimate compensation. But how is an individual, who is responsible for the interests of his group, to justify the sacrifice of interests other than his own? "It follows," declares Hugh Cecil, "that all that department of morality which requires an individual to sacrifice his interests to others, everything which falls under the heading of unselfishness, is inappropriate to the action of a state. No one has a right to be unselfish with other people's interests." (p. 267)

For this reason, students of politics—in the United States—usually argue that in performing a job which is a public trust, it is essential to separate individual feelings and personal interpretations of "right" and "justice" from those of the larger society. This does not mean you should never allow personal values to take precedence over those of the society and political system within which you work; *it does mean that one should have full knowledge of which set of values is being used and what the impact of an action will be on both the individual and the system.*

This was a point often made by Martin Luther King. He told his followers they should understand they were attempting to change the values of individuals in the larger society. Therefore, if they broke a specific law they should be ready to pay the price for having done so. By so doing King and his followers were able to literally change the formal and informal values and rules of society. He obviously understood that, in those cases where he led acts of civil disobedience, the actions of him and his followers would force individuals across the United States to recognize that there was a conflict between many existing laws and a deep-seated value of equality in treatment for all citizens. In the United States, this conflict in values could be forced into people's attention by peaceful demonstration. (The same tactics had worked for Nehru in India, but again he was dealing with a British society that could be touched by such demonstrations.) This tactic worked in a society that believed in the Judeo-Christian ethic and in basic democratic principles. It probably would not work in most authoritarian/statist societies.[5]

In the United States it is considered essential for public servants to have empathy (understanding so intimate that the feelings, thoughts, and motives of one are readily comprehended by another) for the culture, values, and beliefs of others within society; however, that understanding is not supposed to become sympathy (an affinity between persons in which whatever affects one correspondingly affects the other, often leading to devotion, allegiance, and favoritism). Empathy allows sensitivity in judgement while maintaining objectivity; sympathy crosses the border into subjectivity, a dangerous position in which to find one's self. While this assumption that empathy is good but sympathy is dangerous is true across the fields of values, culture, and religion, it is most important in dealing with religion because of the multiplicity and variance of religious beliefs in American society. Problems with a religious base may not appear regularly or often within the realm of the public bureaucracy; however, when they do they must be handled with utmost sophistication and sensitivity, for they touch the core values of the individuals involved.

BASIC VALUES AND THE BUREAUCRAT

While "the law" (discussed in Chapter 4) is always close to the surface of any bureaucrat's consciousness, the culture of his or her society is generally taken for granted. It is easy to go through life in a society and not give much thought to "the rest of the world outside." Within the larger social order, an organization has its own culture, which we will examine in the next chapter, and immersion in that culture can easily blot out consciousness of the same phenomenon on a larger scale. Thus individuals can be doubly influenced by culture and hardly be aware of it. However, the interviews carried out for this research show that all three issues discussed here are addressed, albeit often indirectly. As one of the interviewed managers argued, most successful managers are aware of the impact of culture on actions, but culture does not usually impinge on one's thinking. Instead it creates an environment, a milieu, in which alternatives are imagined and analyzed. We are aware of it only if we stop and think specifically of it. Obviously, to the extent that general values, principles, and perceptions do apply, they must then be translated so they become relevant to the specific issue about which we are concerned.

Translation of the generalities of culture to the concrete actions of administration is the skill most needed by middle managers in the public service, even though they often develop it without immediate recognition that such understanding is growing as part of their arsenal of available tools.

The issue of *religion* appears to be relatively distant for most public managers. Almost none of them addressed religion as a general cultural factor, although it was mentioned as a personal factor affecting decisions (see Chapter 3). However, moral stances closely related to religious beliefs may become excruciatingly important in those cases where public policy and religious beliefs intersect (e.g., the abortion issue or the debate over public support of private education in church–run schools). As one individual in a health policy position noted,

In these cases you are working with "true believers," [she borrowed this term from Eric Hoffer, 1951] and their values become more important than those of society, or they see their values as "right" for society whether others agree or not.

This problem becomes especially difficult if someone with this kind of mentality is appointed to a top position in a public agency. Because of their true believer mentality, they often forget or fail to give credence to policy positions developed through the democratic process and to procedures guaranteeing due process or protection of minority rights. They simply want to act, to carry out a policy, to hire someone, to change a policy because "I am the boss and I believe my decision is right." These people often fail to see the damage they might cause to the democratic system. One manager in this situation who faced a lot of "heat" because of his refusal to obey orders immediately, commented:

One of the hardest parts of doing your job as an upper middle manager is dealing with appointed officials who are brought in because of their personal stand for or against a particular issue. While we as bureaucrats are not supposed to take sides, our superiors occasionally have very strong opinions, in fact are brought in because of their advocacy of a position, and then it is extremely difficult to maintain any equanimity in handling the details of the program. In dealing with the public, we can listen empathetically to both sides and then interpret their desires within the context of the laws and policies that exist. Superiors, because they are often from outside the governmental and bureaucratic systems, do not understand the limits to interpretation and implementation of laws. They simply want something done, do not care how it is accomplished, and are not used to being told "you cannot do that." They are often from business, where their commands are not countered by law or questioned by a watching public. And they do not understand that in these highly emotional cases there is always careful scrutiny from both sides. [The officials], therefore, become very angry at us even though we are keeping them from getting into deep trouble. They do not understand that.

One way this manager handled his superior when the appointed official insisted on "bending the law" to carry out a personally motivated action was by delaying action as long as possible while reiterating that "the boss had a legal right to carry out the action, but also consistently pointing out that there was more to the issue than legality, it was an issue of ethics." Since the superior was new to appointive office and came from a dramatically different environment, he was not sensitive to the fact that the press would *inevitably* get access to the information. Nor was he aware of what the press could and would do with the information.

[Therefore] I thought my major role was to have him try to understand that the public sector was a world of perception, perception was often equal to, if not more important, than issues of legality. I always used with him the phrase, "Does it pass the 'smell' test?" When it becomes public information, will it be perceived or understood by the public as ethical? You can rationalize the manipulating of . . . regulations and law so you can say, "Hey, it really wasn't illegal." But that is not the issue. The issue is, is it unethical? Is it bad public policy?

Ultimately the administrator's actions were appreciated, but only after a lengthy period of intense pressure to "knuckle under" and do what his superior wanted.

Special care both to be and appear to be objective, not directly engaged, and to make it clear that personal feelings were not involved in their decisions, was the general rule when issues as deeply felt as religious beliefs were involved. The consensus of those who were involved in these issues was that neutrality (the separation of personal and official feelings) was the only way to survive and maintain an ability to operate over the long haul in these volatile fields. Surgeon General C. Everett Koop, serving in the Reagan administration, was an outstanding model of an individual who did not try to hide his personal beliefs and values regarding issues he had to deal with, but who also showed he would deal with volatile issues such as smoking, abortion, or AIDS in a clear, objective, and scientific manner befitting someone who must represent the medical profession in a way that served all the people of the nation. While he was reviled by specific groups for his stand on specific issues, the surgeon general was highly respected by the vast majority of the nation because of his ability to separate personal and official duties much in the way described by Niebuhr.

General philosophical tenets were never raised by any of the interviewees in their initial discussion of their cases. When asked about such concepts and whether or not they had any influence, it became obvious that few of the interviewees could discuss philosophical principles on a familiar level, at least in relation to their specific cases; however, they were aware of the basic influence that such principles had in forming the general belief and thinking system that they used. For example, when asked if philosophical principles had any influence on her actions, the lawyer who was faced with the problem of a witness being pressured by his supervisor to change his testimony in a regulatory hearing (see Chapter 7) replied,

I did not think about them at the time. Nothing that cosmic. Now, with several years of experience and responsibility for young lawyers who are in the position I was then, I think about philosophical issues a little more.

What was mentioned by most of the interviewees was a sensitivity to democratic values and the values of society at large. These two factors played a significant role in the decision processes used by most of the managers as they tried to deal with their specific cases. However, they tended to simplify these principles into general categories with which they could deal in the everyday world of organizational decision making.

The word most often heard was "fairness." In almost every case the managers sought to guarantee they were fair in their actions, but that term meant more than just satisfying their own sense of fairness so they could sleep at night. They were interested in a general perception of fairness as defined by others, including the general public. An example of the desire to be fair while carrying out normal managerial tasks was presented by one gentleman who had to deal with a particularly thorny example of a relatively common problem for a manager, "What do you do with a problem employee who has been unloaded on you?"

George Anderson was the supervisor of a team of statistical analysts, all with at least one master's degree, who were responsible for developing evaluation tools, carrying out evaluation studies, and reporting on program effectiveness in the Department of Labor. Early in the spring, George was called into "the front office" and informed that he was being assigned Laura Weston, a young, handicapped lady, who would work with his team. He was informed by his superiors that her only physical impediment was a total loss of hearing, but she was a very good accountant, and they thought she could become a good program auditor. Laura had started working for the Department of Labor a little over three years earlier, as a GS 5, and was now a GS 11. Since his superiors were interested in helping Laura, and since she would need special help in fitting into the new organization, George had carte blanche to spend any money he wanted on getting her trained.

By early summer it became obvious that George had not been given complete information about the young lady now working for him. While Laura tried very hard, she had encumbrances that had not been mentioned. It turned out that she had no short-term recall and probably less–than–average intelligence. She was taking up 25–30 percent of George's time, and if he was not there when she came looking for him she just stopped anybody else and disrupted their work for an extended period of time. She could not come even remotely close to the performance standards for her GS 11 position.

By fall the problem was causing difficulties for the work group, including delays in completing some of the studies; so George decided that it was time to do a little background investigation. First, he went to the front office. They denied any previous knowledge of the additional handicaps and evaded the real issue of what to do with her by simply noting, "Hey, we do not want a problem here. Don't cause trouble." Second, he approached individuals from the office where Laura had worked prior to being assigned to his office, and he discovered there had been similar problems in that office. In fact, it was rumored that she had threatened to commit suicide if she was not given her last promotion; apparently her supervisor took her threat seriously. He gave her a promotion, and then quietly moved her out of the office—and into George's shop—with the help of some friends "up above." Third, George went to the personnel office to find out what the performance and review standards were for handicapped people. Their position was absolutely clear. "Be as helpful as you can; however, the performance standards are the same for all individuals in all positions. If she cannot do the job, fire her."

Finally, he talked to a few of his peers and members of his staff whom he trusted not to spread any gossip about the problem. The general consensus was that "the bosses" would not like it if George made waves. To make it even worse, any action against Laura would probably lead to a law suit which would be almost unwinnable. In such a suit the supervisor would probably get no support from any superiors in the organization and would end up being characterized as "a person in the office who is against handicapped people and who really took it out on this poor lady."

While contemplating this relatively unpalatable set of factors, time ran out. George found in his mail Laura's evaluation and recommendation for an in-grade pay raise. A couple of days later Laura approached him and asked, "When am I going to get promoted?" George had to examine his alternatives and decide what to do.

There were a series of impinging factors. First, George felt sorry for Laura. She had suffered a lot of "rough licks" in life. Second, he had never seen a person try harder and accomplish more given her starting point. Third, in a way it was not her fault that she had been hired to do a job it was doubtful she could ever perform, nor that she had been promoted far beyond her capabilities. Fourth, the people in the front office had made it very clear they wanted no problems.

Basically, five options were open to George:

- Go along and give Laura her in-grade raise and support her promotion. Try to continue working with her.

- Give Laura her raise but suggest that she not be promoted. Try to continue to work with her.

- Do either of the above and try to move Laura to another office—unload her just as had been done when she came to his office.

- Start procedures toward firing her.

- Try to find a position between the two extremes of "going along" and "firing."

George had to act immediately on the evaluation and in-grade raise recommendations, and the recommendation had an important impact on the options open to him later. The easy way out was simply to go along and approve the raise. If he did, he was left with two options.

- First, if he gave Laura a satisfactory evaluation and recommended that she be given her in-grade pay raise, the front office would not even know about it; this would allow him to buy time in order to figure out what he wanted to do. However, if he approved the in-grade, he would undo any case for removal in the future because Laura could use the evaluation as proof of her satisfactory performance on the job.

- Second, if George approved Laura's in-grade, he could then try to get rid of her by pushing her off on someone else. He would be rid of the problem which the front office did not want to deal with. On the other hand, it did not seem appropriate to continue to pass on the problem. If Laura was not able to perform satisfactorily, it was unethical to perpetuate the problem, both from the view of wasting the taxpayers' dollars and from the view of good management and personnel principles.

George decided on a middle-ground solution. He told his superiors in the front office, "I am not going to approve Laura's in-grade pay raise because I think she ought to be fired. I am willing—and I have talked to my staff, who back me—to start the procedures to fire her. Tell me what you want me to do. However, please understand, I will not approve her in-grade pay raise or her promotion."

There was no immediate response. When Laura's in-grade recommendation was due, George again took a middle-ground position. He could have given her all unsatisfactories—which would have put a lot of pressure on the front office. They could not, in that case, get out of facing the problem. Instead, he gave her a low but not completely unsatisfactory review; however, he noted on the review that he was evaluating her at the GS 5 performance level. (Since she was currently a GS 11, George was not sure that his action was actually legal.)

George's "middle-ground action" led to two immediate responses. First George's superiors "got bent all out of shape." No one ever said that what George did was wrong; they were upset because it put them on the spot. Even though George had volunteered to take the heat for firing Laura, they could not bring themselves to tell him to do so, nor could they face the problem of what to do in this very sticky situation.

Second, upon receipt of her rating, Laura spent many hours in George's office weeping and arguing. He could not bring himself to throw her out of his office, but neither was he willing to bend. He would not change the review. Sure enough, she threatened to commit suicide if he did not change his mind. His response to this threat was, "I hope you do not because that would be devastating to me. On the other hand, you are neither stupid nor mentally unbalanced. If you decide to do so, that is your decision and you will be doing it, not me." When her pleas failed, she appealed to individuals in the higher offices, including that of the director.

Shortly thereafter the front office moved Laura to a position in another program. In following the situation, George noticed that Laura again received an unsatisfactory rating and that she was once again moved. He was informed by the supervisor under whom Laura had been moved that, "Since you took the bull by the horns, I felt that I could give Laura an objective [unsatisfactory] rating without getting into trouble." At that point Laura was moved into a position where she could do a minimally proficient job. Even though it was a job rated at a lower GS level, she was protected by the pay rules. The top administrators let her work the minimum time required (five years) and gave her a medical retirement (which was questionable legally because she had been hired with the disability, she had not developed it from or on the job, but no one wished to force that issue).

George, because of the year of pressure and trauma surrounding the situation, moved to a new position that was physically removed from the prior site. He felt that he had to go someplace where he could get away from the immediate environment. Even so, the story had spread throughout the organization. People in the immediate work group, who had been involved in the incident, understood the dynamics of the situation; they had tried to work with Laura. But as the story moved further out in the organization it got twisted. Two years later, when George had a totally different type of problem with a secretary, she brought up the case as a way of accusing him of being unreasonable and "picking on her." It took several years for the story to die down, and there is no guarantee that it might not reappear if it is to someone's advantage to bring it up.

In this case the problem related to the handling of a disabled employee, but that central problem was influenced in many ways by the culture and values of our society. In the first place, based on a set of values that is still evolving, society has established very strict rules relating to the equal opportunity of handicapped individuals and guaranteeing that they are treated fairly by other individuals, especially employers. Everyone, including George Anderson's superiors, recognized the sensitivity of the issue and did not want to face the hard decisions, nor the time-consuming effort involved.

Second, even though George was careful to follow the rules and regulations, he knew that this was a case where he would be "found guilty until proven innocent." Anyone not intimately familiar with the facts of the situation would almost automatically be sympathetic to Laura and that bias would have to be overcome.

Third, even George Anderson's attitudes were influenced by the general societal values. He sympathized with Laura because "she had suffered a lot of rough licks," and he felt that she worked very hard to overcome her problems. Both sympathy for the unfortunate and appreciation of the work ethic influenced him as he had to make his tough decisions.

Fourth, however, he was also influenced by the values associated with his position to work efficiently and effectively: he did not want to "waste taxpayer dollars."

Ultimately the test that he used was that of "fairness." George Anderson noted, "My own personal values informed me of a lot as I went along; however, I wanted to be perceived by the other relevant actors as fair, generous, honest [remember Kaplan's discussion of *fraternity* as an American social and political value]." In order to check the perception of others, he discussed the case with as many other individuals as he could bring into the process without expanding it beyond the range of reasonableness. He used these discussions to construct a perception of what other relevant actors considered fair and used that as a yardstick against which to measure his actions, thereby giving himself an external check of his definition of the term.

Valerie Franklin, in discussing her problem of unserved minority clients, consistently used the term "equity"; however, since it dealt with the treatment of minority individuals and organizations the term was synonymous in many ways with the more general term fairness. She could not accept the unequal treatment, based on irrelevant and biased criteria, of supposedly comparable organizations. The consistent issue for all of the managers as they faced their ethical dilemmas was to come to an understanding of what was "fair" and then to follow the guidelines and limits established by that definition.

A policy of openness and the guarantee of due process was often essential to the concept of fairness. As noted by one interviewee at a relatively high level of his organization,

I think that government ought to be sensitive to notions of fairness. When you are dealing with public business it is important to make sure nothing undercuts confidence because people see business being done for personal benefit. One of the best ways to achieve that confidence is through openness, so there can be no perception of shady deals or special arrangements. I will not argue that policy always should be made in the sunshine, but its implementation must occur in an environment of sharp shadows.

Very closely related is the concept of due process. Managers had to balance their actions in such a way that they could protect the integrity of their organizations while at the same time guaranteeing fair treatment of those involved in the situations under consideration. Due process was a guarantee of fairness for all concerned in the ethical dilemmas.

Central to ethical sensitivity in almost all of the cases was the *learning that occurred through experience and observation*. Ethical maturity, the ability to understand and deal with ethical dilemmas, which might also be defined as "wisdom," increased with time and the opportunity to deal with a variety of ethical situations. The individual who dealt in the greatest detail with the changing values of society and his growing sensitivity to them argued that

There is growth and new inputs with experience and insights. If you are a thoughtful person then you are going to be concerned about "How am I practicing my profession?" There are a lot of environmental influences that work on you. I had a checkered career. I worked in several different organizations (Department of Defense; National Aeronautics and Space Administration; Department of Health, Education and Welfare; the Civil Service Commission), and there is a vast array of values that come into play in your consciousness throughout these experiences.

In the same way I got sensitized to societal values through experience. What happens is our values—and societal values—change over time. I was the person who drew up the separation papers for the homosexual whose case went to the Supreme Court. At that time it was a straightforward case for me; what you do is separate anybody who is "morally unfit." That was the standard. The Supreme Court said there must be a nexus between outside conduct and job performance, and the government could not prove—however one felt about the moral reprehensibleness of the actions of the gentleman—a connection between his performance off the job and performance on the job. The Supreme Court ruled that the only reason to separate anyone was "for such cause as will promote the efficiency of the service." The gentleman was restored with back pay. If you look at the values that were in play—this was back in the early 1960s—we didn't have the appreciation of the problem of sexual preference that we do now. It is very clear, because of that court case, and for other reasons, that society's modal [most common] values have changed with respect to "sexual preference."

In a similar manner due process in security matters has changed dramatically. The 1960 values were loyalty and security, but individuals were deprived of due process. We now tend to believe that an individual's rights as a citizen are much less curtailed by virtue of government employment. I started my career with the traditional view that you have no "right" to work for the government, and if you decide you want to work for the government you give up certain rights. I think that the evolution of civil service law, based to a great extent on changing social values, over the last twenty years has made serious inroads into that position.

I had a lot more ethical problems to deal with when I came to Washington than I ever had out in the field. However, *maybe* that is because I became more sensitized.

Many writers, such as Ralph Hummel (1987) and even including Max Weber (1947), have argued continued existence in the bureaucracy numbs one's sensitivity to, and dulls one's ability to make decisions about, "gray" issues in unclear-cut areas of ethics. We shall discuss this phenomenon more in Chapter 6; however, it is sufficient here to say this charge does not appear to hold as a *universal* assessment of the sensitivity of bureaucrats. For all but one of the individuals interviewed in this study, experience created greater sensitivity to, and ability to deal with, ethical problems. Variations on this theme were regularly presented by our managers. Perhaps this is because they started out with a sensitivity to such issues and that sensitivity increased, whereas others may never have been attuned to ethical issues in the first place. The basic openness to cultural values may have to exist prior to commencing a public career (this is probably true of business also), and if one has no such nature from the beginning it may be difficult to instill it. However, if an awareness of social and political values exists, it can be cultivated and made to play a major role in guaranteeing an ethical public service.

NOTES

1. The three issues mentioned in this paragraph are all addressed in *Federalist No. 51*, written by James Madison, where he notes that adequate power to govern has been granted the new national government, but that power has been divided within the governmental structure so as to limit encroachment on individual freedoms. In order to guarantee that the power stays divided rather than becoming concentrated, the power is distributed between the three branches of government.

[T]he great security against a gradual concentration of the several powers in the same department, consists in giving to those who administer each department the necessary constitutional means and personal motives to resist encroachments of the others. . . . Ambition must be made to counteract ambition. . . . It may be a reflection on human nature, that such devices should be necessary to control the abuses of government. But what is government itself, but the greatest of all reflections on human nature? If men were angels, no government would be necessary. If angels were to govern men, neither external nor internal controls on government would be necessary. In framing a government which is to be administered by men over men, the great difficulty lies in this: you must first enable the government to control the governed; and in the next place oblige it to control itself. (Hamilton, Madison, and Jay 1961, 321–322)

2. I say Kaplan is optimistic because he believes that the American dream can continue and flourish if we want it badly enough. He makes this clear in his conclusion when he says:

My aim [in this book] has been to reinstate the connection between morality and power, to give political force to moral principle. . . . Whatever its shortcomings, it is the old-fashioned American dream that brought America moral greatness. . . .

I am myself an immigrant, from a family of immigrants, and I see America still as those huddled masses saw it—so various, so beautiful, so new. When my father visited Washington for the first time, I stood with him under the dome of the Capitol and watched what he saw of America struggling with what he remembered of tsarist Russia. Then he asked, "Does it really belong to us?" It does indeed—it belongs to the people, to all the people—if we but choose to make it our own. ([1963] 1980, 107)

3. Self-interest, of course, lies at the heart of one of our most popular political/economic theories of the time—Public Choice Theory. Supporters of this theory, like Madison and

his friends at an earlier time, argue that this basic urge can be used or structured to achieve better decisions in politics and government. I suspect Roelofs and his compatriots would vociferously deny that any political structure can be created to guarantee that any combination of "self-interests" will equal the "public interest."

4. Hopefully, the situation is not as bad as Roelofs believes, for he sees little hope of resolving the conflicts he portrays, and he believes those conflicts to be paralyzing in a way that gives us little hope to correct the problems or to deal with the changing world around us. He argues that,

Perhaps America's most pressing need as a political community is to abandon pretense and admit general political incompetence. Until that happens, the American political system will remain a dangerous actor on the world stage and a woefully self-deluding one at home, with unpredictable consequences in both areas. . . .

America's condition is not unique. Recorded history shows numerous examples of societies suffering from the same political immobilism in the face of major problems that afflict this country. We must beware of illusions of freedom. We have no more liberty to make over our future than our history allows us. The past is a prison. If there is to be escape from it, the keys must be found within. Keys of the right size and strength may not exist for us. (1976, 242)

5. Simply stated, "authoritarian" societies are based on the assumption that society cannot survive without a definite hierarchy of authority that usually distributes most or all of the power to the upper classes, and often only to the leader and perhaps his select group of compatriots. "Statist" societies are those where the preservation of the state is considered more important than the preservation of individuals and/or their liberties. These two ideas—authoritarianism and statism—usually go together. Obviously, other factors, such as personal benefit, often are cloaked in such language, but we need not deal with that fact here.

CHAPTER 6

ORGANIZATIONAL DYNAMICS: THE MANAGER'S ENVIRONMENT

The idea of the organization as part of the problem no longer seems novel and farfetched. Much literature argues that a major factor in failing to maintain a humane and ethical bureaucracy is the organization itself. This argument is perhaps most powerfully made by Ralph Hummel who argues, ''[B]ureaucracy . . . has produced [a] dehumanized human fragment—socially crippled, culturally normless, psychologically dependent, linguistically mute, and politically powerless'' (1977, 221). Literature dealing with bureaucracy[1] is filled with discussions of the ways this type of organization can cause difficulties in dealing directly with important issues by focusing attention on means instead of ends, by creating conservative and hesitant attitudes in officials and employees, and by allowing strong personalities to control perceptions and communications in a way that denies realistic appraisals and actions when they are most needed.

Many of the most serious travesties of ethical behavior have been justified on the grounds that the perpetrators of evil were ''obeying the orders of their superiors''; this was the major defense of numerous Nazi war criminals. Such an excuse is a blatant attempt to hide behind the idea of chain of command rather than accepting personal responsibility for unethical actions. There is pressure to conform to group values (Asch 1987). Several of the Watergate participants, *appointed officials* in every case, commented on their willingness to ''go along with the coverup because they wanted to be good team players and not rock the boat'' (Colson 1977; Weisband and Franck 1975). Both Oliver North and Fawn Hall appear to have been swept away by ''I'm a member of the team'' and ''it's us against them'' attitudes during the Iran/Contra affair. In these cases the organizational milieu or environment, in part created by group pressure, led to

unethical decisions, faulty information, misplaced loyalty, and warped perceptions of right and wrong.

At the same time, it is important to notice that, when operating effectively,
the bureaucracy can be a major element in maintaining a balanced perspective
of the world and in seeing that needed tasks are accomplished in reasonable and
equitable but humane ways. Elliott Jacques (1976), in presenting this side of the
argument, believes bureaucracies help human beings achieve their higher goals
while maintaining a sense of community and encouraging pluralism. Certainly,
during the Watergate era, the bureaucracy not only kept the government operating
when most of its leadership was totally distracted, it also operated as a vehicle
of protection for many who would have been improperly swept away in the
struggle between the administration and its accusers (Cronin 1973).

The difference between the negative view of Hummel and the positive
perspective of Jacques depends upon whether or not one believes the bureaucracy can be structured and controlled in a way to focus on ends rather than
means, maintain accountability, and develop a culture of openness and participation by individuals throughout the organization. We will not resolve
that debate here; however, those interviewed as part of this research invari-
ably were forced to consider these kinds of organizational dynamics as they
decided what to do. The impact of those dynamics was sometimes positive,
sometimes negative, and often mixed. However, as bureaucrats embedded
within an organization, there was no way to avoid considering the numerous
facets of the almost all-pervasive milieu, for as Kathryn Denhardt notes, the
organizational context

imposes [and administrators accept] a new set of obligations, pressures and constraints.
The organization will in some ways determine who engages in ethical deliberation, what
is considered ethical, as well as the range of options available to administrators who are
attempting to make the "ethical" decision. (1988, 75)

The important questions public managers considered in trying to develop a
clear comprehension of the organizational impact on their ethical problems were,
"How do the environment, structure, and atmosphere of the relevant organi-
zation(s) affect the perception and interpretation of ethical issues as they arise,
and do these factors place any limits on action that may be taken to resolve
ethical issues?" The questions became important, of course, because organizations limit comprehension of and action on ethical problems. Organizational
influence on an individual's ability to carry out clear and reasoned ethical analysis
can be classified under three general topics—external influences, organization
structure and functions, and organizational culture. All of these topics are of
equal importance, and they constantly interact in real-world situations. If any
one organizational facet is adjusted as part of an attempt to alter, or "correct,"
its influence on the individual, that change will influence all of the other facets
positively or negatively; moreover, because of their interaction, it is possible to
understand why one element of the organization operates as it does only after

all the other units have been examined. Once again, let us lay out the theoretical approach to analyzing this part of an ethical dilemma, and then look at how that model fits the actions of managers in the throes of real-world situations.

EXTERNAL FORCES AND THEIR IMPACT ON ETHICAL DILEMMAS

One of the unique characteristics of the field of ethics *and* public administration is the importance of external groups and the general political environment to the perceptions, alternatives, and actions of public administrators. In the public sector external influences constantly affect one's ability to analyze ethical dilemmas. There is also a certain amount of dependence on external groups—including clientele, legislative bodies, other bureaus, and interest groups—for a variety of elements such as material resources, employees, information (including expertise), and moral support.

For example, the types of clients served influence the amount of dependence or interdependence that a bureaucrat must face in dealing with an ethical problem; they may also determine the amount and sophistication of the information available from themselves and other sources (Rourke 1984; Peters 1989). Some clients can only complain that, "It hurts," because they do not have either the knowledge about their problem or the ability to communicate what little they do know. Bureaucrats find it difficult to know how to help people in such a situation. On occasion this inability to communicate may *create* an ethical dilemma for a decision maker; however, it is more likely to create a *problem in analyzing* an ethical question because of an inability to get needed information on which to base the decision. Likewise, inarticulate clients cannot help in solving problems since they have no political clout (they are not and often cannot be "organized").

Often a greater ethical problem exists, however, when the decision maker is dealing with the opposite type of clients and external groups; when clients are well-organized and articulate in expressing their demands on the system, it is quite possible their desires and the desires of the rest of society (as expressed in law and policy) may differ. When such is the case, it is easy for a public administrator to be placed in a position of trying to satisfy clients or interest groups while remaining within the legal limits of activity, and the pressure increases as the level of dependence on external groups rises (Rourke 1984; Bernstein 1977). Therefore, many public administrators attempt to develop and maintain a measure of independence so they may manage their agencies relatively free of outside influence. At the same time, public agencies may tend to become non-responsive to the citizens they serve if too much independence is obtained.

These problems are constantly faced by regulatory agencies at all levels of government. The question of the strength of ties between top officials of the Department of Energy (DOE) and the major electric power and oil companies, and therefore the danger of DOE policy being controlled by "big oil" or the nuclear power industry, was the main topic of discussion as the new department was staffed. The reason for the debate was the history of other similar agencies (e.g., the Federal Communications Commission, Interstate Commerce Commission), for in numerous cases they had been "captured" by the industries they were supposed to control. In the case of regulatory commissions, for example, the expertise required in the public agencies is usually found among employees of (or professionals retained by) the industries, but it is also essential to maintain both the reality and the semblance of independence from the organizations being controlled in the public interest. Professionals in these kinds of agencies have very special and intense ethical problems because they must balance the public and private interests while "working in a fishbowl."

When an ethical problem appears to have at least part of its basis in, or is aggravated by, the organization, it becomes imperative to examine the position of the organization in relation to its relevant external groups and to ascertain whether or not any of the problem is created by this set of interrelationships. This analysis is doubly important because public administrators often wish to maintain close ties with other organizations and clients so that coordinated action may be taken when necessary ("networking" is an important aspect of public service). However, they still want to be independent so that improper pressure cannot be applied by others. In trying to walk this tightrope, there is a need for constant observation and the ability to make quick, sensitive adjustments in relationships between an organization and its environment.

While external factors are important and play a role in some ethical dilemmas of public managers, the existence and influence of external actors and pressures are considered primarily by decision makers toward the top of the hierarchy, the "policy makers." When such factors did occasionally show up at the middle management and professional levels of the public bureaucracy, as presented in the cases by our interviewees, the role of external actors or forces was usually determined relatively quickly and the managers made adjustments accordingly.

STRUCTURE AND FUNCTION

The more important, more pervasive factor for public managers was the organization within which they worked. Organizational structure influences both the type of ethical dilemmas being faced and one's ability to deal with them. When discussing structure at least four factors must be considered: size, shape of the hierarchy, the dispersion or centralization of activities within the overall organization, and one's location within the organization.

One of the most obvious characteristics of modern bureaucracy is size. To paraphrase a comment about another common subject of discussion, "Everybody talks about the size of the bureaucracies, but nobody can do anything about it." Size, in and of itself, is not bad; in fact, size appears to be one of the natural effects of our technological and interdependent society. As an example of the correlation between technology, interdependence, and the size of related organizations, look at the area of transportation. When transportation was slow and simple, the routes used by the public were generally maintained by the local farmers who occasionally banded together under the guidance of someone like the township trustee to carry out such necessary activities. There was no air travel, little rail travel, and sea travel was the prerogative of those brave enough to face its vicissitudes. Now travel between continents is almost instantaneous, and everyone expects smooth, speedy highways when on the continent; but in order for this to be so, many large, technically specialized, public and private organizations have arisen. In fact, much of our economy (and our style of life) is intimately involved in this system, and it is impossible to separate the benefits of the technology from the organizations that have grown within and around it. We must accept both the technology and the large organizations or agree to the reduction of both.

Ethical problems are not caused by size alone; however, magnitude of an organization can lead to serious difficulties in attempting to analyze such problems. Largeness can create a situation where the decision maker is so removed from "the action" it is impossible to readily understand the organization's objectives and the leadership's program positions. Large bureaucracies also make it easy to forget that all of the activity occurring around you is ultimately meant to maintain a democratic society and its values. Even when you *are* intimately involved with the development of objectives and programs, immensity may lead to a feeling that "it does not matter which decisions are made because they are meaningless within the context of the bureaucracy" (Caplow 1957; Hummel 1987; Presthus 1978).

When an individual works in a large bureaucracy, it is difficult to cut through the "red tape" (people, offices, and procedures) in order to realize the basic reasons for the organization's existence, yet this information is essential when making a rational, ethical choice. This is a special problem for people working in the federal bureaucracy. Departments are a conglomeration of distantly related activities, and it is difficult to decide how agency and department goals coalesce. The Department of Commerce, for example, includes bureaus dealing with international trade, small businesses, the census, the oceans, and the weather.

Departmental size means contact and coordination between people is possible only in specialized areas, contiguous units, or at the highest levels. Again, in the Department of Commerce, neither the largest nor the smallest of the federal departments, the average employee only sees the secretary of the department at honorary, carefully staged functions; even assistant secretaries and deputy assistant secretaries are individuals seldom met but about whom the "grapevine" reports constantly. Managers at all levels are faced with information, coming from above or below, that has filtered through numerous levels of the organization. Likewise, objectives are unclear and often confusing. This leads to feelings of impotence on the part of the employees at all levels of the hierarchy, for they feel that they have no influence on either organizational decisions or actions. (At the top orders are given but little changes in the way the bureaucracy carries out its duties; at the bottom one feels too far removed to have any influence on those giving the orders; in the middle one gets pressures from both directions.) Over time this feeling of helplessness is especially debilitating to individuals faced with ethical dilemmas and who must deal with those dilemmas within the organizational context. It is easy to reach a point where you are convinced that it really doesn't matter what decision is made because it will have no impact.

The issue of organizational size may be aggravated or ameliorated by other structural elements. For example, the shape of the hierarchy within the bureaucracy has a tremendous influence on the amount of freedom you may have in dealing with a problem and the success that can be expected in guiding organizational response once a decision has been made. If a multilayered hierarchy exists, the decision maker is faced with a controlled environment where decisions that do not follow the rules are hard to make. If, on the other hand, there are few layers to the hierarchy, even though the organization is large, it may be possible to move toward a decision with dispatch. In such a situation, the success of an organization depends on a clear understanding of organizational goals by all members, limited but essential coordination and control functions that have been carefully established, and precisely stated rights and duties for all members. When an organization functions in this manner, the ability to carry out meaningful ethical analysis will probably be more available than in other types of situations.

Similarly, the physical or geographic dispersion of an organization may affect an individual's ability to recognize and to analyze ethical problems. While dispersion of activities may be necessary for a variety of reasons (such as proximity to clients or information or quick turnaround on services), it also creates friction and problems of communication and coordination. For example, an auditor in the San Francisco office of the Internal Revenue Service described in her interview the difficulty she had understanding and applying the regulations promulgated in Washington, D.C., to a unique case in Eureka, California. Her proximity to the case was essential, but her inability to have a face-to-face conversation with the rule makers caused serious handicaps in interpreting rules in a fair, objective manner. As another interviewee commented:

It is easy for differences in values and perceptions to occur between regional operations [Boston Region versus Dallas Region], or between regional and central offices. In fact, in at least one case, these differences led to bitter debate in deciding what constitutes "right and equitable" resolution of similar conflicts in the two regions.

When a bureaucrat is faced with an ethical problem, it is necessary to stop and examine how position in the organizational structure influences personal power and perception. Position within the hierarchy also determines how much one knows about the overall activity within the organization (as individuals move higher in the hierarchy they have a more general picture of what goes on in the organization). Therefore it is essential to consider how sheltered, by hierarchical or physical location, one is and how well one comprehends the reasons for decisions and actions taken by superiors. Information critical to a decision is often not received, and if received it is multi-filtered—and we may not even understand where and how this happens. In order to deal with these difficulties an individual must be familiar with both the formal and informal structure of the organization (Homans 1950; Blau and Scott 1962; Downs 1967; Davis 1973). Only by understanding how these issues interact can an individual develop the autonomous, objective stance necessary to make an "independent" ethical decision rather than one dictated by organizational structures.

Closely allied to the influence of structure on the individual is the influence of organizational "functions," or the internal workings of the organization. Of course, what goes on inside the organization is inseparably related to "output" (a product or service) and "clientele" (recipients of that service or product); hence, these factors also must be examined in any consideration of functions. For example, if the output of an operation is a concrete product, it is often easier to maintain a group consensus on objectives than when the output is a service. This is true because it is often more difficult to define: (1) the service; (2) an acceptable quantity and quality of the service; and (3) the expected result of the service on those receiving it. Therefore, when an organization is delivering a service, it is easier for displacement of goals from ends to means to take place (Merton 1968). Likewise, the type of clientele being served may influence the prestige of the organization and, therefore, affect the capacity of its members to influence issues where they believe they have the expertise (and should have the power) to make decisions.

A related factor is the practice of functional specializations and the division of tasks so economies of expertise and scale can be gained. While this allows the organization to run smoothly and efficiently, it often leads to technocratic myopia on the part of individuals in specific positions. In fact, the change in perspective from specialist to generalist is one of the phenomena regularly addressed when anyone discusses the difference between working as a "yeoman" in the organization and filling a managerial position. Managers can no longer zero in on a particular job, technique, or function, but they must instead be concerned with structure, process, goals, and behavior of members in their part of the organization. Rather than seeing only specific tasks and working to perfect them, managers must see organizations as systems of coordinated, productive, and political activities, where personal and group interests, needs, and/or aspirations give rise to bargaining, negotiating, and coalition building in order to achieve the larger goals of the organization (Morgan 1986). Actually, managers must balance their recognition of functional specialization with a generalist view of the organization, so they get torn between the two in a way that is not applicable to individuals at either the top or bottom of the organization.

The only hope one may have of being able to deal with ethical dilemmas which occur in the context of such organizational functions is to develop an understanding of the way the phenomena interact. The appropriate place to start examining this issue is to define the type of organization in which the problem occurs. Harold Wilensky (1967), for example, draws a line between "action organizations" and "knowledge organizations"; he notes that the type of functions, and the pressures under which those functions are performed, varies according to the purpose of the organization. Other writers define organizations according to the types of actions they perform. (For a discussion of organizational structure and design, see Gortner et al. 1987, Chapter 4).

By examining these aspects of the organization, it is possible to comprehend better how the organization's structures and functions are setting the context of the ethical problem and to decide how these might help or hinder proper analysis of the problem. One of the most important questions to be resolved is, "At what point are the decisions and/or actions causing the ethical dilemma occurring in the organization and its processes?" This question may be broken down into two parts. First, is the issue a policy problem for the organization, and if so, at what point are we in the policy-making process? If the problem appears early in the policy-making process—before policies have become too concrete—it *may* be possible to do quite a bit of analysis because most people feel less threatened with immediate and irreparable harm if a decision is not made instantaneously. In addition, the policy may still be flexible because decision makers have not yet had to "take a stand." They will not be made to lose face by "backing down." Such a situation allows much more freedom in arriving at a resolution acceptable to everyone concerned. Obviously, if it is late in the policy-making process all of the opposite problems may exist.

The second part of the larger question is whether or not the issue deals with the implementation of a policy. If the ethical decision applies to an ongoing program, perhaps one established for some time, then the dilemma must be resolved in an environment where there are time pressures—a sense of urgency, a deadline for resolving the problem, or a situation where someone may be affected by inaction. There are also policies already established and accepted by many of the other actors in the system. Any misunderstanding of where the ethical dilemma falls within the total organizational process may lead to the wrong questions and the wrong assumptions as to when, and in what form, decisions must be made.

Another major factor to be considered when examining the impact of organizational functions on an ethical problem is the "centrality" or importance of the function to the continued existence of the organization. When a function is essential to the well-being of an agency, one of two tactics is usually adopted in order to maintain control over that function: The operation is placed in "the center" of the organization and insulated from the environment, thereby letting the function continue in a relatively steady state regardless of its surroundings (Thompson 1967); or, if that is impossible, (for example, an individual works at the periphery of an organization and controls information from the environment that is important to the organization), the organization develops a system of status and rewards which is designed to maintain the loyalty and continued cooperation of those involved in the essential operation (Kahn et al. 1964). If the decision maker is in a sheltered position within the organization, it is highly probable any information is multi-filtered, thus requiring a special effort to get independent, unbiased information. Being in such a position may cause a decision maker to be unaware of conflicts surrounding a decision unless a special sensitivity for such problems is carefully nurtured.

On the other hand, the individual who operates from the periphery of the organization (where there is contact with clients, interested observers, and competitors) must be equally aware of the possibility of ethical conflicts. It is essential to represent properly the organization (the organization has the right to expect cooperation in meeting its objectives) while not allowing loyalty to the organization to blind one to the legitimate demands of clients and other citizens. Thus, the location of an individual within the functional framework of the organization may be the cause of an ethical dilemma and/or create special difficulties in attempting to analyze an ethical problem when it arises.

ORGANIZATIONAL CULTURE

The impact of structure and function on individuals in an organization is widely accepted. At the same time, decision makers often do not consider the culture of the organization within which they work because it develops so subtly, and they are socialized into it so gradually, that its presence is not recognized. While the idea of organizational culture had existed all along—Chester Barnard ([1938] 1979) recognized its existence fifty years ago—the concept actually became important in the study of organizations during the 1960s. The argument of those supporting the study of organizational culture is that the subtlety and totality of the factors making up the organization's culture, and their influence on individuals as they operate within the public bureaucracy, require special attention be given to them; otherwise, a major influence on ethical decisions may be completely overlooked by both the public administrator who is faced with the dilemma and the observer who attempts to study the public administrator's actions.

"Organizational culture" is the organization's "system of knowledge, ideology, values, laws, and day-to-day ritual" (Morgan 1986, 112). Culture includes mores, attitudes, and perceptions that develop through the history of the organization based on the interactions of the group members with one another, and to a certain extent with the outside world. Cultural development may or may not be based on a realistic assessment of the surrounding world. In fact, organizational culture, and the "myths" involved, often help in creating organizational identity, engendering motivation and commitment to the organization, and in general socializing and controlling newcomers (Mahler 1988). Culture and its accompanying myths often include segments developed primarily as defense mechanisms to protect individuals and groups, or structures and processes, from cognitive dissonance related to threatening realities.

A strongly defensive culture can create ethical dilemmas; however, even when an organization has a relatively healthy culture it is still important to be aware of its composition and the effect it may have on the recognition and analysis of ethical problems. The factor to remember is that the group's expectation as to the way an individual will perceive problems, and the range of possible actions available to deal with them, are limiting factors on the freedom of an individual to analyze and correct ethical dilemmas; yet, many group members are not aware they operate in such a culture, and scoff at the idea that it might bias their decision making. Let us look at three major factors helping to create an organization's culture (type of people in the organization, leadership style, and norms and values) as a sample of the way culture affects one's ability to recognize and deal with ethical dilemmas.

Different organizations attract different types of employees; this variation is caused by a set of factors which includes such things as: the physical environment and the effort involved in the job; the ability to advance one's career; the amount of formalized training and professional or technical expertise required; the prestige of the position; and society's perception of a "proper" position for certain individuals. This set of physical, socioeconomic, and intellectual factors play an important role both in who joins the organization and, once individuals join, in influencing or shaping perceptions during socialization and later membership.

The result of this process is a specific socioeconomic composition of employees in any specific organization. Any time an organization is composed of people from approximately the same background, a consensus is liable to develop among the group; there is also a high probability the consensus will be skewed by the group's common set of experiences, views of the world, and training. The classic example of this occurs when an organization is dominated by people from one profession (see Chapter 7). In such cases, there is usually pressure for everyone in the organization to accept the predominant attitudes and habits; this can lead to difficulty in overcoming predispositions when examining a question (it is hard to be objective when steeped in a culture) or when carrying out a course of action once a decision has been made (the organization has a set way of dealing with such problems).

Related to people and culture are the types of personalities possessed by the members of the organization. Both Robert Presthus (1978) and Anthony Downs (1967) discuss the influence between the overall organization and its members' personalities. When organizations are young, vibrant, growing, and "on the way up," individuals are attracted because of the chance to advance their careers. These people do not have rigid views of the world, and they are amenable to trying new ideas; in this way they may be easier to work with when an ethical problem must be faced. On the other hand, individuals attached to an organization because it is dynamic are interested in advancement, and the thirst for personal gain can lead to pressure to accept any decision or action increasing the chance of success, regardless of the other consequences. In this case, an individual who is trying to deal with an ethical problem may be subtly or bluntly urged to compromise on an issue, to "shave the fine points," so the organization can be successful. Such pressure may be very hard to withstand.

Mature organizations, and especially organizations operating from a steady or diminishing resource base, tend to collect or retain individuals who are more conservative in their decision-making and action philosophies (Levine 1978). In steady-state and shrinking organizations, the normal reaction of members is to protect themselves, to react cautiously, and to withdraw from new or "radical" ideas (ideas different from the status quo), even if in fact the only hope for regaining or maintaining organizational vitality may be such decisions, actions, and/or programs. When one is faced with an ethical dilemma in this type of organization, often two problems must be solved; not only must an ethical choice be made, but a way must be found to carry it out in an environment that discourages new or different activities. In fact, this "inability to cope" may be at the heart of the ethical dilemma.

Perhaps the most important element in creating an organization's culture is its leadership. The leadership style of the top people percolates through any organization and plays a major role in deciding how the employees at the lower levels think and act in their daily operation, especially in times of crisis (Gardner 1986; Burns 1978). Since ethical dilemmas can be expected to create a crisis for at least some employees, if not for the total organization, ethical decisions are apt to be influenced by the expected reaction of the leaders. If the managers are authoritarian in their leadership style, the subordinates can be expected to hesitate rather than to strike out in search of a solution to the problem. The subordinates recognize that making important decisions is considered to be the prerogative of the leaders, so action must wait for pronouncement from above. If, on the other hand, the leadership style is democratic, employees may feel comfortable in immediately attacking an ethical problem confronting them because they are used to being given latitude in dealing with the situations they face.

When leaders are adept at identifying the goals and values of an organization and maintaining close adherence to those goals through effective communication and control (they are usually democratic in this case), it is easier for employees to recognize ethical difficulties and to bring the problems into the open (Barnard [1938] 1979). In an agency where clarity of goals exists—remember Gulick's ([1937] 1973a) concept of "leading through an idea"—it is also easier to raise a meaningful debate about important ethical issues and their impact on the organization, for everyone involved in the debate can take significant stands on the relevant topics. This is what Kathryn Denhardt refers to as "enhancing ethical discourse" (1988, 153–156).

Cooper (1986) also argues this is the ideal situation for administrators facing ethical problems, for if administrators know what decisions they can legitimately make, have the ability to participate in the policy-making process, and therefore understand what the goals of the organization are, they will feel free to make decisions and be held accountable for them. If a leader operates in a manner that hides or obfuscates important goals and discourages participation in clarifying them, it is difficult to carry on a meaningful debate because of the disagreement among the disputants as to the organization's raison d'etre, and because the act of bringing an issue into the open may be frowned upon by one's superiors.

Other leadership factors, such as the level of charisma evinced by the manager, the leader's acceptance of conflict (within relatively broad limits) as healthy, and the flexibility or inflexibility of his or her personality, all serve as creators and reinforcers of the doctrines and values held by members of the organization.

From the leadership style and the type of people in the organizations, and many other factors we cannot cover here, come *the set of values and norms under which organizational members operate.* Values and norms decide what beliefs are important or unimportant to people and how they will act by habit (other actions require special thought in order to carry them out). The values and norms, the leadership styles, the characteristics of the individuals throughout the organization, along with the external factors and the structures and functions discussed above, combine to form the total organizational culture. It is almost beyond human capability to measure the impact of this culture upon particular individuals as they attempt to recognize and analyze ethical problems. These factors do play a major role, however, in the ethical dilemmas faced by public managers and their professional peers. Let us look at some of the experiences of mid-level managers in the federal bureaucracy for examples of organizational impact on personal decisions.

WHEN THE ORGANIZATION IS PART OF THE PROBLEM

In the ethical dilemmas faced by public managers it became apparent that some or all of the organizational aspects discussed above either helped cause the problems or complicated their resolution. Since the organization was directly or indirectly involved, it was necessary to understand the role played by these "system problems," as they are often called, and to overcome the difficulty. In many cases all three of the facets examined above (external forces, structures and functions, and culture) came into play. However, occasionally only one or two facets were present, and usually one was preeminent in the situation.

The level of difficulty related to these factors appears to increase as individuals move from facing external forces to dealing with organizational culture. Dealing with external forces is not easy, but the individual may be less threatened because s/he is protected by bureau rules, and members of the agency are not among those the individual must directly confront. Dealing with or changing procedures is often difficult; coping with structural encumbrances may seem excruciatingly tedious and toilful; but attempting to change organizational perceptions and mores is perhaps the most Augean task imaginable for a mid-management public administrator. Given the turnover at the top of agencies and the natural guardedness that often exists between political appointees and the bureaucrats, members of the bureaucracy seldom have a chance to influence or change the style of management or leadership used by the top people.

External Influences

The power (or lack thereof) of external groups, and the influence they had on organizational perceptions and actions, regularly played a role in the cases presented by the public managers interviewed for this study. One example can be drawn from Dr. Valerie Franklin's case when she tried to change the procedures of her agency in dealing with the black land grant colleges. The fact that her constituents in the black land grant universities were unorganized and had not developed any political clout meant they were overlooked as appropriate and significant players in the life of the agency. While Dr. Franklin's struggle was with her supervisor, she would have been greatly strengthened in her cause if the clients who she served had been perceived as more powerful. Dr. Franklin's supervisor did not believe the black universities' requests should be handled by the national office, and they could not organize a meaningful counterargument. The black colleges had little political clout, little support within the state governments, and small and unorganized alumni and constituency groups. Requests from predominantly white universities were perceived as legitimate, and it must be assumed if their demands were not met they had the means to guarantee their desires were heard. Because of their lack of power, the black colleges were not organized in a way allowing them to support Dr. Franklin in her argument that these university programs needed special help. Therefore, she had to carry on her fight alone.

Whereas Dr. Franklin's problem was exacerbated by the lack of power among her constituents, when David Weathers found that access to energy reserve data bases had been breached he faced a powerful constituency who limited his ability to act. The external constituency was not a direct actor in the drama, and for a mid-level manager this was not surprising. External constituencies are much more likely to be involved with higher level administrators. Nonetheless, the presence of such constituencies had to be considered as decisions were made about ways to handle the case. David recognized that the situation he was dealing with involved powerful industries in the energy field, and at the time this case occurred energy was a major political issue.

When faced with the reality of "politicization" in such a case, the responsible bureaucrats must quickly weigh the costs of giving in to political pressure. A decision not to participate in the politicization often sends a strong signal to other participants in the process that "he or she cannot be bought or bullied."

Such a stance, firmly taken, often brings with it a reputation that keeps the situation from recurring. Several interviewees noted they only had to make it clear two or three times that they would not bend to political pressure, and attempts to influence them stopped. For example, one individual, a winner of several awards for excellence in service, when asked to describe an ethical dilemma that he had faced, immediately responded he had not faced any. After some discussion about what was meant by the term "ethical dilemma," he agreed he had faced a few situations early in his career. One example involved attempts by congressional aides to influence some of his personnel appointments. He then went on to describe how he had firmly but politely squelched the first couple of attempts by these individuals. After those cases the word apparently got around, for he was no longer approached on such issues.

It is relatively common for governmental organizations to have a concern about maintaining the cooperation of particular industries in the daily work of the agency. In most situations the government cannot successfully carry out its mission unless it gains and maintains the trust of those whom it is regulating or serving. For example, acceptance of the regulatory process as fair and equitable by all actors guarantees greater voluntary cooperation and less confrontation in the hearing and rule-making process. In David Weather's case the corporations had cooperated well beyond what was required by law in turning over to the Department of Energy information that they considered to be top secret. Therefore, David had to be especially careful not to destroy the level of trust, tenuous at best, which had slowly developed between the government and private industry.

David Weathers felt relatively certain he faced a second kind of external power, that of another part of the government. Public programs seldom involve only one specific office or agency, and this case was a perfect example. Individuals in a separate part of the executive branch, in this case members of the Office of the President, were involved because of their desire to get the National Energy Policy finished as quickly as possible. David had no way to contend with the power of the people in the executive office; therefore, a confrontation was out of the question. Nothing could be gained and much could be lost, so any resolution of the problem had to sidestep that issue.

Several interviewees noted they sometimes faced ethical problems related to relationships with other government departments or agencies. A tremendous amount of coordination of goals and activities must be carried out in the federal government because of its size, complexity, and overlap in mission between agencies. A particular problem often faced related to the fact that individuals had transferred from one agency to another and then were placed in a "boundary-spanning" situation between the two organizations (dealing with projects involving both organizations and requiring the individuals to play a role representing one agency against the other).

This dilemma was resolved in three ways. One alternative is to ask to be relieved of the responsibility, explaining the conflict that is faced. This request is often granted. In many situations the individual is able to resolve the issue of conflict of interest in his or her mind, and in such cases an individual may be able to represent his or her current agency in the negotiations from a position of power since s/he knows the people with whom s/he must negotiate. In more than one case individuals reported they were able to use this knowledge to arrive at solutions that were advantageous to both organizations. One individual who was interviewed (Jim in the case presented in Chapter 3) did not think through the impact of his unique situation and the result was a failure in representing his current agency.

Structural/Functional Influences

Structural and functional questions, and the fact that the individual faced with the dilemma was "in the middle" of the bureaucracy, were recognized regularly by the managers. Most of the situations described by mid-level managers involved a smaller milieu. They recognized that the case they were dealing with was important only to a limited group and in a "linking pin" way because of its impact on a specific portion of a program or organization. The impact probably would be noticed only in their workgroup and those immediately below and above. Robert Fellows, for example, commented that his action in the specific case of an unqualified supervisor probably was relevant only to his operation and the one to which the gentleman might move. He recognized, however, that his actions would have an impact on the morale of his subordinates, and he felt responsible for guaranteeing the improved efficiency and productivity of his office, especially since those factors had been a major reason for his appointment to the position.

Position was also important, but in a different way, in a case related to stolen entrance examinations that was presented by one of the interviewees in this study. That case presents several interesting insights into the influence of the organization on the perception and resolution of a complex ethical problem, therefore let me present it here.

During 1985, it came to the attention of the executives of a federal agency, which operated under exempt civil service status, that the entrance/selection examination for professional employees within that agency had been compromised. A number of clerical and support workers within the agency had gained unauthorized access to the examination. These employees had taken and passed the entrance exam; a few had been hired, and several were on the current eligible lists. The associate commissioner in charge of this area of operation was on temporary leave of absence, so his subordinates proceeded vigorously to investigate this cheating scandal.

A number of the suspected individuals, when confronted with the evidence, admitted they had cheated and implicated others. It was decided that those who had originally been suspected, and the additional people who were implicated by confessed cheaters, would be given polygraph tests to determine if they had cheated on the exam. As each individual was brought in, he or she was presented with a choice by the investigators. If the implicated persons would withdraw their names from the eligible list, it was agreed that no inference would be made from that action and they would be free to retake the test—which by now had been rewritten—and they would be reinstated on the list according to their score. If the individuals chose not to remove their names, the investigators maintained the right to go ahead with the polygraph test if they so decided.

Several people agreed to retake the entrance examination; however, quite a few people took the polygraph. Half of those who took the polygraph test were judged to be telling the truth; half were judged to be showing deception. Of those who were judged to be showing deception, about half immediately admitted they had cheated and half admitted nothing.

Before the polygraphing was completed, the associate commissioner returned from leave. He immediately ordered that the polygraphs stop. He felt that it would be best to put a cap on the situation. He did not want a highly publicized "West Point style" cheating scandal to break into the news and damage the reputation of the agency. It was obvious that a number of recently hired professional employees had gotten their jobs by cheating, and there was no way to know exactly how many; so the decision was made to "stop at that point rather than try to catch everyone who had broken the rules." Only those who were not yet officially hired were investigated.

The individuals who had failed the polygraph but had not admitted guilt (approximately twenty-five) began an appeal process on the grounds that the polygraph was not admissible as evidence and that it was unfair and arbitrary to use it on some individuals and not on all hired during the time in question. Since this was an "exempt" service—outside the regular civil service—these appeals were reviewed by individuals in the executive branch of the agency. In each case the reviewers of the appeals had recommended against the appellants. The rulings consistently found that the individuals appealing should not be allowed to retake the examination and that they should not be considered eligible for the entry position.

However, these appeals kept popping up, especially requests for reconsideration, and the problem had continued for about three years. At this point Jeanne Pope was given the task of looking at these appeals and drafting a policy that would resolve the remaining cases. She was given no specific directions. She was simply told that "When this goes to the commissioner, he goes crazy. He does not want to see it any more." This was not uncommon. In fact, it was commonly known that the commissioner was "the outside man" of the agency, and the associate commissioner for administration really ran the internal operation of the organization (perhaps having more to do than there was staff to do it properly). In part that was how the procedures of investigation had given rise to the current problem in the first place. No one had gone to the commissioner with the problem and the associate commissioner had been on leave; therefore, the actions had been taken without the full implications being considered by one of the top administrators of the agency. Now Jeanne's job was to fairly, finally, and permanently resolve this issue so that it could be put to rest and the organization could move on to other matters.

It was obvious to Jeanne that several ethical decisions had already been made by administrators. She was being asked to "clean up the loose ends" of what had been a traumatic situation for many people in the organization. Perhaps those who had previously made decisions, and reviewed and made recommendations about appeals related to those decisions, had not even seen the problem as having an ethical content. However, it appeared to her that she faced an ethical dilemma based on several factors.

Jeanne wanted to protect the organization. The integrity of the organization was extremely important. Without that quality, and equally important, without the appearance of that quality to the public, it could not carry out its task. The professionals being hired through this examination must work with a tremendous amount of autonomy, regularly dealing with issues affecting national security. Everyone had to have absolute trust in these employees. It seemed equally valid, on a personal level, to deny entrance to anyone who had cheated.

On the other hand, Jeanne wanted to be fair and guarantee at least a minimum of due process to the people who claimed to be innocent and had stayed with the organization throughout this long and frustrating procedure. They had at least shown some loyalty to the organization and some stamina in a difficult situation.

Jeanne knew none of the individuals personally, nor would she necessarily ever meet any of them. She had to act objectively and rationally from within the hierarchy of the organization, yet try to place proper emphasis on due process and individual rights. This had to be done at her own personal instigation because there was no special pressure on her to maintain a particular bias, or lack of bias, in her decision. Jeanne surmised that since others had been given a shot at this problem before, the boss might be looking for something different in this report; but that was not certain. Her decision would almost certainly be accepted as the final statement on the issue if it showed any semblance of rationality.

It rapidly became apparent to Jeanne that the prior reviewers of the appeals had not gone back to examine the procedures used in making the initial decision as to whom was placed on the suspected list, investigated, and ultimately asked to take the polygraph. Their decisions had been based on a superficial examination of the issue and, probably, their personal feelings about "people who were cheaters." Before making any final determination she decided she should look into this matter. It was possible to go back through the records of the agency and recreate the complete process from the beginning of the cheating scandal. Jeanne found out that the initial decision about possible suspectability was made by a man in a relatively low-level position within the personnel department. He had, on his own, prepared a list of questions that he used in reviewing the cases. These factors—and how many of them were met in a particular case—determined whether or not individuals were suspect.[2] The list seemed appropriate; so Jeanne, for the sake of consistency, and after making clear what she was doing, applied it in her own decision process.

Upon reviewing all of the pending cases, based on the original list of characteristics that pointed to suspicion, Jeanne found that the appellants fell into two categories. Twenty-two individuals met several, and in a few cases all, of the criteria. Where that was so, it was recommended that the evidence appeared to be weighty enough that those individuals' scores should be discounted and they should be removed from the eligible list. If they wanted to retest, they would be allowed to do so.

On the other hand, in three cases only one criteria (dramatically increased score) fit. Statistically it was unlikely that the individual could score that much better without cheating, but Jeanne hated to depend totally on statistics. At the same time, it had been three years since they had taken the test, and that seemed to point to a reasonable solution to the problem. Based on the delay between testing and placement, it appeared appropriate to require data based on the new test before considering these individuals for employment. Therefore, Jeanne's recommendation was almost the same, but with a significant nuance added. These three individuals *should be encouraged* to take the new test. Their old scores had to be discounted due to both the problem of cheating and because of the delay in hiring, but they should be given a show of support from the organization in their effort. That seemed to be as far as the organization could go at this point, and while it would probably not satisfy these appellants, it appeared to be the fairest alternative available in the situation.

Jeanne's recommendation was accepted by the administration of the agency. While she had wondered how those who had prepared the prior decisions would react, they accepted her recommendation readily. It was not very far from their original decision, although it was more carefully thought out and did make a few changes in individual cases. While she felt a strong ethical dilemma while determining the case, no one else seemed to realize that fact. As far as her superiors were concerned, this was just one of many issues Jeanne had to deal with, and nothing was ever said to her about it after a few weeks. She had successfully fulfilled one of her numerous charges as a special assistant.

Jeanne was right in guessing that not all of the appellants would be happy. One person in particular had been pushing the issue with the support of her bureau director. The bureau director called the appellant aside, at this point, and told her, "Listen, they have bent over backwards for you. I am aware of the effort that has gone into this decision. You had better back off." That individual took the new test (which was supposedly of approximately the same difficulty as the old, compromised test) and did poorly. With this final action the case came to a close.

In this case a special assistant on temporary assignment from a field position was asked to resolve an issue that had the potential for serious agency damage. This is not uncommon; situations that appear to have great impact to the individual involved are shrugged aside as one of many such issues by the organizational administration. Jeanne Pope was "plunked down" in a situation with a rather lengthy history and asked to "resolve it." She realized the information she received was multi-filtered because of her position within the associate commissioner's office and her time of entry into the case. She was assigned the case only after several others had examined the situation, so they had interpreted the information prior to her receiving it, and they probably had colored the attitudes of others in the administration.

What she also found out was that the earlier examiners of the problem had not made any attempt to go back and collect information for themselves; they had accepted what was given to them as all the information either available or necessary to resolve the dilemma. Jeanne was

appalled that no one had checked in the bowels of the organization and found either the man who decided which individuals were "guilty" or the criteria by which he had made the decision. Here an important decision for the organization was actually delegated to a very low-level individual pretty much unbeknown to anyone. There was too much inattention to detail this time.

Only after doing some additional checking and finding the source of the criteria originally used to make the decisions as to who was under suspicion and who was not, was Jeanne able to establish a decision model that allowed her to resolve the case in a way acceptable to her and to the other members of the organization.

Jeanne was also sensitive to the impersonality of such a large organization. She knew none of the individuals being charged and had no reason to believe she would ever meet them. She occasionally heard about specific individuals involved through "the grapevine." While she was making her decision in Washington, D.C., many of the people affected were stationed in distant offices. Therefore, she felt a special responsibility to compensate for this environment.

In her mind this could only be accomplished and the case permanently laid to rest if everyone involved came away from her decision with a sense that it had been fairly resolved.

The case of George Anderson and his unqualified employee also shows how one's position in the organization often makes decision making and action much more difficult. George realized he was caught in the middle, his bosses wanted "no trouble," and Laura had unrealistic expectations and, as a disabled employee, had the natural sympathy of any unknowledgeable observer. Therefore, before George took any action against Laura he turned to those parts of the organization that could help him determine what he should do and how he should act. One major source was the personnel office, a staff office supposedly expert in handling such cases. First he found a stunning ignorance about Laura's disabilities; no one in the personnel office could give him any information about what kinds and levels of disability she had. He said,

I had to force the personnel people to confront the realities of the situation. When they did examine her abilities and her performance, both the central office and the division office said, "Fire her." But then they would always end up whispering, "the boss ain't going to let you fire her."

While officially there were special parts of the organization available to help him, in reality these offices could not or would not do so; therefore, he had to take care of the situation alone and then take the heat. Thus, structure and function were important to understand, but they did not answer all of the questions.

Finally, even though mid-level managers seldom make major policy related to the ultimate goals of the organization, the impact of their decisions may be dramatic anyway, especially their impact on morale, efficiency, and effectiveness. And the decision may be quite germane to the overall success of the organization. A nutrition program cannot be considered successful if it is not serving that portion of the population most in need of its services. Energy companies must cooperate if a national energy policy is to be realistic and have any meaning. Trust in the recruiting policies of a major agency must be maintained if employees and the citizenry at large are expected to believe the organization has top quality people chosen in an objective and equitable way. Ethical decisions are important at all levels of the policy process; no particular part of the process can be denigrated and considered unimportant. All of these issues relate, in part, also to the culture of the organization.

Organizational Cultural Influences

Each of the managers interviewed was sensitive to those organizational factors we have called "culture." Each individual also had a unique view of that culture, not necessarily one shared by others in the same organization; interpretation of such phenomena takes on a distinctively personal cast, and it is sometimes difficult to tell who is right or wrong. Such a result is unavoidable, and perhaps it is appropriate because we are dealing with human beings, not pieces of inanimate machinery. Each individual also believed his or her decisions and actions were influenced by that understanding of how the organization, primarily its leaders but often coworkers, perceived the problem and what alternative courses of action were acceptable to the organization. In Dr. Franklin's case she became convinced that, at best, the organization was insensitive to racism on the part of her supervisor and, at worst, it condoned his actions. David Weathers had observed the behavior of his superiors in similar situations, and he decided, given their values, he dared not take the customary first action in such cases— he could not go to his boss with his problem.

A lawyer involved in a situation where her prime witness was pressured by his boss to change his testimony (see Chapter 7) gave one of the more interesting descriptions of the formal structure of her organization versus the informal realities with which she had to work. The staff office within which she worked was supposed to be an independent group of legal advisors to the technical staff as opposed to a legal staff for the commission (later on that separation of functions was formalized in the rules). However, political considerations permeated the actions of the agency, and she could not ignore them. Neither did she think she could allow them to dictate her actions. Therefore, she made a judgement about the management style of her supervisor, assumed that he would support her in whatever action she took, and acted upon it. Luckily she was right, both in her judgement and in the way the other threatening supervisor reacted, therefore the case was resolved satisfactorily. Not everyone is that lucky.

One of the managers who had changed agencies numerous times noted he had worked for the Department of Defense, the National Aeronautics and Space Administration, the Department of Health and Human Services, and the Office of Management and Budget.

There is a vast array of values that come into play in your consciousness. Part of being a success in such a variety of agencies is individual growth, new inputs with experience, and insights that come with each new environment. Not only does the successful manager adapt to the values, mores, and goals of each organization, but he or she adds each new experience to his or her bank of knowledge, and that hopefully leads to greater sensitivity and sophistication in handling the ticklish situations.

Finally, in none of the cases studied did the managers start out with the idea of remaking or revolutionizing goals, structure, function, or culture of the organization. While that occurs in a few cases, such is not usually the goal of managers. Instead they try to do their job in an efficient and effective way, and revolution is not primary in their mind. Yes, they have their own ideas about good government and the political battles of the day, and they are committed to the democratic values on which public administrative ethics must be based, but they see their job as keeping the government running on a day-to-day basis. Above all, they recognize the possibility of becoming socialized into the organization to such a degree that they lose their own identity and personal values. This they consistently resist.

NOTES

1. Writers throughout the twentieth century have described the evils created by organizational life (Thorstein Veblen 1915 and 1924; William Whyte 1956; Bendix 1977; Bennis 1966). The latest of these exposes is by Robert Jackall (1988), in his study entitled *Moral Mazes: The World of Corporate Managers*. However, while not belittling the importance of these studies, I believe they are examples of researchers asking questions that determine what they find. If you start out looking for negative aspects of bureaucracy you will find innumerable examples. On the other hand, this is not the only face of bureaucracy. The effects of its existence have improved the lives of countless people and societies: Are the lives of individuals better in those societies where bureaucracy has existed—even though it has been used to accomplish evil by many? Would we prefer the Middle Ages with the lack of bureaucracies in most aspects of life? Would we be able to live the full and long lives that we do without it? Would we, as individuals, be happier working in non-bureaucratic situations? The answer to these questions is not clear. Could not stories of the success of bureaucracy—even in making the lives of individuals within the bureaucracy more rewarding than they would have been in lone endeavor—be discovered if that question were asked instead of the questions asked by the authors above? Individuals do survive in the bureaucracy as healthy, mature, sensitive, and productive personalities. I found many of them. (Admittedly I also found a few of the types of individuals described by Jackall, Whyte, and Hummel.) In order to balance the discussion of bureaucracy it is important to also look at Mosher's *Democracy and the Public Service* (1982), and Goodsell's *The Case for Bureaucracy* (1983).

2. Some of the most pertinent questions asked were:

• Did an individual work in the specific office where security related to the examination had been breached?

• Was the individual a certain type of support employee prior to taking the test? (Certain employees had easier access to such information.)

• Had the individual participated in specific training programs where the examination had been distributed to some of the trainees?

• Had the individual come into contact with certain agency employees who were known to have distributed the exam to some people?

• Had the individual's score risen dramatically upon retaking the exam? (Test scores normally remained approximately the same even when retaken.)

CHAPTER 7

PROFESSIONS, PROFESSIONALISM, AND ETHICS

We live in a "professional society." Most educated people, if not part of a profession, wish to become members of one, and it seems any career group requiring special training wants to be recognized as "professional." Professions play a major role throughout the public service. A large number of those who move to higher levels in the federal civil service begin their career in one of the professions (e.g., law, medicine, accounting, engineering); at the other end of the public service spectrum, many city managers at the local level of government are members of the International City Management Association. Fritz Mosher and Richard Stillman (1982) have pointed out the existence of professions which are located entirely or almost entirely within public agencies (e.g., public health, foreign service), and in numerous situations these professionals tend to dominate their bureaus.

Any individual who belongs to a profession and attempts to operate in a "professional" manner will undoubtedly turn to that affiliation as a source of values and practical guidance when faced with an ethical dilemma. This is as it should be; however, the values embedded within a profession, and the practical guidance that comes from the interpretation of these values, must be carefully examined. In the first place, the values held by society at large and those of any profession are inevitably different in small or large ways. Second, charges are regularly leveled against the professions and those who consider themselves members in good standing, because outsiders see the actions of those organizations and individuals to be narrow-minded, self-centered, damaging to society, and inimical to the very values they claim to uphold. This feeling is perhaps best expressed by the playwright and social critic George Bernard Shaw's comment, "All professions are conspiracies against the laity."

A third reason for the conflict between professions and the larger society is related to the changing role of the professions and, to a certain extent, flies in the face of the charge of narrow-mindedness. The increased virtuosity in practice that technology allows has greatly broadened the ethical scope considered by professions; however, the new areas of ethical consideration are not recognized by many people in the general public. As Franz J. Ingelfinger notes about the medical profession,

[T]he doctor today is less concerned about the possibility of fee splitting by a colleague than about the fact that a terminal patient is being kept alive, day after day at great expense, with no ultimate hope for life. Confidentiality has also become a serious issue in view of the many agencies that have access to patients' records. Thus, although medicine has become more commercialized, it has at the same time become more sensitive to ethical dilemmas more profound than financial gain or loss. (1975, 25)

Dr. Ingelfinger might also have pointed out that many of the new ethical questions address inter-individual relationships, those of which patients are aware and about which they care. The practice of medicine is seldom simply a matter of the relationship between doctor and patient. As the practice of medicine has changed, the new ethical questions in the profession address problems related to multiple relationships in a complex, technological, impersonal operation that has impact far beyond any one doctor and patient.

The change in medicine is a classic example of what is happening across the professions. It is probable that ethical values are changing—and the level of sensitivity increasing—across most professions, but such a statement is not easily proven or disproven. No objective data exists to test it. In the public sector any shortcomings among professionals tend to be exaggerated by reporters and politicians (although politicians have had little time to point fingers at others lately), with the rare sensational event being stressed rather than the important but routine fulfillment of professional obligations by the vast majority of actors. The sensational sells newspapers. Likewise it gains votes.

[I]t is politically more expedient for a public figure to dwell on what's wrong rather than on what's right. . . . Interestingly enough, many of the charges made in the media or on Capitol Hill are based on self-criticism by members of the [profession involved]. (Ingelfinger 1975, 25–26)

For responsible individuals the key is to recognize their profession's strengths and limitations as they work in the larger public arena. In this chapter we shall attempt to address this issue by defining the generic characteristics of professions, examining what it means for an individual to be a "professional" and to have a sense of "professionalism," and looking at how both of these roles help and hinder one in making ethical decisions. Finally we shall look at the impact of the professions, and especially of the "professional state of mind," on mid-managers in the federal bureaucracy.

THE "PROFESSIONS" AND "PROFESSIONALISM" AS ETHICAL ANCHORS

Central to understanding how professionals deal with ethical problems is a knowledge of those characteristics that "ideal model" professions have in common—and how these characteristics lead to the development of particular values in their members—those values which are often described as "professionalism."

The term "ideal model" is used here to point out the fact that no profession meets all of the characteristics in a perfect form. A few professions important in the public sector come close. Numerous other occupations refer to themselves as professions even though they stray relatively far from the ideal. The professional title is beneficial to members of these occupations for many reasons (status within the community, limitation of membership into the occupation, control of membership behavior, control over pricing of services, etc.), but to the extent these factors are the bases for claiming professional status they are the proof those occupations are *not* what they claim to be.

Status as a profession is actually granted from society, not claimed by an occupation. When an occupation is deemed by the community to be so essential to its well-being that the populace grants the members of the occupation status and privileges not generally given, especially including internal determination of who is qualified to be considered a member in good standing and what is proper behavior as a member of the group, that occupation moves into the category of "profession." Traditionally, this type of internal control has been granted to only a limited number of occupations, with the original three being medicine, law, and the clergy. The current professions vary in their knowledge bases, technological skills, political power, codes of ethics, salary/compensation, and overall public acceptance. However, "ideal" professions have the following characteristics.

1. The professional practice is based on a body of abstract knowledge which to be adequately mastered requires a lengthy period of education, training, apprenticeship and/or internship.

2. Standards for preparatory training, entry into journeyman status, and continuing competence are established and enforced by the profession.

3. The sternest measure a profession can take against one of its members is expulsion from the profession.

4. The profession's primary purpose is to serve a given societal need, and practice of the profession is done under the legitimization of that society.

5. Members of the professions are bound by an oath and/or ethical code which places altruistic service and the good of society among its goals.

6. There is a collegial sense among the members of the profession, where each is subject

to the dictates of the profession, yet charged with insuring the integrity of it at the same time. One's behavior is controlled by rules made by his or her compatriots while at the same time each individual, as part of the larger group, is prescribing and monitoring the behavior of colleagues with whom they share a professional and, not infrequently, a personal bond.

7. Viewed in the strictest sense, members of a profession must be prepared to make the supreme sacrifice when their society is in chaos. (taken in part from Fragola 1984)

When fulfilling these roles the professions play an important part in maintaining society, for they serve as an anchor *and* guide for society in areas of extreme consequence when stability or positive change is needed. These roles also grant *status* to professionals and often allow them to play an important role in several parts of the policy process. At the same time these characteristics are central to the development, among members of the profession, of a sense of "professionalism."

Everyone in the profession is unique "as an individual"; however, within the profession per se, some of that individualism is given up for the overall goals of the profession. Each individual reaps rewards commensurate with the contributions made to society; nonetheless, the *altruism/service ethos* is supposed to remain foremost in the priorities of the individual as a professional. And there should be rewards, for a commitment and, in a way, a sacrifice is made because "when someone seeks to enter what might be termed a profession, that person sets himself aside from all the luxuries of other states in society and takes on added responsibility" (Fragola 1984, 555).

Central to that individual's priorities is a set of values which make up that which we call professionalism. They are:

1. Belief in the need for *expertise* in the body of abstract knowledge applicable to the profession.

2. Belief that professionals should have *autonomy* in work activities and decision making.

3. *Identification* with the profession and fellow professionals.

4. *Commitment to a life's work* in the profession as a calling.

5. A feeling of ethical *obligation to render service* to clients without self-interest and with emotional neutrality.

6. A belief in *self-regulation* and collegial maintenance of standards, that is, that fellow professionals are best qualified to judge and police each other. (Filley, House, and Kerr 1976)

It is inevitable that such a set of values should develop among professionals given our knowledge of socialization. In fact, one of the major tasks of professional schools, whether they admit it or not, is to carry out the first major steps in socializing future members of the profession at the same time those future members are learning the knowledge and skills that they will use in their professional roles. Professional education includes more than the learning and mastery of skills, it also involves an habituation into an ethos, an acceptance of common values, and an identification with appropriate role models. In most cases this is not explicit; teachers, role models, and peers generally are not aware of, or do not think about, the socialization as they go about their jobs of teaching, training, and collaborating. Nonetheless it occurs and influences one's perceptions, habits, and even how one measures "success." Thus professional education has a moral element in that it shapes character and inspires commitment. The questions that must be asked about professional education are how and to what end are the students influenced (Laney 1985).

This socialization into the professions and professional values is the occurrence that creates both strengths and weaknesses for professionals as they try to weigh important social issues and to make ethical decisions. Professionalism helps an individual to break away from some of the limiting factors in ethical decision making. In fact, Michael Bayles (1989) argues four issues encompass the problems faced in professional ethics, and the determination of these four issues ultimately shapes the values and roles of professions within the larger society. These issues are: (1) the goal of equal service for all; (2) the relationship between clients and professionals; (3) the effects on others of professional conduct on behalf of clients; and (4) the professional's status as an employee. Note the similarity between these four issues and the professional values noted by Filley, House, and Kerr. The interpretation of these values in relation to the four issues leads to either strength or weakness in the position of any profession and its ability to help its members.

Equal service for all who need it is probably an unachievable goal; however, acceptance of and an attempt to achieve such a goal inasmuch as possible will lead to numerous ethical conflicts over such issues as the legitimacy of advertising, the cost of services, and the arbitrary restriction of practice to certain individuals. The relationship issues—between clients and professionals, and professionals' responsibilities to the larger public—raise innumerable value conflicts. And the pull between professional and organizational loyalties is a long-recognized area of ethical conflict. For example, it is taken for granted that a professional orientation is inversely related to organizational loyalty. A professional has the ability, indeed the need, to look at an ethical problem from at least two perspectives—that of the organization within which s/he works *and* from that of the profession to which s/he owes loyalty.

Most professions have formalized and verbalized their values in a code of ethics, and that document serves two functions. First, it is understood that beyond the educational arena professional values continue to evolve, and the end toward which those values hopefully develop is presented in the code of ethics of the profession. Second, it describes to the public, those not privy to the mysteries of the profession, the basis upon which interactions should take place between outsiders/clients and members of the profession, thus establishing an objective set of minimum standards or principles of behavior. The code can be "used rather mechanistically to give the answers to specific moral problems or . . . as signposts pointing to the direction of their right solutions" (Blake 1966, 5).

PROFESSIONALISM AS AN ETHICAL STATE OF MIND

There is an increasingly important interrelationship between the professions and the political sector of society. Modern society, in order to maintain some control over the professions, requires governmental recognition and authorization for their existence, and it places constraints on where and how they operate. In return, many professions play an active role in the political process, attempting to influence the powers and constraints placed upon them by government. Within the government, public administrators are often "professionals" in that they identify with and have been educated/trained in one of the occupations recognized by society as a profession. In fact, as noted earlier, several professions work almost exclusively in government. In this case, according to Mosher and Stillman (1982), separating "the profession" from "the government" has become increasingly difficult in modern society.

To the extent professionals work in the government, they are placed in a situation of divided loyalties and values: They are supposed to (1) protect and further the "public interest," (2) accomplish the goals of their organizations, and (3) achieve their professional ends. Most of the time these three goals are similar; occasionally they end up being at odds. When they are at odds, the attempt to consider and coordinate these varying goals creates special pressures, often in the form of ethical problems, especially since they must be faced in a public arena "where 'truth' is elusive, where values are more compelling than facts, and where professionalism is likely to have a significant impact on the perceptual context in which beliefs are developed and decisions made" (Feldman 1982, 93). On the other hand, in such an environment the state of mind that *should* be generated within a professional is precisely the desired approach to an ethical problem. Why is this so?

Ideally, professionals are taught to question all assumptions related to their work and their findings. Thus a frame of reference toward the world is created that leaves one open to challenging that which is accepted as normal and correct. When dealing with important issues, even if something appears to be obvious and must be acted upon, it should never be taken for granted. Advances are made within general knowledge and the practice of the profession when conventional wisdom is questioned and proven wrong. Therefore, the professional, while continuing to act—since action must be taken—will always be sensitive to anything appearing to be incongruent with his or her sense of balance. Included in this questioning is one's own perception of the problem being considered. This is important because the way one initially interprets the problem or situation often determines the ultimately accepted solution. Two individuals looking at the problem from different but equally rational points of view may arrive at different, equally supportable solutions.

This kind of questioning and self-analysis, while occasionally generating serious problems for the questioner, may sometimes also open new vistas, and the new ways of perceiving the world may create changed assumptions and, ultimately, improved theories about how to deal with the problems being faced. This experience, while often traumatic for an individual, is necessary for both the resolution of specific problems and for ethical growth.

The result of such an approach to the work environment is that tension is likely to develop between loyalty to the organization within which one works and to the profession with which one identifies. Such a situation has long been called by sociologists "role conflict." This happens for two reasons. First, bureaus may demand that an individual perform specific tasks or interpret/categorize situations, cases, or clients in ways that do not appear to be appropriate from a professional perspective. At this point one can hopefully use "the professional state of mind" to step back, analyze the bigger or more basic problem, and try to find a constructive way to handle the dilemma. It is important to remember that the professions exist to "serve the public." Of course, it is also necessary to recognize the difference between the professional and the administrative frame of mind.

The professional has a value system and orientation, influenced by a process of formalized education and socialization, that leads to expected patterns of behavior anytime or anywhere the sets of problems appear that are regularly dealt with by that occupation. Professionals are worried about specific problems or functions within the larger society. The generalist administrator is influenced by a process of education and experience to think in procedural, resource, and logistic terms and to apply that learning in a particular organizational setting. Administrators are worried about funding decisions, program priorities, efficiency of process, and their effectiveness in achieving specific ends, organizational stability, relations with the legislature, threats from interested external parties, and other similar factors.

The two perspectives and backgrounds lead to natural tension. In examining and evaluating the work of professionals, administrators will attempt to measure competence and diligence, honesty and candor, and the proper use of discretion *from the perspective of the organization*. Professionals focus on the impact of ideas and technology on the generic field within which they work. They worry about prescriptive/corrective decisions and actions and define competence and diligence, honesty and candor, and the proper use of discretion *from a client-centered perspective*. Only secondarily do they dwell on how those factors will affect the specific organization for which they work.

These perspectives should not change; such tension, within limits, is healthy. However, in such a situation the individual professional must be at least minimally aware that his decisions may have a long-term or more universal impact on the organization within which he works, and he must understand there is a cost to the bureau in any attempt to change current procedures or to follow his professional instincts instead of the rules of the bureau. Likewise, the administrator must be aware of the tensions created for professionals working within the bureaucratic structure. And for the administrator who has moved to that position from a profession, a relatively common phenomenon, there must be a special sensitivity to the fact that his professional value system and perspective may get in the way of his ability to clearly and logically evaluate the impacts that changes in priorities or procedures have on the organization and on the fulfillment of the formally established public policy. Such sensitivity on the part of all actors does not ease decision making, but it leads to the understanding of the public interest, broadly defined, and wiser actions based on this knowledge.

Second, organizations demand loyalty. What is organizational loyalty, and are there times when such loyalty may very well work against the greater public good? Bayles notes that "The obligation of obedience has two parts: (1) to act as one's employer directs and (2) to act only as one's employer directs" (1989, 140). Coordination of diverse activities is a basic assumption and function of managers within organizations. As long as an order is legally and ethically permissible individuals are expected to do what they are told and *not to assume they should do more.* Herein lies another tension between organizational and professional perspectives. Professionals are trained as individuals to use discretion within their level of competence, but the organization expects them as members of a larger group, all of whom are working toward common goals, not to step beyond the directions given by superiors.

At this point the issue is not one of private, personal preferences or beliefs, but one of professional standards/ethics and community or social good. Professionals have an automatic check on total, blind, organizational loyalty, and they are sometimes forced to face situations where they must determine if it is disloyal to dissent, if the refusal to "go along" is insubordination, and if it is proper or even essential to work against the objectives of one's own organization. At the same time, disloyalty to an organization is never taken lightly by a profession. Unless benefits from such an action can be clearly identified it is doubtful any profession will honor any member guilty of organizational disloyalty.

However, there will be rare occasions when one must follow the dictates of his profession even though it places him in a vulnerable position from the point of view of the bureau. In many, but not all, such situations the profession will rally behind the individual member and add its voice and weight to his defense against the many powerful forces that can be utilized by the bureau. This is precisely the role that a profession can and should play when its canons are violated and its professionals are forced to act against their professional values without proper cause.

The major factor, although obviously not the only one, that can justify such a stance is clear evidence that such an action is necessary in order to maintain basic democratic values. The larger political focus on democratic values, however, is not at the center of most professional value systems; they focus instead on narrow relationships and goals related to their area of specialty. This failure to address broader social values is one of the reasons the American Society for Public Administration has attempted to fill the apparent void. Democratic values, for example, are at the heart of the code of ethics developed within the American Society for Public Administration. Organizational disloyalty is acceptable if it occurs for reasons that clearly relate to society's democratic processes because

organizational disloyalty can be constructive if it promotes an adversarial process that results in the critical scrutiny of government policy and an opportunity to express diverse points of view, including the self-interest of outside groups. While it complicates the decision making process, professionalism can substantially improve the quality of the product. (Feldman 1982, 93)

What is at issue here is guaranteeing that the democratic political process works at least at a minimal level. "Proceduralism," as this concept is referred to by Chandler, "is necessary because in a pluralist pressure system an article of faith must be that from the clash of opposites, contraries, extremes and poles will come not the victory of any one, but the mediation and accommodation of all" (1982, 370).

In cases where there is a conflict between the ethics of the profession and the rules and regulations of the bureau, the first question asked by a professional tends to be, "How does my professional code guide action in the area where the ethical dilemma exists?" The answer to that question is usually in favor of the public interest because those codes almost always center on the concepts of denial of self-interest, service for the public good, and proper procedures for achieving both.

Still, the perspective taken by any code is peculiar to its profession and may be misguiding, as far as the public interest is concerned, in particular cases. Therefore, it is necessary for professionals to remember Eugene Carson Blake's comment that a code serves as both an *absolute answer* and as a *signpost*. He was specifically addressing the problem of a code of ethics for public life, both the standard professions and public administration in general. In giving answers the code of ethics is *absolute*; it tells one what is right and what is wrong. This is necessary because

the driving force of self-interest will not in fact be sufficiently restrained for a decent civil life without the conviction that there is in every circumstance a right and a wrong, and that these are ultimately based upon an absolute that transcends the built-in relativism of all kinds of humanism. (1966, 8)

However, the absolute right or wrong must be determined in the whole context of the decision and not by applying some pious moral principle which does not recognize the complexity and variability of human life.

On the other hand, Blake argues that the code of ethics in public life must be seen as a *set of signposts*, as relative, because many of the worst evils in human life have occurred out of arrogance on the part of those who were convinced they knew what was "the right." Actually, the only way to achieve the public good is through compromise—one is reminded of Willbern's comment that "it is necessary upon occasion to rise above principle and make a deal" (1984, 108). However, Blake points out that "compromise is not the same as appeasement. . . . Only a man of moral principle can compromise" (1966, 9). The code of ethics serves as a set of checks as one moves through the compromise. It can tell an individual if he is moving in the right direction and help to set limits on the compromise—to keep him from going too far. The code also gives an individual a "moral support" if he needs it for any reason; a reasonable claim can be made that "the code of ethics of my profession will not let me do that." And such a claim may be useful if not overdone.

To the supporters of the professions, ethical professionals are part of the backbone of a democratic society. Professional training brings out the best in individuals and the continuing professional association helps to nurture and support these individuals as they face the numerous situations where ethical choices must be made for the good of clients, organization, and the larger society.

PROFESSIONALISM AS AN UNETHICAL STATE OF MIND

In speaking to the legal profession, James Laney argues that there must be an aspect of nobility about its activities or else it becomes "a collection of individuals and firms who are little more than 'hired guns' " (1985, 503). For public sector professionals, that nobility comes from a constant recognition of the importance of the public interest, with its basis in our democratic values, in all that they do. As can be implied from Laney's comment, however, there are numerous individuals who feel the professions fail to always keep the social good and public interest in mind. They also believe professionals may hide their political activities behind a mantle of objectivity and nonpartisanship. For example, many "realists" in political science argue that when applied to city managers, "the very term 'professional' simply disguises one of the best politicians in town," and the term is actually "meaningless and deceptive [because it] fails to describe a manager's 'real' activities and functions" (Stillman 1982, 29). If the "professional/politician" can maintain an ethical balance that keeps in focus the public interest such a charge does not matter; if they cannot maintain an ethical balance professionals/politicians can seriously undermine public trust in the democratic values and process. The central factor in the case of city managers, and in all of the other professions acting in the public sector, is *how they use their power*.

Power is neutral—it is neither good nor bad. Its normative character is determined by how it is used. This is especially true in public management, where the use of power cannot be avoided. Professions rightly demand to certify those fit to practice because the members best know who should be allowed to use the power gained through professional knowledge and status. The members must also have the power to protect members against wrongful external criticism. However, on occasion this self-policing leads to "overidentification" with the profession. In this case individuals within the profession set themselves apart from the society they are charged to serve and identify with the field rather than the public interest. When this happens the individuals' values and actions become synonymous with protectionism for the profession, inflexibility in viewing the environment, and/or unwillingness to realize the need for change. If this approach has become the norm for all members of the occupation, it is using its power improperly and has lost its right to be considered a profession. Usually, however, this charge can be made against only a small portion of the total group. If, as is usually true, the profession can still claim its right to acceptance as such, then the members guilty of the protectionist stance must answer some questions that are really charges of wrongdoing.

Is this [inflexible, protectionist] stance part of the code of ethics or oath of office of the . . . profession, or is it the bleating of individuals who have not committed themselves as servants of society? Is this a chorus for sacrifice, or one for self-reward? Is it an acceptance of responsibility or the avoidance of it? (Fragola 1984, 557)

These problems sometimes exist among even the oldest professions. In such situations the ethical professional may have to choose a singular route that denies his or her background and ties, and this is not an easy task. Sometimes, but not often, the individual may have to strike off alone in an effort to create change. In many cases it is possible to look to one's organization for support. The organization may be right in what it wants, or it may see the correctness of the stance of its professional member. Hopefully the bureau can be flexible enough to allow innovation in the delivery of services, and the professional will look diligently for ways to resolve the conflict between the organization and the profession. There is no guarantee of such flexibility on the part of either group, however, and one's professional ties can make it even harder to carry out the public interest.

All too often the failure of a profession to maintain a focus on the public interest can be traced directly back to the education and socialization of its members. Both the educators and the socializers have probably forgotten the moral dimension of the profession and, instead, placed primary emphasis on "being the best and brightest," in doing "the task well, regardless of the kind of person one is, where the task itself is defined as *what the client wants*" (Laney 1985, 501, emphasis added). In the rush to guarantee competence, in the face of the ever-enlarging universe of knowledge that must be mastered in any profession, in the desire for the bottom-line ethic of business (which we are told is "good for government"), we have often allowed "a diminishing emphasis upon the larger sense of professionalism, leaving little time or inclination for 'soft' concerns such as character, virtue, and commitment to the public trust beyond self-interest'' (ibid.). Yet the public's trust is probably the most valuable asset possessed by any profession.

It is at this point that an individual, if he or she is so inclined, might best attack the problems within his or her profession. Reinhold Niebuhr's comment that the collapse of a society may be traced to the sins of the "good people," rather than to the criminal activities of "bad people," applies especially to the professions in the public sector.

THE PROPER BALANCE: PUBLIC MANAGERS AND THEIR PROFESSIONS

There has been a lot of muckraking lately in relation to the professions, and rightly so; however, things are not as bad as modern yellow journalism would make us believe. Rather than proving that all professions and professionals are bad, what has been shown is that the dilemmas faced by professionals working in the public sector are more complex, and usually of more importance to society, than those faced when dealing with individual situations. In addition to worrying about the outcome for one's self, it is necessary to also think about the larger universe. Therefore,

we have discovered that the ordinary systems of morality which function so well in most decisions in our personal lives break down when we consider the very complex moral decisions in the professions. (Losito 1983, 24)

In many cases the two systems of morality are supportive. Another example taken from the cases related by public administrators in this research, in this case by a professional in a regulatory agency, helps to show how professional and public administrative morality do support one another.

Staff attorneys have a great deal of discretion in how they prepare and prosecute cases that go before regulatory commission hearing judges. However, they must balance the law, commission policy, and office policy. This can become difficult.

After spending two years at the agency, Sarah Underwood was a GS–13 attorney in the Federal Energy Regulatory Commission. At this point she was given the kind of case about which every young attorney dreams. She was the staff attorney assigned to a hearing dealing with certification for a $500 million pipeline project. The case was politically sensitive, and it was drawing close public attention.

There was a team of ten staff witnesses who were involved in analyzing the case. Sarah's responsibility was to put these individuals on the stand and have their findings included as part of the environmental impact statement required under the National Environmental Policy Act of 1968. One staff witness—Dr. Jones, a Ph.D. statistician—had completed an exhaustive environmental impact study, based on a new computer modeling program he had developed, and his results showed the impact of the project to be significantly detrimental to the environment. Based on these studies, and his experience, Dr. Jones was convinced that it would be wrong to certify the project as it was currently presented. That recommendation, along with other team testimony, which was in part based on his findings, was central to the final recommendation of the staff that major modifications should be required prior to granting the certification being sought.

The staff and Sarah had jointly worked out the trial strategy. Dr. Jones would be placed on the witness stand first, and he would present his findings and recommendation with all back-up materials. The other witnesses would follow. Both Dr. Jones and Sarah informed their supervisors of the planned approach to the case.

At this point the trial was well along; the petitioner and the interveners had presented their cases to the judge; staff testimony began the next day. That afternoon Dr. Jones was informed by his superior, a GM 15 division chief, that he could not file his testimony, or if he did, he had to alter his ultimate conclusions. He had to reinterpret his data to come up with the opposite conclusion. (Neither Dr. Jones nor Sarah Underwood ever knew what drove the division chief to make that call, although everyone knew the case was receiving a lot of attention from the commission, the industry, and the press.)

As soon as Dr. Jones became aware of this development, he approached Sarah and informed her that there was a problem. Dr. Jones explained what had happened. He was not afraid of losing his job if he disobeyed his supervisor, but he was afraid that his performance appraisals would suffer and that the type of assignments he received in the future would also be seriously affected. There sometimes is a fine line between a direct threat and intimidation. Dr. Jones identified what had happened as the latter. He felt strong professional pride because a portion of his model was central to the testimony of the other staff witnesses. He came to Sarah as his attorney and basically asked, "What should we do with this?"

Sarah's personal reaction was quite negative to the kind of pressure that Dr. Jones was being subjected to, but because of her position in the bureaucracy, her options were limited. She reported to her boss that one of her witnesses was being pressured to change his testimony. Her boss said, "Look, it's your case. Fix it. You do what has to be done in your case." Sarah, seeking some further and more precise guidance, responded, "This is a big case. A lot of people are watching. I want you to know what is going on." He repeated, "I am aware of what is happening. Fix it. Do what has to be done."

Sarah had no choice but to fish or cut bait; no direction was going to come from her boss. She suspected that this might be a test by her boss to see how she would react. This was an on-the-record proceeding, and as an adversarial process it could only go one way or the other. It was not like a "rule-making" where there could be a lot of input from many different sources, and where compromises were expected. Since the trial was quite advanced, she could not ask for a delay. Sarah had to make a quick decision.

As Sarah pondered over what to do she reflected on an ethics course that she had taken in the last semester of law school. The thought that constantly came back to her was that she was an officer of the court. As such, she had an obligation not to present evidence that she knew to be false, nor could she suborn perjury (allow a witness to be forced to give evidence that he could not swear to).

On the next morning, fifteen minutes before testimony started, Sarah went to Dr. Jones' supervisor and told him it was her intention to put Dr. Jones on the stand. If Dr. Jones was not allowed to testify, Sarah was going to introduce into the record as "item by reference" (therefore making them part of the trial record) the studies that Jones had done. She would apprise the judge, as part of what she considered her ethical responsibility as an officer of the court, that Jones had been placed under pressure to alter what Sarah knew to be his ultimate conclusions in the case. Sarah stated that she would note that he—the supervisor—was the individual responsible for the change because he had requested the ultimate recommendations be changed. She would suggest to the judge hearing the case that he compel the supervisor to testify, in place of Dr. Jones, and explain why he ordered the changes in the studies. Finally, Sarah bluffed, but in a way that she felt was safe, by informing Dr. Jones' superior that she had the complete backing of her supervisor. (He had told her to "fix the situation," and she believed that he would support her even though she had not asked him specifically if he would do so given this scenario.)

Dr. Jones' supervisor had approximately twelve minutes to think about the situation. He backed down, saying he would take care of it at a higher level after the judge had rendered his decision. Sarah never had to put anything about the situation on the record; Dr. Jones testified; the judge ruled with the staff; the project was not approved; ultimately, the changes suggested were required prior to certification. When the case got to the commission, the judge's ruling was upheld.

While Sarah was somewhat worried about what the ramifications of this situation would be, it had no direct effect on her career. Life went on as usual and as if the case had never occurred. Although he never directly addressed the case in his discussion with her, Sarah's boss was apparently satisfied with her handling of the situation, and she regularly moved up through the organization to positions of greater authority. (Shortly before this book was finished, Sarah was promoted into the position held by her supervisor when the case occurred.) Nothing further was ever said to Sarah by the supervisor of Dr. Jones, and to her knowledge he made no future attempts to influence testimony by the staff. However, Sarah suspected that he tried to influence the assignment of some cases in order to guarantee their handling by other staff attorneys. Staff morale was improved because they knew what had happened and knew that their professional independence and objectivity had been protected in a very touchy situation. Dr. Jones was able to continue to function effectively within the staff.

Sarah Underwood was able to turn to both her education and the ethics of her legal profession for a clear definition of the problem and grounds upon which to act. It quickly became obvious she had to make the crucial decision. "I knew it came down to me. It was my call." The boss had said he was aware of the problem and Sarah should "fix it." The ethics of her profession were important in her decision.

When I faced the problem of the lawyer's responsibility, I went back to notes from the ethics class that I took in law school. I also researched the American Bar Association Canon of Ethics and the laws of the State of New York where I was admitted to the bar. All made it clear that I should not, could not "suborn perjury" from a witness—"force a witness to give evidence he could not swear to."

Her professional attachment and values fit her initial feeling that what was being demanded was against the public interest. However, Sarah was functioning as a professional, a lawyer, in this case. She was not a manager. Now that she is a manager, Sarah attempts to help young lawyers recognize such situations, even if not as clear cut, and she emphasizes to them the importance of following the professional code of ethics because she is convinced of its supportiveness of the public interest and the development of public trust in the regulatory process.

The problem can be complicated for professionals if they are in an organizational culture that is not, for whatever reason, sympathetic to the professional values and mores. Valerie Franklin felt she had to be sensitive to, and true to, the values of her profession, but she also had to be cognizant of the bureaucratic environment in which she worked. That environment was inimical in some ways to professional values as they were stated earlier in this chapter, and her attempt to change the values and mores of the organization created serious trauma for her and for the bureau. Dr. Franklin was relatively new to the organization, and she maintained a high level of commitment to the individuals who were the end users of the overall programs administered by the organization. Without being able to prove any such statement, it appeared that other members of the organization, especially Dr. Franklin's superior, had been influenced by the bureaucratic context and their loyalty had shifted from the poor and vulnerable citizens, who were the ultimate recipients of aid, to the bureau, the state universities who received money and program assistance, and the processes that were considered inviolable.

Dr. Franklin's case was the only one in the relatively small universe of this study to reach such a level of tension; however, lesser levels of tension were regularly recognized by individuals who were "managing within their professions," or working as managers in organizations where their professions played a major role in the policy-making and the implementation/operation of their program. Robert McGowan points out that such cross pressure is normal and usually healthy because

the public professional, to function properly, must . . . integrate professional goals with those of the organization. This individual must continually update skills as the technology changes and must have some understanding of formal and informal networks. In addition, he or she should develop proficiency in developing support at the program and policy levels and become adept in the use of extra-governmental channels. . . . The distinguishing element for the public professional is "publicness" and understanding all that this involves. (1982, 348).

In such a case there is a good deal of stress and internal conflict experienced by the committed professional who works in a public organizational context (Rainey and Backoff 1982, 326–328). And there will always be some percentage of any group who cannot or will not wrestle with the more weighty and serious problems. They will fail their fellows either because they interpret the ethics of the profession too superficially, they ignore them, or they cannot handle the complex yet subtle political aspects of professional ethical dilemmas in the public context.

To an individual, those interviewees who had started their public careers in one of the professions (law, accounting, engineering, medicine, etc.) but had moved into managerial positions recognized they had moved from the special environment of the profession to the more general environment of management, and they generally found the mores and values of their new positions different from those of their original professions. Most of them found the ethics of their profession either irrelevant or inadequate to deal with the problems they faced as managers. "Ultimately," said one manager in a health agency, "while my profession and my professional values are important in my calculation, I cannot depend on them for answers to the ethical dilemmas that I face. My 'professional side' is only one of the many factors that plays a part in guaranteeing my 'ethical anchor' when facing the everyday work world."

Another top-level manager in the Department of Commerce noted the same problem, only put it more strongly.

My profession as accountant has had little to do with my *management* function. It applies to those few actions I still take as an accountant—the development of accounting and reporting systems, systems for collecting overdue accounts, etc.; but my much greater role as manager primarily deals with organizational structure, planning and implementing programs, and dealing with personnel issues. While it sets a proper general tone for behavior, the accounting code of ethics does not deal with those issues.

For those managers who worked in occupations only peripherally considered to be professional, the question of professional values and ethics was important but had to be addressed differently. These individuals made no pretense about being professional in the traditional sense; however, they were sensitive to the values and attitudes attached to the professions, and they strove to fulfill these values in their more general world. Many of the management fields in which these individuals labored (e.g., personnel, budgeting, planning, policy analysis) have developed codes of ethics, but the emphasis on that code was much less, nor could the professional organizations to which they belonged control actual behavior of their members. For example, Robert Fellows has been a lifelong member of professional organizations related to personnel management; yet he argued that the code of ethics of the profession had no influence on him at all in his decision on how to handle the specific situation he faced with his incompetent subordinate. On the other hand, he was aware of what it meant to be a professional, and he attempted to function daily according to such standards, especially when ethical problems arose.

I perceived myself as a professional. (I have always perceived myself as ethical.) But the professional code of ethics, although on my wall, I perceived as a motherhood statement without all that concrete meaning for me.[1] It belabored the obvious. I never recall having tested a decision on that code of ethics. But I try to make "professional" decisions. I believe the frame of reference attached to professionalism is appropriate for public managers as they try to serve the larger society.

Another interviewee noted she used the code of ethics in her profession only when it helped her make an argument against doing something she felt was improper.

If I needed additional support for my stance and could not dissuade those putting pressure on me, which seldom happened, I sometimes used the code of ethics as a baseline for my argument. I do not ever remember using the code of ethics to support an argument *for* doing something.

Thus, there was a constant thread of consideration or thought about what the concept of professionalism meant within the context of management. (Can there be such a thing as a "professional public manager"?) And this effort to wrestle with the ideals and values surrounding the concept were important to the maintenance of an objective approach to ethical problems across the board. When the public managers faced an ethical dilemma they consistently tried to act in a professional way.

As George Anderson described his thought processes and his attempt to determine how to handle his dilemma with Laura (the handicapped employee), he stated that on more than one occasion he came back to the same set of questions:

What are managers? What do they try to do? What is professionalism? What do professionals do in a circumstance like this? Maybe management is not a profession, but can we learn from the questions they [the professions] ask and the stance they take?

What he was doing was making sure he approached the issue, to the extent possible, from an objective, disinterested viewpoint so his personal feelings would not get in the way of rationality combined with fairness and an attempt to act in the long-term public interest. This kind of application of professionalism, which regularly appeared, is a positive sign for all concerned. It shows that public managers are cognizant of the importance that professional values have, and they are attempting to utilize the positive aspects of professionalism when possible. The "professional yardstick" is regularly used by public managers as one more test of the appropriateness of their response to ethical dilemmas.

Frederick Mosher has noted that "for better or worse—or better *and* worse— much of our government is now in the hands of professionals"(1982, 142). The responses of the managers interviewed for this study make one believe that the positive far outweighs the negative. Professionalism helps to raise the level of ethical sensitivity and sophistication among those doing the public's work.

NOTE

1. Sadly, the reaction toward the American Society for Public Administration code of ethics was similar. None of the interviewees volunteered the ASPA code as a relevant factor in their decisions. Few of them knew of its existence.

CHAPTER 8

ANALYZING AND RESOLVING
ETHICAL DILEMMAS

Most of the problems public managers face in their daily work are not of great complexity nor is it monumentally difficult to figure out which actions are appropriate to their bureau or the public interest/trust that they and their bureau serve. Thank goodness this is so; otherwise little would be accomplished. On the other hand, ethical issues regularly arise requiring careful analysis and conscientious effort on the part of the decision maker in order to guarantee that personal, organizational, and societal values are protected. It is difficult to fulfill the specified mission of an agency from within the middle of the bureaucracy and at the same time to keep in mind the protection of the public interest, justice, fairness, and ultimately the maintenance and development of democratic principles. Factors such as democratic principles seem far removed from efficient and effective management; however, there is an ultimate connection between the two when we peel back the layers of rules, regulations, procedures, and inter-organizational politics so often covering up the basic but most important elements of what it means to be a "public servant."

When ethical issues are important, we must be prepared to sort back through the levels of interest and organizational politics in an intelligent and effective manner. Our most basic responsibility—once we get past the immediacy of our job, our peers, and the rules and regulations by which we live our organizational lives—is to guarantee the values of our society and political system. Individuals do count; due process is essential to guarantee justice and fairness; change can occur peacefully; democratic government, while imperfect, is the best system discovered so far to protect all of us in our daily lives; bureaucratic decisions, even those made in the apparently routine life of the middle manager, ultimately have an impact on public trust in the political system.

Sensitivity and wisdom are needed when we face ethical dilemmas, but there is little evidence of serious attention to preparation for these situations on the part of the bureaucracy. Few managers receive any deliberately planned help in preparing to face ethical dilemmas, so they must take it on themselves to prepare for such situations; otherwise, any thought given to such issues will occur as an accident or afterthought.

The last five chapters have discussed both theoretical approaches to public administrative ethics and practical approaches taken by managers working in the public bureaucracy. Both of these perspectives give us important insights into understanding and dealing with ethical dilemmas when we face them as managers in a public organization. As these ways of examining ethical dilemmas are considered, it also becomes increasingly clear that no one approach can give us all of the insights and answers we need. While we may all believe in certain ultimate and immutable ethical laws, we must interpret them to meet myriad different situations. In any particular situation only one or two of the several approaches to ethical analysis that we have examined are likely to apply, and even those approaches have to be adjusted to address the unique characteristics of the case at hand. Therefore, it is time to pull the information together in summary form, and in a way allowing us to apply the proper analytic tools to the situation we face. Table 7 summarizes the many issues presented in this study as potentially important in a thorough analysis of ethical issues, and the following pages briefly discuss these questions and how they might be addressed in an orderly fashion when such investigation is necessary. After that we will look briefly at the kinds of options available to an individual in a managerial position when he or she "tries to do the right thing," and we will also address the possible results of such actions. But first, let us think a moment about how the analyst should approach his or her task.

ANALYSIS MUST BE THOROUGH AND OBJECTIVE

In order to deal with analysis and decision making in an ethical dilemma, it is necessary to carry out the analysis carefully and thoroughly; and central to the process of thorough analysis, of course, is the ability to be detached and objective. Pure objectivity is never possible, but one should strive to minimize subjectivity.

Over the last two or three decades there has been a recurring proposal from some academicians in public administration that public servants become advocates for one party or the other—usually "the underdog"—in public disputes. Another group, primarily composed of some economists and political scientists, advocates that all public decisions should be approached with a presumption that government intervention in any activity is bad and that public choices should be made through the application of certain economic tools and/or market devices.

Either approach to ethical dilemmas appears to be an invitation to trouble. If ethical issues are analyzed with such bias, the result is a foregone conclusion and the process is a charade.

Issues requiring careful study do so precisely because the various facets of the questions shade into one another, and this subtlety of meaning and causation can easily lead to misunderstanding. Objectivity is difficult but essential in such situations; however, it does not guarantee success in winning over others or in gaining their acceptance when decisions are made and actions taken. In fact, public managers involved in ethical cases commonly expect misunderstanding even when, or especially when, they are objective. Therefore they look for ways to make it clear their judgments and actions are nonbiased. They are aware that other people's preconceived ideas or inclinations cause the subtleties of the issue to be lost. As one respondent working in an intermediary role noted,

It was obvious that the other primary actors in [the case] had strong opinions firmly set, and if I disagreed with their decision I would be charged with bias no matter how carefully I documented my facts and reasoning. My only choice was to document and move ahead in a way that would satisfy those individuals who might see my report and were not so personally involved in the case, especially individuals at a higher level in the organization.

Victor Thompson speaks directly to this point when he argues that law students, as future professionals, must learn the importance of objectivity.

One of the hardest lessons for a young law student to learn is that he must give up his . . . interest in the outcomes and dispositions for the actual persons involved in the cases he studies and that he must concentrate on the principle of the law involved. . . . This skill in impersonality is a necessary prerequisite to the successful practice of a profession [such as] the giving of good legal advice. (1975, 114)

Only objective analysis can give an answer uncluttered by personal opinion or biased evaluation.[1] It does not matter who is being served, it is impossible to serve them well without a good analysis of the situation; biased analysis may lead to the greatest disservice of all because it will lead to the wrong conclusion and an inappropriate alternative selection. The probability of unanticipated consequences related to the best possible choice are great enough without exacerbating the problem. Ethical dilemmas require a clear head, a clean slate, and openness to a variety of ideas about the facts of and actors in any situation.

ASKING THE RIGHT QUESTIONS

It is impossible to know the answers to ethical problems in advance. Ethically mature individuals know what they believe is right on a general scale; however, that standard must then be applied to the specific situation being faced at the moment, and general rules seldom fit specific cases. This is why we must have courts of law in which to decide the numerous cases brought before them.

If general rules must be applied to specific situations, then we must develop

Table 7

A Framework of Analysis for Ethical Dilemmas

First it is necessary to make sure that the problem faced is an ethical dilemma. In order to verify this fact there must be a positive response to the questions:

--Are important values in conflict in this case?

--Can those values be identified, and/or must additional effort be made to discover them?

--Is it necessary to analyze, calculate, reason about, which of the competing values must be served?

The recognition of the ethical dilemma <u>and</u> its analysis require sensitivity to, and ability to understand the factors influencing, <u>at least</u> the five following areas.

I. THE LAW--What can relevant laws tell me about what I am expected to do in this case? (The term "law" includes established rules and regulations interpreting the substance <u>and</u> process of more general statutes.)

    A.   What does the statute say, both the specific language and the context?

    B.   What does the statute <u>not</u> say, and is there any hint as to why that was left unsaid?

    C.   Is it possible to go beyond the specific words of the law and understand what the "intent" of those establishing the law was?

    D.   What do I do if the law is wrong or does not apply to my case?

II. THE PHILOSOPHICAL AND CULTURAL SETTING--Can I learn important factors about this situation by examining the basic philosophical and cultural elements that create ethical perceptions and determine what responses are acceptable?

    A.   What can an understanding of the culture tell me about the way significant others perceive the issues I face and what their expectations are?

    B.   Do the tenets of political philosophy on which our expectations are founded help to clarify the values that are important to the dilemma at hand, and can they help me frame the proper questions to ask?

    C.   What are the basic American political values, and how can I guarantee that I stay true to them in my decisions and actions?

    D.   Do the principal actors in the case at hand interpret the political values in the same way, and if not, what are the differences in interpretation?

    E.   How have society's values relative to this issue changed over the immediate past, and will change continue to occur?

    F.   Must I take into account other factors, such as religious or political beliefs, in order to understand the values at play in the issue?

a way of analyzing the situation so we may interpret our basic beliefs and values as they fit the dilemma we face. We cannot know the right answer, but hopefully we can know the right questions to ask. Rather than dealing with important ethical problems from a single focus, perspective, or vantage point, it is necessary to use a multifaceted approach so we make sure we do not overlook significant but obscured factors influencing the situation. As a minimum, I have argued that everyone, in order to make a well-informed decision, should examine those ethical dilemmas requiring serious analysis from at least five viewpoints (see Table 7).

The order in which the five areas are considered may not matter, and it may become clear rather quickly that one or more of the subjects is not relevant to the issue at hand. Still, if the issue is important it is essential to look at these five areas, even if the decision is that a particular issue is not important in the

Table 7 (Continued)

III. PROFESSIONS AND PROFESSIONALISM--Does my professional training or my broader sense of "professionalism" help me to understand what I should do?
A. By remembering the characteristics of a "profession," can I better picture how I should approach and resolve this dilemma?
B. Is this a problem regularly faced, in some similar form, by members of my profession, and if so, how is it regularly resolved?
C. What professional values can serve as a guide to action?
D. Is the conflict between my role as a professional and my role as a bureau member?
E. Am I "hiding behind" my profession so as to avoid decisions and actions?

IV. ORGANIZATIONAL DYNAMICS--Is the organization in which I work, or my relationship with that organization, a part of the problem?
A. What external forces related to the organization might be influencing the questions and alternatives that I face?
B. Does the structure (size, type of hierarchy, centralization or decentralization, etc.) of the organization either cause all or part of the problem or affect my ability to resolve it?
C. Do the functions (procedures, outputs, etc.) carried out by the bureau cause or help solve the ethical dilemma?
D. Does the organizational culture (values, rituals, etc.) influence the type of ethical dilemma I face and the possible alternatives available to resolve it.

V. PERSONAL ASPECTS--What do I need to know about myself in order to adequately deal with this ethical dilemma?
A. What about my personal background (family, religious and political beliefs, education, etc.) influences my perception and attitudes toward the ethical dilemma I face?
B. How do my personality characteristics affect my ability to deal with complex ethical problems and the people with whom I must interact?
C. At what level of maturity and sophistication do I deal with ethical dilemmas, and do I understand the maturity level of the others with whom I must deal in this situation?

present case. This procedure will guarantee the problem is addressed from a variety of viewpoints and no important factor is overlooked through carelessness or negligence. This is known as guaranteeing analytic and intellectual rigor.

Personal Aspects

For a public servant to be able to deal with all of the ethical issues facing him or her in an effective manner, s/he must have developed a high level of "self-understanding." Ultimately our interpretation of all other factors is enhanced or limited by our own development into a sensitive, mature, sophisticated interpreter of values (what people desire), reality (what really exists), and perceptions (what people believe exists) around us. Perfect self-understanding is probably impossible; however, our level of sensitivity and sophistication is greatly enhanced if we seriously attempt to know all we can about ourselves and understand the impact of our personality, management style, and moral maturity on our ability to deal with any specific ethical dilemma. We also need to know about the same factors as they relate to those about us—the individuals most intimately involved in the problem currently being faced—because the answers about their levels of sensitivity and sophistication tell us how we must deal with them as we try to resolve the problem. Therefore, three questions about one's self need to be addressed, and then those same questions may need to be asked about those significant others involved in the dilemma.

First, I need to understand how my personal background (family influence, religious and political beliefs, educational history, etc.) have had an impact on my perceptions and attitudes toward the ethical dilemma I face. Families from different social, economic, and ethnic backgrounds, for example, may interpret specific actions or situations in dramatically dissimilar ways. Democrats and Republicans can apparently look at the same record of a potential public official— for example, ex-Senator John Tower when he was nominated to be secretary of defense—and arrive at dramatically different conclusions as to his competency to serve. Public managers often note their tendency toward conservatism or liberalism and try to take their personal political philosophy into account as they serve their present appointed master. Religious background influences how questions related to ethical dilemmas are framed. Such influences cannot be avoided, but they can be recognized and compensated for when necessary.

Second, each individual has a unique personality. It determines how problems are tackled and what decisions and actions are likely to follow. These personalities are described in many ways. People are often referred to as ''Type A'' and prime candidates for heart attacks, or as assertive, docile, logical, creative, and so on, and each term refers to a personal style of dealing with reality. We need to understand how we tend to deal with our world. Do we confront issues or avoid them? Do we rush to judgment or do we tend to delay decisions beyond a reasonable time? Do we insist on the facts and search for a logical decision or do we tend to play our hunches? Do we understand how the other actors in our drama play their roles? Any increase in knowledge about these factors will improve our chances of resolving the ethical dilemma in a constructive way.

Third, and this issue deals directly with the question of personal sophistication, how do I define what is an ethical dilemma? Am I able to deal with ethical issues at a sophisticated level that includes larger community values and general concepts of right and wrong? Definitions and resolutions of ethical dilemmas cannot be based simply on what is accepted practice or peer pressure, nor can issues always become ''personalized'' because individuals rather than concepts then become the center of attention. More basic and general concepts and values must be considered. It then becomes extremely important to understand the level of moral maturity of significant others in the conflict. Different levels of moral maturity can be compensated for if they are understood; it is especially important to be able to approach other individuals in the conflict in a way they will understand and to which they can react.

The Law

Once the ethical dilemma itself becomes the focus of the public manager, the obvious first place for managers, because of their position in the organization and their role in implementation of policy, to look for guidance is the law (often more specifically interpreted to apply to a program or agency through statutes, rules, and regulations developed for the bureaucratic actors). What does the statute say, both the specific language and the context of the legislation? This question is vital because we have sworn to uphold the law and because the law creates the parameters within which we must operate. Many problems can be quickly resolved by making sure we clearly understand what the appropriate statutes say. Legislators often attempt to anticipate the major questions that will arise in relation to a statute, and questions that appear unique and original often turn out to have been thought of, and answered by, those who originally wrestled with the policy under consideration.

On the other hand, legislators often do not deal with specific issues, and the language they use may not answer the question at hand; therefore it is important to understand what the statute does *not* say, and to look for any hint as to why it was left unsaid. In fact, legislators sometimes avoid the hardest issues, the seemingly unresolvable ones, and leave them for the bureaucracy to wrestle with. In this case it is the duty of the appropriate bureaucrats to resolve the matter in as equitable a manner as possible and then be prepared to defend their decision. At the same time, it is in this area where public administrators often have to be most skilled at bargaining and compromising because they are attempting to deal with issues found to be unresolvable in the political arena of the day. In this case it is especially important to decide if it is possible to go beyond the specific words of the law and understand what was the "intent" of those establishing the law.

If the law does not apply to the issue at hand, develop the best case possible for whatever action one takes. This should be done *before* the action is taken, not after, because most defenses developed after an action is taken are "rationalizations" (self-satisfying but often incorrect sets of reasons for one's behavior) rather than rational analyses (thought processes manifesting or based upon reason and logic).

The most serious problem arises, however, on those *few* occasions when the law appears to be wrong. At this point, one must guarantee that (1) the assumption the law is wrong is correct and (2) any action taken helps to improve the overall situation by leading to a correction in the law so that *political/societal*[2] values are properly reflected. The most serious challenge faced in this situation is to guarantee that any action taken will lead to an improvement in, commitment to, and application of the democratic values central to society. How can anyone be sure their values are "better" than those of society as a whole, and, therefore, they have the "right" to disobey the law? This question is, at the same time, central to any justifiable action and extremely hard to answer.

The central issue in this case is to decide "how to break the law." Any action must lead to improvement in society, not to the destruction of its fabric, otherwise the individual involved has moved *outside of society* and the issues involved are greater than any ethical decision about a specific law, rule, regulation, or action that might follow from them.

When dealing with the law it is usually possible to get help from competent outsiders. Most agencies have legal counselors as part of the staff, and if insiders cannot help there are plenty of "outside" lawyers available who can advise one on the fine points of the law. Such help must be used wisely; it is sometimes possible to find two lawyers who will give approximately the opposite advice based on the same facts, but even such opposing opinions can prove useful since the arguments behind such views can help to educate any action that is finally taken.

The Philosophical and Cultural Setting

The more basic the issue, the less likely we are to be aware of it. That thought is epitomized in our cultural and philosophical underpinnings on which our values, perceptions, and actions are based. On occasion it may prove worthwhile to back off from a problem and take time to review the set of questions surrounding our most basic assumptions about society. When we do review these assumptions, it may become clear that we are "creatures of our culture" and not at all the free agents we believe ourselves to be.

In the first place we need to realize that what we consider an ethical problem may not seem so to others playing a significant role in the situation. This difference in definition may occur because people are either insensitive or their backgrounds cause them to interpret facts and actions differently than do we; therefore it is useful to understand what an examination of the culture tells us about the way significant others perceive the issue we face and what they expect. The conclusion reached will occasionally be quite different than expected, and it is in precisely these cases that further analysis of cultural and philosophical factors must be carried out. This is especially true when working in an international or intercultural situation; even in the United States the differences brought on by geography, economics, history, religion, and ethnic background can lead to dramatic variations in interpretation of the same set of facts. An understanding of these differences is necessary in order to talk to one another intelligently, to bargain, and to compromise in a meaningful way.

Once an understanding is developed it is possible to begin examining the tenets of political philosophy on which our expectations are founded in order to clarify the values that are important to the dilemma at hand and to help frame the proper questions. In most cases we are talking about basic American political values, and it is important we remain true to them in both decisions and actions. However, even on this supposedly common ground there will be differences of opinion about the interpretation of our democratic values as well as which values are more basic.

Hopefully, intelligent conversations about these issues can help all parties in a dispute to arrive at a common ground; however, that does not always happen. In such a case it is necessary to go one step further and determine what other factors, such as religious and/or political beliefs, must be taken into account in order to understand the values at play in the current issue. Some issues, such as the debate over abortion (right to choice versus right to life) go beyond politics to issues such as religious beliefs. Such factors must be taken into account insofar as possible, or there will be no resolution of the ethical dilemma. However, there will always be some point at which one's personal, carefully developed, and deeply held understanding of cultural and philosophical beliefs and values must be obeyed. The important issue is to make a special effort to comprehend the perspectives and attitudes of those who hold other views.

There is no easy way to guarantee an understanding of the philosophy and culture of a society; it can only come from lifelong experience, individual openness to ideas and perspectives, serious effort, and a willingness to turn to philosophers, anthropologists, sociologists, political scientists, economists, theologians, and any other thoughtful individuals who work in this broad field. Hopefully, this kind of time and effort leads to "wisdom" (common sense, sagacity, and good judgement) which we *assume* develops as individuals move up through their organization into increasingly more critical positions. It is the need for this form of wisdom that leads us to desire in our leaders both a depth and breadth of experience and the willingness to learn from it.

Organization Dynamics

Public administrators spend a very large portion of their time in an organizational context, mostly in the particular bureau with which they are attached. The important word here is bureau. We must remember the characteristics of a bureaucracy as spelled out by Max Weber (1947), and discussed by almost every organization scholar since, and the tremendous influence that these characteristics have on many aspects of our lives—often carrying over into other parts of our daily existence. It is impossible to spend large amounts of time in such an environment without it having a tremendous impact on the way we perceive, define, and think about the larger world. And the demands made upon us by our organization are sometimes at odds with demands from other parts of our world. Therefore, our ethical dilemmas are often generated by a conflict between our organization and our identity with profession, political philosophy, religious beliefs, family, friends, or society.

The organizational context within which we work often causes the conflict of values. Therefore, one question to *always* ask when faced with such a dilemma is whether or not the organization within which I work, or my relationship with that organization, is a part of the problem. If so, and it often will be, the next step is to examine five major factors, any one of which can be further broken down as necessary.

First, are the goals of the organization clear, and are they understood by all actors in the situation being faced? In many cases problems for individuals arise because there is disagreement about the ends of the organization. Clarifying and achieving consensus on the goals can often resolve seemingly insurmountable conflicts.

Second, organizations do not operate in a vacuum; external forces related to the organization might be influencing the questions and alternatives. *Public* bureaus exist within a political environment that can be highly volatile. Powerful external actors influence perceptions, definitions, decisions, and actions related to problems within the organization. These external pressures must be understood if they are related to the current ethical dilemma although they may or may not change one's action; however, a comprehension of the political pressures will undoubtedly help create a more intelligent response.

Third, each bureau has its own unique structure. Bureaus do not come in prefabricated, standardized forms. Organizational structure (size, type of hierarchy, centralization or decentralization of decision making, etc.) may cause the problem and/or can be used to help solve it. A public manager who is very sensitive to his or her position within the larger bureau system can understand the strengths and weaknesses that are attached to his or her position. Those facts place specific parameters on how much one usually knows about the "big picture" (the larger view held by superiors) of the organization and on what one individual at a specific point in the hierarchy can hope to accomplish.

Fourth, we must go beyond the structure of the organization to determine if the functions (procedures, outputs, etc.) carried out by the bureau cause or help solve the ethical dilemma. An organization may have well-defined, worthwhile goals but the procedures may diminish the ability of everyone to achieve those ends; or the procedures being used may fail to take into account the fact that the bureau is operating in a democratic system that emphasizes openness, due process, individual dignity, and other similar values; a failure to recognize such values can lead to conflicts between means and ends. In other words, individuals within the bureaucracy may have suffered "displacement of goals" and forgotten the primary reason for the existence of the bureau. If such are the problems, procedural adjustment may solve the ethical dilemma, and in many cases this kind of adjustment is easier to deal with than changes related to individual personalities or organizational culture, both of which may involve deep-seated attitudes and values that are difficult for people to recognize, admit, and change.

Fifth, and hardest to deal with in many cases, is the role organizational culture (values, rituals, etc.) plays in determining the type of ethical dilemma faced and the available alternatives. Organizational culture plays an important part in people's reactions to any situation, and the less people are aware of the organizational culture the more influential it will be in their actions. That culture, whatever it is, probably has developed from the top down in the organization—the top managers/leaders[3] in the bureau help to create and reinforce values and behavior; therefore, it is often difficult to deal with problems in this area. On the other hand, ignorance of culture in organizational life is a guaranteed recipe for disaster.

Professions and Professionalism

Many managers in public organizations have professional backgrounds—in addition to their operation and existence in public bureaus they are trained in and identify with a profession. The fact that a large number of professions are represented broadly throughout the bureaucracy is one of the elements guaranteeing at least minimal representation of diverse viewpoints and values in the pluralistic system within which public policy is formulated and implemented. Whatever the particular profession under consideration, identification with it

requires continuing professional education and training, involvement in professional associations, regular attention to professional literature, and a sense of responsibility for the [professional] role. Without these a public administrator is cognitively disadvantaged in dealing with organizational definitions of public problems, appropriate administrative conduct, and the purposes of government. In the absence of professional identity the organization's definitions tend to occupy the entire field; vision is narrowed to the organization's interests; responsibility shrinks to the boundaries of the organization; obligation is restricted to the chain of command. (Cooper 1986, xvi)

The "professional viewpoint" existent within most of these individuals helps to guarantee that issues are examined in some depth and blind obedience is not the order of the day. However, we as individuals must closely examine our professional training and sense of professionalism in order to guarantee it remains a viable tool for the public interest. After all, professions are a means to an end, not an end in themselves; professions exist to guarantee that people receive the best possible care or service in a particular, critical part of their lives, and balance must be maintained between that part of their lives and the many other parts that coexist. Therefore, we must remember the central characteristics of a "profession" and see if those attributes give us a better picture of how to approach and resolve any ethical dilemma we face.

Another factor related to the professions is that most of the problems faced by any member are not unique; therefore, often insight and help can be gained from professional experience and the codes of behavior springing from these recurrent problems. We should regularly search for knowledge and wisdom, related to the problem at hand, developed within our profession (if we belong to one) or coming from the professions in general (if we do not belong to one). Each profession has a recurring set of dilemmas, many of them ethical, that "come with the territory," and we should not kid ourselves into believing we often face new situations since there are not that many new things in the world. In most cases it is possible to find relevant, thoughtful advice to apply to the problem at hand.

We should especially understand our professional values. Even though the socialization into these values is often relatively subtle, anyone in a profession is influenced by them. Even if the reaction is revulsion, which seldom occurs, it is still a reaction to a set of values inculcated through training, socialization, and continuing peer pressure. Hopefully, these values can help to solve the dilemma we face; however, resolution may come through four kinds of recognition and concomitant action. We may find these values offer understanding that helps us to solve the problem in what would be considered a professional manner. We may find we are "hiding behind" our profession so as to avoid or rationalize decisions and actions. In this case we must "break out of our professional mold" and approach the ethical dilemma from new and different perspectives. We may discover the ethical dilemma is caused by a conflict between our professional values and the values of the bureau. And finally, we may find that, as *managers*, the ethical guidelines of our profession are not directly relevant to the issue at hand; however, the professional values and viewpoint usually will be useful.

If all of the questions in these five areas discussed above are seriously and objectively considered by anyone facing an ethical dilemma, the probability for a satisfactory ultimate decision will be greatly increased. Being correct does not always solve the problem however; it is still necessary to take action, and that must be done in an environment that does not always welcome the "right answer" to an ethical dilemma. Therefore let us look at the issue of how to go about taking action.

TAKING ACTION: DOING WHAT SHOULD BE DONE

It is one thing to know what is right and another to do it. In every interview carried out for this study, the managers came to clear decisions about what was "right" in their situations. The major problem faced was deciding how to do what they thought was right in an environment that did not guarantee cooperation; in many cases others in the environment seemed determined to remain neutral at best and at worst to work against the managers.

Examining other attempts at dealing with similar ethical problems may prove useful; nevertheless, it is a direct road to disaster to *assume* that any such knowledge learned from comparison can be transferred into a different situation or organization. Therefore, it is often necessary to look for a solution specifically for the problem at hand, but to arrive at this solution through a "standard operating procedure" for approaching ethical problems. In a few cases it may be necessary to step outside the standard operating procedures spelled out here; however, these situations probably arise much less often than we believe.

In this study, managers looked, above all, for a solution that allowed the situation to be resolved without undue conflict. Their first goal was to *minimize conflict as much as possible*. Part of "being right" included allowing others, whenever possible, a chance to save face, to look good to the public, to learn and change. Being right did not require a public recognition of the holiness of their cause nor an award for excellence in public service.

On the other hand, they recognized that it is useless to believe that conflict can always be avoided. In general, organization therapists argue that a certain level of conflict, defined as tension, is probably healthy. And the total lack of conflict in the cases faced by these public managers would have meant there was no ethical dilemma in the first place.

Possible Levels of Response

Ethical dilemmas faced by public managers occur within an organizational context; these are not issues faced in a vacuum. Generally we should start at the lowest level of confrontation, involving as few people as possible, maximizing the opportunity for agreement and minimizing the loss of face, and then expand the range and intensity of the conflict as it becomes necessary. Stated in another way, in order to minimize conflict we should start any actions at the level allowing the least amount of "disturbance" to the individuals and organizational units involved, and escalate carefully only when it is clear the current level of confrontation is not working. Individual and organizational response to conflict is related to the provocation or danger they see; therefore, at each level of escalation it is increasingly harder to achieve closure on the conflict because the process of coming to agreement, or resolution, involves more individuals, requires more steps, and may force individuals to publicly admit they were wrong (not always an easy task). This was the general approach of most of the managers interviewed, and in those cases where such tactics were not followed there was usually a recognition that failure to act that way exacerbated the problem. As one individual put it:

I learned a lot from the experience I went through. I would never change my decision, it was right. But I would attack the problem differently, trying to find a way that would not lead to the almost immediate confrontation that occurred in my case. Perhaps the conflict would have reached the same level of intensity, but I would simply feel better in knowing that I had done everything I could to keep that from happening.

March and Simon (1958) argue there are four levels of conflict within an organization. If we can deal with the dilemma from a *problem-solving* mode, where it is assumed we share objectives and values, then our decision-making activity is to identify a solution satisfactory to our shared criteria. In this case we will need to assemble information and look for alternatives that fulfill our jointly shared desires. (If, for example, everyone agrees that one of the goals of the regulatory hearing process is to give all competing parties a chance to be heard, such agreement will resolve any problems arising in regard to the admissibility of expert testimony; such testimony allows the presentation of the best possible case by all sides, and therefore, all expert witnesses should be given an unfettered opportunity to present their findings. In this case we are all operating from a common set of principles. We may have to look for a unique or new way to accomplish this goal, but we are in agreement on the goal to be achieved.)

Even if we do not share the same specific goals, we can still probably resolve the ethical dilemma in a relatively nonthreatening way if we can trace our separate goals back to more general ends on which we can agree. In such a case we agree on the more general and basic goals; therefore, we can compromise or find an integrative solution,[4] because we have found common ground at a more basic level that helps us to define and analyze our subgoals. We find that common ground through what March and Simon call *persuasion*, or by showing the other party how we do ultimately share a common goal even though it is not immediately ascertainable. (If two individuals in a regulatory agency disagree as to the admissibility of the testimony of a specific government expert, and one individual feels he has the right to order his subordinate to alter his testimony, it may be necessary to point out there is a more basic political goal—the guarantee of due process in all regulatory hearings—which overrules the particular organizational, hierarchical mores. If the more basic political goal is understood and agreed upon, the rules surrounding the admissibility of evidence become much clearer and easier to administer. In a way, however, we have appealed to a set of rules that expands the arena—from the internal, hierarchical principle to a social, political principle—within which the controversy is being settled.)

If persuasion does not work, then we may have to resort to *bargaining*. In such a case it has become apparent there is disagreement over goals, and we must try to achieve a resolution of the conflict through other means; however, we do not want to appeal to parties outside those immediately involved in the confrontation. It is our hope, in this case, to appeal to a sense of "fairness" or "rationality" or some other basic value shared by all even though it is more general and perhaps not specifically related to this case. On the other hand, our competitors may depend on persistence, hierarchical position/power, or other similar characteristics to win, in which case rational factors may be useless. (If it becomes clear that the individual with whom we are in conflict does not agree with our definition of due process as applied to the case in hand, we must then bargain with him. We may appeal to other factors that we believe will influence his ultimate decision; these may include his sense of general "fair play" even if he believes the letter of the law does not apply in this case, or we may threaten him with public disclosure of his attempt at changing testimony. If he accepts our appeal to fair play, fine. If not, we threaten and see if he is willing to face the music. In the case of Sarah Underwood, the threat was sufficient to carry the day.)

Once bargaining fails, the final choice is to resort to *politics*. In this case we expand the field of the conflict by bringing in other allies who can help us fight the battle. This probably also means we lose some control over the situation; therefore, this can be a dangerous tactic. Even if the conflict stays inside the organization, it is no longer possible to control the outcome; the case may become bigger and have different repercussions than we ever thought or desired. (If we appeal to our superior, he will ultimately decide how far the issue is pursued, and if we carry through our threat and inform the judge about the witness tampering, the judge will have the same power. In either case the impact on the individual with whom we are in conflict, *and on our organization*, may be greater than we wish, and we cannot be sure what the ultimate impact will be on our own peace of mind and/or career. In diplomatic terms ''we have just declared war, our allies have joined, and now we no longer control exactly when or how the war will end.'' Luckily, in the Sarah Underwood case, this step was not necessary.)

Each of the steps above (problem-solving, persuasion, bargaining, and politics) is an expansion of the level of conflict. However, none of the steps may go outside the organization. At the fourth level the probability of expansion outside the organization becomes high, therefore it becomes important to weigh carefully every option (your control over it plus its ability to meet the goals or end results you desire while minimizing the potential costs or negative consequences that might occur) available. Dr. Valerie Franklin, in the case of the unserved minority university programs, ultimately had to move to the political level and open the case outside the organization by hiring a lawyer, going to court, and leveling a charge of racial bias against her supervisor (and, therefore, the organization) before her case could be resolved. However, the level of confrontation also made it extremely difficult to resolve the issue in a way that would allow individuals to continue in their prior relationships. It took time and, ultimately, the movement of people within the organization to heal the wounds and allow the activities of the organization to continue—admittedly in an improved way.

Dennis Thompson says there are four useful categories or levels of dissent available to members of a bureaucracy. In summary, these categories of dissent are:

1. *Protest within the organization* but still help implement the policy, or (a slightly stronger measure) ask for a different assignment in the organization;

2. With the knowledge of, but against the wishes of superiors, *carry the protest outside the organization* while otherwise performing assigned jobs satisfactorily;

3. *Openly obstruct policy*—officials may, for example, withhold knowledge or expertise that the organization needs to pursue the policy, refuse to step aside so that others can pursue it, or give information and other kinds of assistance to outsiders who are trying to overturn the policy; or

4. *Covertly obstruct policy* (perhaps the most powerful and dangerous)—unauthorized disclosure (the leak) is the most prominent example. (1985, 557–558)

The first and fourth levels of dissent suggested by Thompson may be used while the conflict is still operating at the three lower levels spelled out by March and Simon; however, the two middle levels of dissent automatically involve the bureaucrat in politics, and the fourth level of dissent will become a political conflict the instant such action becomes known, especially if it can be traced to its perpetrator. It should be understood by individuals using Thompson's fourth approach that their actions will almost certainly be considered illegal by their superiors. The obstructor is working directly to stop public policy as interpreted by his or her superiors; therefore, anyone participating in the covert obstruction of policy should understand the seriousness of his or her action and be prepared to pay the price if/when found out.

Moving from Analysis to Action

The analytic process arriving at the final action plan (which may contain several of the levels of response noted above over the life of any situation) must deal with five steps or issues. Once again, we are looking at ethical dilemmas occurring within the bureaucracy. Clarifying each issue or answering each question guarantees that the decision about handling the ethical dilemmas fulfills the desire of minimizing conflict while accomplishing the goal of maintaining ethical balance. As the situation progresses it may be necessary to go through some of these steps more than once.

When defining the problem, be specific. Ambiguous attacks accomplish nothing. In fact, if you cannot clearly and precisely define the issue, interested individuals, especially organization members, are invited to discount the whole affair as the maudlin maunderings of "another fuzzy-brained do-gooder," albeit one on the inside this time. Therefore, analyze the problem thoroughly and pinpoint it clearly for all to understand. Especially clarify the role that the organization plays if it is guilty of helping to create or exacerbate the problem. And be prepared to offer at least one *workable* (given the usually extremely complex individual, organization, political, and societal realities) alternative with a high probability of solving the problem.

Decide whether or not it is possible to be "loyal to the team" for one cannot be almost loyal; it is often impossible to "play ball" with both sides on important questions. This was precisely what got one interviewed manager into trouble; Jim, as I referred to him in Chapter 3, tried to please both sides and failed miserably to please anyone, himself included. At the other extreme, no one should be blindly loyal. An individual can empathize with people on the opposing sides of propositions. It is proper and possible for an individual to work out meaningful compromises and innovative, integrative solutions (Follett 1940). However, for an individual to maintain a record of meaningful attainment in solving ethical conflicts, it is essential that s/he compromise from a firm and well-understood position.

If your position is in basic alignment with the organization in which you work, even if there are some serious difficulties, it makes sense, for two reasons, to work within and through the context of the organization: (1) if the issue is primarily individual, and does not involve larger "affairs of state," it is necessary to continue to exist within the context of the bureaucracy, even if not in the current organization; a record of working as a part of the team is essential to success in that environment and should be given up only after considerable soul-searching; (2) for larger, policy-oriented, non-personal issues, it is usually necessary to have the support of some group (preferably including your immediate working group) in order to have an impact on the larger public-policy systems. These are the systems that must be changed if such large ethical impasses are to be resolved. If it is possible to declare and maintain loyalty to the organization, then the decision has been made as to the power base one is going to attempt to influence, change, and stimulate into action.

If it does not appear possible to declare and maintain loyalty to the organization as it presently exists, then there are two major questions to be answered. Is it possible to influence the organization enough, thereby creating at least minimal essential changes, that one can hope to continue working in and through it? Is the only alternative to leave the organization and work to resolve the problem from another base of operations? If the answer to the first question is affirmative, it is probably wise to continue working through one's organization. If the answer to the second question is affirmative, then it is time to start looking for a way out, and the only issues to be resolved are "how long I can stay here without unduly compromising my position on this issue" and "where I can go." If the answer to the first question is negative *and* the answer to the second is negative, there is a high probability that the individual facing the dilemmas is not being rational *or* it is time to go back to the beginning and work through the steps of analysis more carefully in order to increase or broaden understanding.

In most cases "managerial" ethical dilemmas do not lead to leaving the organization. However, the issue of loyalty can be a recurring one if you decide to stay in the organization and you are facing a critical issue. It may be necessary on several occasions to re-evaluate one's relation to the organization; this is not an issue that can be settled once and for all time.

Whether staying in or leaving the organization, there will be a need to go ahead and examine the three related issues yet to be discussed. At the same time, do not overemphasize the importance of the issue being considered. Most ethical dilemmas are related to managerial functions and decisions, and in this case it is properly difficult to generate a lot of interest outside of the organization. The public expects bureaus to work out such problems without turning them into community-wide free-for-alls.

It is time to start seeking support once the decision has been made as to whether or not to remain in the organization. For the individual operating within the bureaucracy a search for support is basic in the attempt to resolve an ethical dilemma, or to create change, regardless of one's position.

Supporters may exist within or without the organization. The first place to look for support is among the organizational leaders. The most immediate individual to try to win over is your supervisor, then if it is possible to work up through the hierarchy every effort should be made to do so. If your superiors can be convinced of the correctness of a particular ethical stance, an obstacle to change is converted to a force for change. Top administrators generally control resources, guide organizational effort, maintain appropriate external contacts, and influence political peers and superiors, so the task of rallying advocates for a cause is greatly simplified if the leaders can be co-opted.

However, in many cases it may not be possible to gain the backing of all the top management. It should be remembered from our case studies that leaders often did not wish to become personally involved in the ethical dilemmas of their subordinates. In most cases they either said "fix it," or "I do not want to know," or they helped create at least part of the problem because of their inappropriate attitudes or demands for action. In such cases it is necessary to take note of which superiors can and cannot be counted on, and then tactics must be worked out that take into account these realistic evaluations of where power lies on each side of the issue.

Once every effort has been made to gain the support of the leadership, it becomes important to look for other groups that will lend their names and efforts both to resolving and attempting to change the circumstances that cause the ethical problem. Your immediate coworkers comprise the most obvious group that will often lend support because they are familiar with the world in which you work and the pressures that exist. They also probably understand the particulars of the case because it is similar to their own activity. In the case where the decision was made to break the letter of the law because it was deemed in the public interest to move funds from one account to another in order to maintain a program, the decision was made by a small group of immediate peers and supervisors who thoroughly discussed their dilemma and possible options before taking any action.

There may be formal groups that can be recruited to help in protecting ethical individuals and/or fighting for change. Other groups will be informal, and it may be necessary to recruit individuals almost on a one-by-one basis. It is not uncommon in a large bureaucracy for groups of employees who have common concerns to join together either formally or informally. If these individuals all work in the same organization, and can be convinced that it is in their interest to rally round a specific ethical issue, it is possible to establish a communications network and a system of mutual support that can have a tremendous impact. Another variant of this idea is the professional society that meets regularly and can deal with a particular issue or area of interest. In this case, the participants may be drawn from a cross section of organizations; this can be beneficial because it is possible to broaden the support for an issue over a wider range. The broader base of support becomes especially important if it is necessary to move the arena of debate outside of the originating organization and into the larger political system.

Within the federal government there is a variety of formal actors who may be of interest to anyone facing an ethical problem. It is the official duty of a part of the Merit System Protection Board to work with whistle-blowers and protect their rights (however poorly that office may be able to carry out its function). Each federal department has an Inspector General's Office that is interested in ferreting out any illegal action by members of the bureaucracy at any level; however, they can only officially move against "illegal" acts, and many times "ethical dilemmas" do not involve illegal activities. Remember, illegal acts are seldom seen as "dilemmas" although the set of actions surrounding, but not directly involved in, the illegal act may raise many ethical questions. Audit or review agencies, such as the General Accounting Office, may also be of help, but they obviously cannot take on every individual case where someone feels that an ethical issue is at hand. Some states and localities have similar auditing organizations or offices that may be of help, and many jurisdictions and agencies have an ombudsman's office which may be able to listen, give advice, and perhaps play a positive role in resolving sticky problems.

One particular group, the union, needs to be considered very carefully when looking for support because it can be a valuable ally, but may not be an appropriate or interested party in many ethical battles. If the issue is of interest to a union, it will often be one of the strongest allies that can be gained; however, before expecting to gain the backing of a union in an ethical battle it is important to understand why a union exists, who it represents, and what types of issues are likely to gain its support. *Unions exist to protect and champion the rights and material well-being of their members.* Unions usually represent *nonmanagerial* employees. If the ethical issue happens to impinge on this area of interest (i.e., the issue happens to affect the health, working conditions, or general well-being of an employee or a group of employees), and the resolution of the issue appears to bode positively for rank-and-file union members it is possible that a union, or several of them, may join in the effort to correct the predicament. If, however, the ethical debate does not involve an issue that is of importance to the union (e.g., its members), there is no reason to expect anything beyond pro forma support.

This is not an indictment of unions, nor does this idea apply only to unions. It is a statement of the reality of life. The same kind of analysis of organizational goals and processes must be carried out whenever support is sought from any external source. The interesting aspect of this analytic process is that, if it is equally applied to all organizations with an interest in a particular issue, policy, or process, allies may appear in unexpected places. Often, when dealing with a particular issue rather than broader policies, it may be possible to enlist support from organizations that are direct competitors for resources and programs; these competitors may be interested in resolving a specific dilemma because they recognize its relationship to their programs and processes. Since they work in the same general area they can often see the utility of resolving these issues so that they are not faced with similar problems.

Generally, support is accepted from any source. However, there are some sources that are so odious, or so pernicious, that their support is damaging rather than helpful (e.g., the support of the Mafia or the Ku Klux Klan); in these cases it is necessary to divorce one's cause from such support if it cannot be discouraged or forestalled. An example of refusing support deemed inappropriate occurred when the public radio stations in Alaska refused an Exxon donation to help support their coverage of the Exxon Valdez oil spill in Prince William Sound. Nevertheless, support from most groups can be utilized in some fashion even though the members have widely divergent reasons and contrasting ideas about ways to support a cause. In fact, since we operate in a pluralist political system, and with an institutional arrangement that allows multiple access points to the public policy process, it is often possible to utilize these divergent groups to gain the ear of particular actors in the public policy system who could not be reached by any single organization. Therefore, when properly orchestrated and conducted, the support of a variety of groups can be a powerful tool.

After all possible support has been gathered, *a decision must be made about whether or not to make a public move to bring about the needed change.* This step can be taken once the amount and type of support that can be mustered is clear. In "making a *public* move," some specific action is taken with the intent of changing the policy, or the organizational structures or processes, in a way that will alleviate the current ethical problem and keep it from recurring in the future. The period of analysis—of waiting—is over and action is commencing. However, making a public move does not necessarily mean that a broad appeal is being made to the citizenry-at-large; the action may be taken on a purely internal basis in an individual's bureaucracy.

Even if staying in the organization, the situation may call for going public with one's information or accusation. "Whistle-blowing" (Nader, Percas, and Blackwell 1972; Westin 1981), as this activity has come to be known, is a necessary step in selected situations, but it should be understood as an activity that can be "dangerous to your health." The costs and benefits of such an action must be measured as carefully as possible. Above all, it should be recognized that in only a few cases will whistle-blowing make a major difference—people are familiar with the few cases where the whistle-blower has gained notoriety (while many times, at least initially, still losing his or her job), but in most cases there is no such public outcry of support. In other words, it may be necessary to blow the whistle, but do not naively expect people to accept you as a hero and to rally around you. Instead weigh the potential costs and benefits, and gather your allies very carefully before doing anything—especially going public with your information.

If, on the other hand, it is necessary to leave the organization in order to resolve the problem, one must decide how and when to quit and what to do afterward. Should you leave quietly and work for change from outside the organization? This is undoubtedly the most common choice. Should you refuse to follow an order or carry out a duty, perhaps forcing someone to fire you (as done by Elliot Richardson during the "Saturday Night Massacre" related to the Nixon/Watergate investigation), and thereby trying to force others to examine the reasons for protest (but take the chance of being held responsible for insubordination)? While this particular method of carrying the protest into the public, suggested by Dennis Thompson (1985) among others, may generate some publicity, it is doubtful that your particular case will generate enough publicity for people to notice. And the effort is probably not worthwhile unless there is a way to pique public interest in the issue. Actually, this alternative is little different from that of openly obstructing policy, also suggested by Thompson.

Should you go public while resigning, thereby attempting to sway the populace on the issue? Weisband and Franck (1975) argue that the political and public-policy-making system would benefit greatly from increased openness and debate over ethical, philosophical, and political differences that cause top officials at the cabinet and sub-cabinet level of the federal bureaucracy to quit their jobs. Regardless of one's opinion on this issue, the situation is decidedly different for civil servants at lower levels of the bureaucracy; they do not automatically generate news media attention and, therefore, cannot be assured that their message will be received or considered as important by the public. In addition, the "big guns" can be called into action against lower level civil servants if they threaten the programs or political lives of their superiors (or ex-superiors). All of this does not mean that one should always go quietly; indeed, there are undoubtedly times when the public should be informed about ethical dilemmas that are not being faced or are being covered over. However, it is wise to weigh the costs and consequences of "going public." Above all, remember that few martyrs become saints; most become statistics.

When the issue is made public to the appropriate audience a commitment to see it through to its conclusion has been made; therefore, it is of utmost importance to carry out the steps described earlier, and to choose the appropriate time and place to initiate action in order to make the strongest case possible. The types of resolution that occur, the ability or inability to compromise or find an innovative solution, are often set by these initial steps in the process; thus, the ultimate success of any individual in dealing with an ethical problem rests on the groundwork done before attempting to bring about change.

The final step is to *carry the action to its conclusion.* Hopefully, there is some understanding of what level of conflict (problem-solving, persuasion, bargaining, politics) will be required and there is an openness to face-saving and compromise if no innovative/integrative solutions can be reached. No matter how carefully one plans, the actual development of a situation can never be forecast; therefore, it is necessary to re-evaluate constantly all aspects of the situation and to adjust one's demands and expectations accordingly.

While there are basic values that must be upheld at all times, it is almost never possible to achieve absolutes; there are no "final answers" that make everything "right." It may be possible to solve the current dilemma, and therefore, to move on to new problems that have heretofore been unrecognized or ignored because of the press of the current issue (Follet 1940). But it is also true that almost every solution creates new problems; the cycle will recur, but hopefully at a new level of conscience, ethical awareness, sophistication, and action rather than at the same point where prior controversy occurred. To the extent this is true, you will have served as a "transformational" leader, raising the general ethical plane of those around you, as described by James MacGregor Burns (1978).

RESULTS: RETRIBUTION OR REWARDS

We are taught by our religious leaders that righteousness is always rewarded. The corollary does not follow in the political world. Ethical behavior is *not* always rewarded; in fact, it should not be assumed that ethical behavior will be rewarded for at least three reasons. Ethical behavior is expected as the norm, and we usually only reward people for performing above the norm. What is so special about acting ethically? Is that not what we are supposed to do? In a similar vein, since we are discussing ethical dilemmas, we have admitted that in many cases there may be honest disagreement about real cause, proper action, and possible effect. There is a "grayness" in interpretation of ethical issues that opens the door to disagreement and dispute. Finally, one individual's ethical behavior often creates problems (properly or by chance) for others who may or may not appreciate the attention brought to their actions for a variety of reasons varying from shyness to culpability in crime.

All too often ethical behavior leads to retribution. The retribution, of course, will be directly related to the importance or significance of the ethical issue involved and its impact on those affected by the situation. Most ethical dilemmas are not earth shattering; they have a direct impact on only a few people, and consciousness of the issue will often fade away relatively quickly after it is resolved. Therefore, in most cases this means that the only retribution felt by individuals is that they may, for some time, be made uncomfortable by their superiors and/or peers because of the ethical decision and action. Superiors and peers may be embarrassed or inconvenienced as their established perspectives, unquestioned values, or working routines are challenged by the ethically sensitive worker. These individuals may be challenged to change, and change is both inconvenient because it is necessary to "learn" new behavior and threatening because people are never quite sure what the results of change will be. A recurring theme among superiors in the cases studied for this work was that superiors did not want to know about the problem, did not want to deal with it, and therefore told the employees to "take care of it," or were upset that the employee created a "problem" by insisting on doing something the superiors did not want done, sometimes even to the point of disobeying superiors' orders. The frequent result in such cases is to take out the resulting frustration on the "perpetrator" of the situation—the ethical individual who "rocked the boat."

Recent history is full of cases where the ethical individual paid a dear price for his or her adherence to high principles. Referring back to the discussion of whistle-blowing earlier in this chapter, even though the Office of Special Counsel was established in the Federal Merit System Protection Board with a specific charge to help protect whistle-blowers, the director of that office, in 1984, recommended that people think carefully about such actions before carrying them out because he could not help most of them in their battle with their agencies, peers, and bosses. K. William O'Connor, then head of the Office of Special Council, said in an interview in the *Washington Post*:

I'd say that unless you're in a position to retire or are independently wealthy, don't do it. Don't put your head up, because it will get blown off. . . . If you get your head above water, you're very likely to be recommended for criminal prosecution by the very entities and organizations on which you're trying to blow the whistle. (Kurtz 1984, A17)

This was certainly true of Dr. Valerie Franklin when she turned to the inspector general *within* her organization. She immediately had charges filed against her that led initially to her removal from the civil service although that action was overturned shortly thereafter.

There are few places to turn for support when an individual carries out such an act, even when the information released is correct, corroborated, and critical to fulfilling the public trust. This does not mean that public servants should not fulfill their public trust and maintain a high standard of values, beliefs, and behavior for themselves and those surrounding them in the public bureaucracy. It simply means that decisions about actions should not be taken in a naive belief that the decision maker will be appreciated and rewarded for that behavior.

In most cases the decisions made by individuals in the public service, as is undoubtedly true everywhere, received no great attention, caused no important reactions, and were forgotten as particular incidents within a very short time. The individual often developed, over time, a reputation for ethical beliefs and behavior, and this is perhaps the greatest reward these individuals can receive. They soon come to be known as individuals of whom you do not ask questionable favors, special treatment, or loose interpretations of rules and regulations. Again, let me remind you of the individual who upon being interviewed said he had no ethical problems while serving in the federal civil service. He immediately turned down the first few people who asked for favors; he never even saw those situations as ethical problems—the requests were outside his interpretation of his position and power; the message quickly got around that he "was not for sale," and the requests quickly died away.

Likewise, Sarah Underwood, the lawyer in the regulatory agency, noted that she was never again placed in a situation where her witnesses were pressured to suborn testimony. That might be coincidence; but the opposite would not be. If she had agreed to the changed testimony she almost certainly would have been seen as an attorney who would "play ball" and the situation would have arisen again and again. It is much more likely that her reputation was made in that case, and no one was willing to take the risk of approaching her or her witnesses again in the future. As she said, "The offending supervisor may have made sure that certain cases were not given to me—although I doubt that he had such authority—but, whatever the reason, he never again messed with any of my cases." As a public manager it is essential to remember that you are responsible for other individuals in the organization. Your decisions should consider how those other individuals will be affected by your action. You are, in some small or large way, creating the "management style" of the organization when you respond to ethical challenges.

In a similar vein, a city manager related to me how his chief building inspector commented that builders were suddenly much more brazen in their attempt to bribe him to overlook certain building code violations. The city manager's response was, "Are builders really suddenly different? Maybe you are doing something that suggests to them that you may be approachable on the matter of taking bribes." A few weeks later the building inspector came back to the city manager and said, "You were right. I have carefully considered my actions, and I was suggesting to the builders that I might be approachable even though I do not want them to think so. I have changed my behavior, and the result has been that such approaches have ceased. Thank you for pointing out to me that such situations are two-sided." One of the benefits of operating at a high ethical level is that you are placed in fewer situations where ethical questions are liable to arise.

So what if your ethical behavior is not publicly noticed and rewarded? Individuals who are sincerely interested in performing ethically are not disturbed by a lack of attention or reward. These individuals have a commitment to democratic principles and to serving the public in a manner that leaves no doubt about their loyalty to the public interest. The knowledge that they have helped in some small but steady and significant way to build and maintain public trust in the government, its policies, and its bureaucracy is reward enough for "doing the right thing." Public recognition of ethical behavior is welcome, and perhaps there is an increasing understanding of the positive force such recognition can have in focusing public attention on the importance of ethics in public life and in encouraging individuals throughout the public sector to hold fast to the values of democracy and public service. But public recognition is only one of the significant factors in maintaining an ethical public service. Commitment to ethics on the part of each public servant as an individual is the key to increasing and strengthening the public's trust in the public service.

NOTES

1. It is important in this discussion to remember the difference between "empathy" (understanding so intimate that the feelings, thoughts, and motives of one are readily comprehended by another) and "sympathy" (a relationship or affinity between persons in which whatever affects one correspondingly affects the other, therefore often leading to favoritism, loyalty, devotion, or allegiance between the persons). Empathy is an important part of objective understanding of many situations, sympathy destroys the possibility of objective understanding.

2. I emphasize "societal" because it is easy, but dreadfully mistaken, to assume societal values equal or mirror personal or organizational values. *Very careful validation* of such an assumption must be completed before it can be the basis of any action.

3. In public bureaus, culture is influenced by the politically appointed head of the organization; however, that individual is usually a "short timer" and any influence .is often passing. Instead, the culture of the bureau often may be generated by the top managers for whom this is their permanent home. In such a case the existent culture may be intermittently appropriate or inappropriate as political regimes come and go, or it may be permanently favorable or inimical to those political leaders.

4. Mary Parker Follett (1940) argues conflicts end in one of three ways: (1) domination—in which one side wins and the other loses, and the issue will be rejoined once the loser believes his or her power is great enough to force a more satisfactory resolution; (2) compromise—in which case both sides have given up something desired, and once the balance of power changes the issue will arise again; or (3) integration—in which case both or all of the combatants have found a satisfactory solution where neither side has had to sacrifice anything of value. In this case the particular conflict is *resolved* and the actors can move on to other issues.

APPENDIX: RESEARCH METHODOLOGY AND INTERVIEW INSTRUMENT

Interviewees for this research were drawn from federal employees who were in GS 15 positions or higher (including the Senior Executive Service), or from retired federal employees who had held similar positions while with the federal government. While the identities of the individuals must remain secret, they chosen from a cross-section of employees from that relatively selective universe. Four major reasons were behind the definition of the universe. First, these individuals came from a relatively similar background and brought to the interviews experiences from a single level of government. That removed the different perspectives that might be introduced by the demands of state and local government service. Second, most individuals at this level in the federal service had a relatively lengthy experience in government; therefore, they could choose incidents from different points in their careers. Third, even though the sample was limited to members of the federal service, it included individuals from a variety of positions in that service, thereby allowing situations in a variety of professional paths/positions to be included in the discussions. This helped create a balance between homogeneity of careers and diversity of experiences and perspectives. Fourth, limiting the universe to the federal service made the study manageable for one person. In the future the study can be expanded in a variety of ways.

Interviewees were chosen from careers in the following areas of the federal service:

regulatory agencies

service delivery organizations

staff functions

—personnel offices

—budget office

—procurement offices

—auditing offices

—liaison offices (working with Congress, other agencies, and/or clientele and outside group)

The approach used in the interviews was the "critical incident" approach. This method was used in order to guarantee spontaneity from the interviewees and to allow the opportunity to choose incidents from various periods of their careers. Anonymity was guaranteed. Interviews were structured according to the interview checklist presented below. The structure was established to guarantee that the interviewers would describe their ethical dilemma in full before the following, more specific questions influenced their thinking.

Interview Checklist

Name_____

Number of years of federal service_____

I am carrying out some research on how civil servants approach ethical problems when they face them on the job. I would like for you to think back through your career in the federal government. Choose the one incident in your career that created the most serious ethical dilemma for you. I would like to discuss that situation with you in some depth.

A. Background

--How do you define, or what do you mean by, an "ethical" problem or dilemma?

--What was the specific problem you faced?

--When and where did this take place? (You may skip this, or generalize your response, if it is sensitive.)

--What was your position and grade at the time the incident occurred? (Again, you may skip this if sensitive.)

--Who were the other major actors? (You may use only positions, if you wish, instead of names.)

--Are there other general background factors that are important to the incident?

AT THIS POINT I WOULD LIKE FOR YOU TO DESCRIBE THE TOTAL INCIDENT WITHOUT MY INTERFERENCE--SO THAT I WILL NOT BIAS YOUR DESCRIPTIONS OF THE SITUATION. AFTER YOU HAVE FINISHED I WILL ASK YOU ANY QUESTIONS THAT I HAVE ON MY CHECKLIST THAT YOU HAVE NOT COVERED.

B. Recognition of the problem

--How did you become aware of the problem?

--Did (do) you have some special "trigger mechanisms" that help(ed) you recognize the presence of an ethical problem?

C. Analyzing the problem

--What were the major issues you faced in the specific case we are addressing?

--How did you go about analyzing all of the issues in this case?

--Did (do) you have a "standard operating procedure" for analyzing problems you recognize(d) as "ethical"?

--To what extent did the following areas play any part in your analysis?
     -the law.
     -your profession(s) and its(their) code(s) of ethics.
     -general organizational dynamics, such as the organization's structure, standard operating procedures, the general organizational environment or milieu, etc.
     -democratic values or general philosophical principles.
     -your own personal characteristics.

D. Resolution

--How did you resolve the problem?

--Why that particular resolution?

E. Results

--What were the results of that choice for the organization?

--What were the results of that choice for yourself?
   -How were you treated by the organization? by the individuals involved? by individuals personally close to you? by outsiders?

--Were you surprised by the reactions of the various actors mentioned above?

F. General questions

--Looking back on this case, what were the most important factors that influenced your overall actions?

--Could you have been better prepared for handling the situation? How? Who/what could have helped?
   -your education.
   -your profession.
   -the organization itself.
   -the government.
   -the law.
   -other factors not included here.

--What advice would you give to others who are faced with an ethical dilemma similar in difficulty/importance to the one we have been discussing?

BIBLIOGRAPHY

Adams, Sam. "Vietnam Cover-Up: Playing War with Numbers." In *Public Administration: Concepts and Cases*. 4th ed., edited by Richard J. Stillman II, 262–277. Boston: Houghton Mifflin, 1988.

Anderson, Hurst R. "Ethical Values in Administration." *Personnel Administration* 17 (1): 1–12 (1954).

Appleby, Paul H. *Morality and Administration in Democratic Government*. Baton Rouge, La.: Louisiana State University Press, 1952.

Aram, John D. *Dilemmas of Administrative Behavior*. Englewood Cliffs, N.J.: Prentice Hall, 1976.

Asch, Solomon E. *Social Psychology*. New York: Oxford University Press, 1987.

Bailey, Mary Timney. "Psychological Development of Adults: A Comment." *Public Administration Review*, 47(4): 343–345 (1987).

Bailey, Stephen K. "The Relationship between Ethics and Public Service." In *Public Administration and Democracy: Essays in Honor of Paul Appleby*, edited by Roscoe C. Martin, 283–298. Syracuse N.Y.: Syracuse University Press, 1965.

Barnard, Chester. *Functions of the Executive*. 1938. Reprint. 40th anniversary ed. Cambridge, Mass.: Harvard University Press, 1979.

Bayles, Michael. D. *Professional Ethics*. 2d ed. Belmont, Ca.: Wadsworth, 1989.

Beauchamp, Tom L., and Terry P. Pinkard (eds.). *Ethics and Public Policy: An Introduction to Ethics*. 2d ed. Englewood Cliffs, N.J.: Prentice Hall, 1983.

Bendix, Reinhard. *Max Weber: An Intellectual Portrait*. Berkeley, Ca.: University of California, 1977.

Bennis, Warren. *Changing Organizations: Essays on the Development and Evolution of Human Organization*. New York: McGraw-Hill, 1966.

Bernstein, Marver H. *Regulating Business by Independent Commission*. Westport, Conn.: Greenwood Press, 1977.

Blake, Eugene Carson. "Should the Code of Ethics in Public Life Be Absolute or Relative?" *Annals of the American Academy of Political and Social Science* 363: 4–11 (January 1966).

Blau, Peter M., and W. Richard Scott. *Formal Organizations: A Comparative Approach.* San Francisco: Chandler, 1962.

Bolles, Blair. "Correctives for Dishonest and Unfair Public Administrators." *Annals of the American Academy of Political and Social Sciences* 363: 23–27 (January 1966).

Bowman, James S. "Whistle Blowing: Literature and Resource Materials." *Public Administration Review* 43(3): 271–276 (1983).

Burns, James MacGregor. *Leadership.* New York: Harper and Row, 1978.

Calabresi, Guido, and Philip Bobbitt. *Tragic Choices.* New York: W. W. Norton, 1978.

Caplow, Theodore. "Organizational Size." *Administrative Science Quarterly* 1(4): 484–505 (1957).

Caro, Robert. *The Power Broker: Robert Moses and the Fall of New York.* New York: Vintage Books, 1974.

Chandler, Ralph C. "The Problems of Moral Illiteracy in Professional Discourse: The Case of the State of Principles of the ASPA." *American Review of Public Administration* 16: 369–386 (Winter 1982).

———. "The Problem of Moral Reasoning in American Public Administration: The Case for a Code of Ethics." *Public Administration Review* 43(1): 32–39 (1983).

Colson, Charles W. *Born Again.* New York: Bantam Books, 1977.

Cooper, Terry L. *The Responsible Administrator: An Approach to Ethics for the Administrative Role.* Rev. ed. New York: Associated Faculty Press, 1986.

Cronin, Thomas E. "The Swelling of the Presidency." *Saturday Review of the Society* 1: 30–36 (February 1973).

Davis, Keith. "The Care and Cultivation of the Corporate Grapevine." *Dunn's Review* 102(1): 44–47 (1973).

Dawes, Charles G. *The First Year of the Budget of the United States.* In *The Administrative Process and Democratic Theory*, edited by Louis C. Gawthrop, 86–97. Boston: Houghton Mifflin, 1970.

Denhardt, Kathryn G. *The Ethics of Public Service: Resolving Moral Dilemmas in Public Organizations.* New York: Greenwood Press, 1988.

Dewey, John, and J. H. Tufts. *Ethics.* New York: Henry Holt, 1932.

Downs, Anthony. *Inside Bureaucracy.* Boston: Little, Brown, 1967.

Dvorin, Eugene P., and Robert H. Simmons. *From Amoral to Humane Bureaucracy.* San Francisco: Canfield, 1972.

Ellis, Tottie. "USA Won't Miss Koop; He Abandoned Principle." Editorial in *USA Today*, July 17, 1989, p. 8A.

Feldman, Saul. "Conflict and Convergence: The Mental Health Professional in Government." In *Professions in Government*, edited by Frederick C. Mosher and Richard J. Stillman II, 91–96. New Brunswick, N.J.: Transaction Books, 1982.

Filley, Alan C., Robert J. House, and Steven Kerr. *Managerial Process and Organizational Behavior.* Glenview, Ill.: Scott, Foresman, 1976.

Fisher, Roger, and Scott Brown. *Getting Together: Building a Relationship That Gets to YES.* Boston: Houghton Mifflin, 1988.

Fisher, Roger, and William Ury. *Getting to YES: Negotiating Agreement Without Giving In.* Boston: Houghton Mifflin, 1981.

Follett, Mary Parker. *Dynamic Administration: The Collected Papers of Mary Parker*

Hoffer, Eric. *The True Believer: Thoughts on the Nature of Mass Movements*. New York: Harper and Row, 1951.

Homans, George C. *The Human Group*. New York: Harcourt, Brace and World, 1950.

Hrezo, William E., Mona Harmon-Bowman, and David L. Robertson. "Public Administration: A Personalized Approach." *Virginia Social Science Journal* 22: 25–35 (Spring 1987).

Hummel, Ralph P. *The Bureaucratic Experience*. New York: St. Martin's Press, 1977.

———. *The Bureaucratic Experience*. 3d rev. ed. New York: St. Martin's Press, 1987.

Ingelfinger, Franz J. "Medicine: However Well People May Speak of Their Individual Doctors, the System of Health Care has a Bad Name." *Saturday Review* 3: 25–27 (November 1, 1975).

Jackall, Robert. *Moral Mazes: The World of Corporate Managers*. New York: Oxford University Press, 1988.

Jacques, Elliott. *A General Theory of Bureaucracy*. London: Heinemann, 1976.

Jones, Garth N. "Rise and Fall of a Professional Ideal: Particulars Concerning Public Administration." *American Review of Public Administration* 16: 305–319 (Winter 1982).

Jung, Carl. *Psychological Types*. New York: Harcourt Brace, 1923.

Kahn, Robert L., Donald M. Wolfe, Robert P. Quinn, and J. Diedrick Snoek. *Organizational Stress: Studies in Role Conflict and Ambiguity*. New York: John Wiley and Sons, 1964.

Kaplan, Abraham. *American Ethics and Public Policy*. 1963. Reprint. Westport, Conn.: Greenwood Press, 1980.

Keirsey, David, and Marilyn Bates. *Please Understand Me: Character and Temperament Types*. Del Mar, Ca.: Prometheus Nemesis, 1984.

Kohlberg, Lawrence. "Children's Perceptions of Contemporary Value Systems." In *Raising Children in Modern America: Problems and Perspective Solutions*, edited by Nathan Talbot, 98–118. Boston: Little, Brown, 1976.

Kurtz, Howard. "Friendly Advice: 'Don't Put Your Head Up.' " *The Washington Post* A17 (July 17, 1984).

Laney, James T. "Moralizing the Professions: Commitment to the Public Interest." *Vital Speeches of the Day* 51: 501–503 (June 1, 1985).

Levine, Charles H. (ed.) "A Symposium: Organizational Decline and Cutback Management." *Public Administration Review* 37(4): 315–325 (1978).

Levinson, Daniel J. *The Seasons of a Man's Life*. New York: Knopf, 1978.

Leys, Wayne A. R. *Ethics and Social Policy*. New York: Prentice Hall, 1941.

———. *Ethics for Policy Decisions: The Art of Asking Deliberative Questions*. 1952. Reprint. New York: Greenwood Press, 1968.

Lindblom, Charles. "The Science of Muddling Through." *Public Administration Review* 19: 79–88 (Spring 1959).

Losito, William F. "Is Ethical Conduct Among Professionals Attainable?" *USA Today*, 111(2456): 22–24 (1983).

Maccoby, Michael. *The Leader: A New Face for American Management*. New York: Simon and Schuster, 1981.

Mahler, Julianne. "The Quest for Organizational Meaning: Identifying and Interpreting the Symbolism in Organizational Stories." *Administration and Society* 20: 344–368 (November 1988).

Follett, edited by Henry C. Metcalf and Lyndall Urwick. New York: Harper a
Brothers, 1940.

Fragola, Albert T. "Professions: Have They Become Un-American?" *Vital Speeches*
the Day 50: 555–557 (July 1984).

Frankena, William K. "Value and Valuation." In *The Encyclopedia of Philosophy*, edi
by Paul Edwards, 229–232. New York: Macmillan, 1967.

French, Wendell, and Cecil B. Bell, Jr. *Organization Development: Behavioral Scie*
Interventions for Organization Improvement. 4th ed. Englewood Cliffs, I
Prentice Hall, 1990.

Fuller, Lon L. *Anatomy of the Law.* New York: Praeger, 1968.

Gale, Raymond F. *Developmental Behavior: A Humanistic Approach.* New York:
millan, 1969.

Gardner, John W. *Tasks of Leadership.* Washington, D.C.: Independent Sector, I
1986.

Gilligan, Carol. *In a Different Voice: Psychological Theory and Women's Develo*
Cambridge, Mass.: Harvard University Press, 1982.

Golembiewski, Robert T. *Men, Management, and Morality: Toward a New Or*
tional Ethic. New York: McGraw-Hill, 1965.

Goodnow, Frank. *Politics and Administration: A Study in Government.* 1900. I
New York: Russell and Russell, 1967.

Goodsell, Charles T. *The Case for Bureaucracy: A Public Administration I*
Chatham, N.J.: Chatham House, 1983.

Gortner, Harold F. *Administration in the Public Sector.* New York: Macmillan

Gortner, Harold F., Julianne Mahler, and Jeanne Bell Nicholson. *Organization*
A Public Perspective. Pacific Grove, Ca.: Brooks/Cole, 1987.

Gould, Roger. *Transformation: Growth and Change in Adult Life.* New Yor
and Schuster, 1978.

Gulick, Luther. "Notes on the Theory of Organization." In *Papers on the .*
Administration, edited by Luther Gulick and L. Urwick, 1–45. 1937
Clifton, N.J.: Augustus Kelley, 1973a.

————. "Science, Values, and Administration." In *Papers on the Science*
istration, edited by Luther Gulick and L. Urwick, 189–195. 1937. Repri
N.J.: Augustus Kelley, 1973b.

Hamilton, Alexander, James Madison, and John Jay. *The Federalist Papers.*
The New American Library, 1961.

Harmon, Michael M., and Richard T. Mayer. *Organization Theory for Pi*
istration. Boston: Little, Brown, 1986.

Hart, David K. "Social Equity, Justice and the Equitable Administrator." *P*
istration Review. 3(1): 3–10 (1974).

Heclo, Hugh. *A Government of Strangers: Executive Politics in Washington.*
D.C.: Brookings Institution, 1977.

Henry, Nicholas. *Public Administration and Public Affairs.* 4th ed. Engl
N.J.: Prentice Hall, 1989.

Hersey, Paul, and Kenneth H. Blanchard. *Management of Organizatic*
Utilizing Human Resources. 5th ed. Englewood Cliffs, N.J.: Prent

Hickson, D. G., and M. M. Thomas. "Professionalization in Britain:
Measurement." *Sociology* 3: 38–53 (June 1969).

March, James G., and Herbert A. Simon. *Organizations*. New York: John Wiley and Sons, 1958.

Marini, Frank (ed.). *Toward a New Public Administration: The Minnowbrook Perspective*. Scranton, Pa.: Chandler Publishing, 1971.

McGowan, Robert P. "The Professional in Public Organizations: Lessons from the Private Sector?" *American Review of Public Administration* 16: 337–349 (Winter 1982).

Merton, Robert. *Social Theory and Social Structure*. New York: Free Press, 1968.

Mitchell, Greg. "Blowing the Whistle." *The Washington Post Magazine*, 12–19 (August 12, 1979).

Moore, W. John. "The Office of Government Ethics: Vigilant Watchdog or Toothless Terrier." *Government Executive* 22–25 (October 1987).

Morgan, Gareth. *Images of Organization*. Beverly Hills, Ca.: Sage, 1986.

Mosher, Frederick C. *Democracy and the Public Service*. 2d ed. New York: Oxford University Press, 1982.

Mosher, Frederick C., and Richard J. Stillman II (eds.). *Professions in Government*. New Brunswick, N.J.: Transaction Press, 1982.

Nader, Ralph, Peter J. Perkas, and Kate Blackwell (eds.). *Whistle Blowing: The Report of the Conference on Professional Responsibility*. New York: Grossman Publishers, 1972.

Niebuhr, Reinhold. *Moral Man and Immoral Society: A Study in Ethics and Politics*. 1932. Reprint. New York: Scribners, 1960.

Ouchi, William G. *Theory Z: How American Business Can Meet the Japanese Challenge*. New York: Avon Books, 1982.

Payne, Roy L., and Roger Mansfield. "Relationships of Perspectives of Organizational Climate to Organizational Structure, Context, and Hierarchical Position." *Administrative Science Quarterly* 18: 515–526 (December 1973).

Peters, B. Guy. *The Politics of Bureaucracy: A Comparative Perspective*. 3d ed. New York: Longman, 1989.

Piaget, Jean. *The Moral Judgement of the Child*. New York: Free Press, 1932.

———. "The General Problems of the Psychobiological Development of the Child." In *Discussions on Child Development: Procedures of the World Health Organization Study Group on the Psychobiological Development of the Child: 4*, edited by J. M. Tanner and Barbel Inhelder. New York: International Universities Press, 1960.

———. "Intellectual Evolution from Adolescence to Adulthood." *Human Development* 15: 1–12 (1972).

Pound, Roscoe. *An Introduction to the Philosophy of Law*. New Haven, Conn.: Yale University Press, 1954.

Presthus, Robert V. *The Organizational Society*. Rev. ed. New York: St. Martin's Press, 1978.

Rainey, Hal G., and Robert W. Backoff. "Professionals in Public Organizations: Organizational Environments and Incentives." *American Review of Public Administration* 16: 319–336 (Winter 1982).

Rittel, Horst W. J., and Melvin Webber. "Dilemmas in a General Theory of Planning." *Policy Sciences* 4(2): 155–169 (1973).

Roelofs, H. Mark. *Ideology and Myth in American Politics: A Critique of a National Political Mind*. Boston: Little, Brown, 1976.

Rohr, John A. *Ethics for Bureaucrats: An Essay on Law and Values*. New York: Marcel Dekker, 1978.

Rossiter, Clinton. *The American Presidency*. 2d rev. ed. New York: Mentor, 1962.

Rourke, Francis E. *Bureaucracy, Politics, and Public Policy*. 3d ed. Boston: Little, Brown, 1984.

Sarkesian, Sam C. (ed.). *Presidential Leadership and National Security: Style, Institutions and Politics*. Boulder, Colo.: Westview Press, 1984.

Schott, Richard L. "The Psychological Development of Adults." *Public Administration Review* 46(6): 657–667 (1986).

———. "Psychological Development of Adults: Further Reflections and a Rejoinder." *Public Administration Review* 47(4): 345–346 (1987).

Segal, Julius, and Herbert Yahraes. *A Child's Journey: Forces that Shape the Lives of Our Young*. New York: McGraw-Hill, 1978.

Shartel, Burke. *Our Legal System and How It Operates*. Ann Arbor. Mich.: University of Michigan Law School, 1951.

Singer, Peter. *Democracy and Disobedience*. New York: Oxford University Press, 1974.

Stillman, Richard J., II. "The City Manager: Professional Helping Hand, or Political Hired Hand?" In *Professions in Government*, edited by Frederick C. Mosher and Richard J. Stillman II. New Brunswick, N.J.: Transaction Books, 1982.

Thompson, Dennis. "The Possibility of Administrative Ethics." *Public Administration Review* 45(5): 555–561 (1985).

Thompson, James D. *Organizations in Action: Social Science Bases of Administrative Theory*. New York: McGraw-Hill, 1967.

Thompson, Victor A. *Without Sympathy or Enthusiasm: The Problem of Administrative Compassion*. University, Ala.: University of Alabama Press, 1975.

"USA Will Miss Koop, a Man of Principle." Lead editorial in *USA Today*, July 17, 1989, p. 8A.

Vaillant, George E. *Adaptation to Life*. Boston: Little, Brown, 1977.

Van Riper, Paul P. *History of the United States Civil Service*. Evanston, Ill.: Row, Peterson, 1958.

Veblen, Thorstein. *The Theory of Business Enterprise*. New York: Scribner, 1915.

———. *Absentee Ownership: The Business Enterprise in Recent Times: The Case of America*. London: Allen, 1924.

Weber, Max. *The Theory of Social and Economic Organization*. translated by A. M. Henderson and Talcott Parsons. New York: The Free Press, 1947.

Weisband, Edward, and Thomas M. Franck. *Resignation in Protest: Political and Ethical Choices Between Loyalty to Team and Loyalty to Conscience in American Public Life*. New York: Grossman Publishers, 1975.

Westin, Alan F., Henry I. Kurtz, and Albert Robbins (eds.). *Whistle Blowing: Loyalty and Dissent in the Corporation*. New York: McGraw-Hill, 1981.

Whyte, William H., Jr. *The Organization Man*. Garden City, N.Y.: Doubleday Anchor, 1956.

Wilensky, Harold L. *Organizational Intelligence: Knowledge and Policy in Government and Industry*. New York: Basic Books, 1967.

Willbern, York. "Types and Levels of Public Morality." *Public Administration Review* 44(2): 102–108 (1984).

Wolin, Sheldon S. *Politics and Vision: Continuity and Innovation in Western Political Thought*. Boston: Little, Brown, 1960.
Zaleznik, Abraham. *Human Dilemmas of Leadership*. New York: Harper & Row, 1966.
Zelermyer, William. *Legal Reasoning: The Evolutionary Process of Law*. Englewood Cliffs, N.J.: Prentice Hall, 1960.

INDEX

ABOUT THE AUTHOR

HAROLD F. GORTNER is Associate Professor of Government and Politics at George Mason University. He received his B.A. from Earlham College and his M.P.A. and M.A. and Ph.D. in Political Science from Indiana University. Dr. Gortner is the author of *Administration in the Public Sector* and the coauthor of *Organization Theory: A Public Perspective*. In addition he has published articles on public policy implementation, personnel administration, and public administration ethics in a variety of professional journals and anthologies.